What Did the Baby Boomers Ever Do For Us?

Why the children of the sixties lived the dream
and failed the future

Francis Beckett

First published in Great Britain in 2010 by
Biteback Publishing Ltd
Heal House
375 Kennington Lane
London
SE11 5QY

ISBN 978-1-84954-026-1

10 9 8 7 6 5 4 3 2 1

A CIP catalogue record for this book is available from the British Library.

Set in Joanna by SoapBox, soapboxcommunications.co.uk
Printed and bound in Great Britain by TJ International Ltd, Padstow, Cornwall

Contents

Author's note and acknowledgements

The precise definition of a baby boomer is disputed, but I have defined it as anyone born between 1945 and 1955. David Willetts in his book *The Pinch* defines it very differently, as people born between 1945 and 1965, but he is quite wrong, because this period contains not one but two baby booms, separated by a small slump. The classic baby boomers, born between 1945 and 1955, were a completely different sort of generation from those born at the start of the sixties.

The complaint may be made that I have not written an objective history of the sixties, but have selected those events and quotes that bear out my thesis. I have a ready answer to this, which is: yup, that's what I've done.

I have told the story of the baby boomer generation partly through the lives of individuals. Among many others, I have made use of the lives of the only two baby boomer Prime Ministers Britain has ever had, or is ever likely to have, Tony Blair and Gordon Brown; of the singer Marianne Faithfull, whose autobiography *Faithfull* is full of insights into what the children of the sixties thought they were, and what they really were; of the student-Trotskyist-turned-far-right-commentator Peter Hitchens and of Paul Mackney, student Trotskyist who kept the faith and became an important and successful trade union leader; and of Greg Dyke, representing that part of the baby boomer generation which made a fortune in business, in a peculiarly sixties way. I'm particularly grateful to three of them – Greg Dyke, Peter Hitchens and Paul Mackney – for long and illuminating interviews; and to Gordon Brown for an interview while I was writing his biography, which has helped me here too.

Other baby boomers make occasional appearances, and some of them have been kind enough to read and comment on certain passages and chapters, or to help with information. They include Eddie Barrett and Tony Russell, who between them – or so it seems to me – know everything there is to know about popular music (and this book was completed in Eddie Barrett's charming house in Calabria, looking out at islands and mountains). They also include the playwright Steve Gooch, and old university friends who were especially helpful on 1968: Mike Brereton, Malcolm Clarke, Marshall Colman, John Howkins, Marina Lewycka, Linden West and Martin Yarnit.

I also want to thank the readers of U3A News, the magazine of the University of the Third Age, and the best place in the world for anyone writing about events in the last fifty years or so to find people who will remember them.

Among the generation betrayed by the baby boomers, I would like to thank in particular two Leeds University graduates in their twenties for information and insights: my son Peter Beckett, now a political lobbyist, and the former National Union of Students president Kat Fletcher.

Introduction

The baby boomers saw themselves as pioneers of a new world – freer, fresher, fairer and infinitely more fun. But they were wrong. The world they made for their children to live in is a far harsher one than the world they inherited.

The first of the men and women born in the baby boom that followed the Second World War started to come of age in the radical sixties. Not since 1918 had the young talked serious revolutionary politics as they did in the sixties.

But in 1918, the men who came back from the war knew that the world was amiss, and knew what they wanted to do about it. So when at last the generation that fought the First World War came to power, in 1945 under Major Clement Attlee, they changed the world. The 1942 Beveridge Report had called for the abolition of the 'five giants' – Want, Ignorance, Disease, Squalor and Idleness – and between 1945 and 1951, despite a war-ruined economy, the Attlee government set about a systematic and remarkably successful assault on those evils.

Exactly fifty years later, revolutionary talk was heard across the land again. But the generation of 1968 was not at all like the generation of 1918. Sixties radicalism decayed fast. It decayed, not because it was groundless, but because it was not grounded. What began as the most radical-sounding generation for half a century turned into a random collection of youthful style gurus who thought the revolution was about fashion; sharp-toothed entrepreneurs and management consultants who believed revolution meant new ways of selling things; and Thatcherites, who thought freedom meant free markets, not free people. At last it decayed into New Labour, which had no idea what either revolution or freedom meant, but rather liked the sound of the words.

The sixties really began in 1956 with John Osborne's *Look Back in Anger*, but few people noticed until the Beatles released 'Love Me Do' in October 1962. By then the oldest of the baby boomers were fully seventeen years old, and within three years they were to know everything there was to know, from the secrets of the universe to the correct way to roll a joint.

The short sixties – from the release of 'Love Me Do' to the student sit-ins and the Paris *événements* of summer 1968 – was a wonderful time to be young. People took the young seriously for the first time, which was good. But the young took themselves seriously, which was less good. The young thought New Jerusalem was round the corner, its arrival hindered only by the conservatism of Harold Wilson's Labour government. They did not realise that they were living in New Jerusalem; that it would all be downhill from then on; and that their generation, which benefited from this dazzling array of freedoms, would, within twenty years, destroy them.

Nor did they realise – for they had never heard of Tony Blair – how lucky they were to have Wilson to hate. Without Wilson, the baby boomers might well have had to fight and die in Vietnam, for a lesser Prime Minister could have been cowed by President Lyndon Johnson and America's power to cripple Britain's economy.

For the first time since the Second World War, there was money, there was safe sex, there was freedom, and no one bothered to stop and think with what misery these things had been bought by earlier generations, for the baby boomers rather despised the past, a small faraway country of which they knew little. Most of the baby boomers hardly realised the privations of their parents, and the struggle that had taken place to ensure that they were not equally deprived.

Before the First World War, 163 of every 1,000 children died before their first birthday. The figure was twice as high for working-class children. It is 15 per 1,000 today. Of those children that survived, a quarter did not live beyond the age of four. In the early weeks of the National Health Service in 1948, consultants reported shoals of women coming in with internal organs that had been prolapsed for years, and men with long undiagnosed hernias and lung diseases.

In the thirties, my grandmother, widowed by the First World War, kept a tin on a shelf, into which she put every spare coin she could, against the day when one of her children might need the doctor. She was a rather wise old lady, so I felt a sense of shock when, as a teenager, I received a letter from her, and realised she wrote like a five-year-old. Like millions of her generation, she was never taught to write properly.

Working-class children in the thirties seldom had enough to eat and received just enough education to equip them for routine work. A father out of work meant a family near starvation. My parents assumed that a working-class child was smaller than a middle-class child, for want of good food. Most of our parents came out of the Second World War determined to change all that.

And that is why the Attlee settlement of 1945–51 gave working people leisure, healthcare, education and security for the first time. In the fifties, older children, especially those at work, had disposable income. Young people became, for the first time, serious consumers, able to make choices and support those choices with cash.

We were the first generation for which university education was not a privilege of wealth. In the sixties, for the first time, proletarian and regional accents were heard throughout the British university system, and (except in a few ancient institutions) their owners were no longer made to feel out of place. We grew up at the time when – as he famously told the Labour Party conference – Neil Kinnock was 'the first Kinnock in a thousand generations' to have a university education. The idea that one might have to pay for education, at any level, seemed to us primitive.

How quickly these things get taken for granted! All previous generations thought of free health care as nothing short of miraculous, but the baby boomers casually assumed that it was the ordained order of things. It was not until the eighties that they started to see how privileged they were, and the National Union of Public Employees produced a T-shirt for them, proudly bearing the slogan 'Born in the NHS'.

Their parents and elder brothers and sisters had battled for health care, for education, for full employment and economic security. These battles having apparently been won, the baby boomers fought for, and won, the right to wear their hair long and to enjoy sex. Proud of having conquered our inherited inhibitions, in our foolishness we thought there was little else to conquer.

Our conviction that everything was easy received repeated boosts when the battlements of the fifties collapsed as the sixties generation approached them, without having to be stormed. National service ended in 1961. The contraceptive pill arrived. There was full employment. People stopped being so frightened of the boss.

So the baby boomers set about destroying the old certainties. These included some reactionary prejudices, but the certainties of the Attlee settlement – that no one should be allowed to die of a treatable illness, that no one should starve, that everyone should get education – were in the firing line at least as much as the certainty that the British class system was the right and natural order of things.

Even the certainties of post-Hitler liberalism – for example, that torture is always, under all circumstances, wrong – even these, if you are questioning everything, have to be questioned. So today, with the sixties certainty that there are no immutable truths about morality, elegant columnists and smartly tieless politicians of the baby boomer generation put up elaborate scenarios in which torture can be justified, and explain how a truly swinging government can be quite relaxed about the fact that Britain is now routinely complicit in torture; and I feel like pulling their fingernails out, very slowly, one by one.

While the philosophy of the sixties seemed progressive at the time, it was really symbolised by the television picture from 1968 of a flower child in a flowing skirt, dancing in a circle and singing, 'Down with police, down with income tax'. It was the direct intellectual predecessor of the Thatcherite view that there is no such thing as society. The children of the sixties were the parents of Thatcherism.

The baby boomers we remember are not the political reformers, but the millionaires. People like Richard Branson, who made his first fortune with Virgin Records; Tony Elliott, who founded Time Out; Felix Dennis, who became a multimillionaire magazine publisher; Greg Dyke, who made a fortune in commercial television before becoming BBC Director General. All these four came straight out of sixties rebellion, and Elliott and Dennis from sixties 'alternative' publishing. Dennis, now a powerful commercial mogul, was a sixties hero who went to prison in 1971 as a co-editor of Oz magazine after the longest conspiracy trial in history. There is no contradiction between his rebellion then and his eminence now. He has not sold out. There was nothing to sell.

The baby boomers destroyed their inheritance, and declined to show the same benevolence to the next generation as was shown to them. They benefited from the victory over Nazism and the Attlee settlement. As teenagers they had spare cash, and fun ways to spend it – things that their parents and grandparents could only dream of. As students they had grants, and the taxpayer picked up the bill for their education. A phrase often heard among their parents was: 'I want him [and increasingly her] to have the opportunities I never had.' Our parents may have grudged us our freedom, but they never grudged us their money, even though most had little enough of it.

Now the children of the sixties are parents, there seems to be a special venom in the loathing they show to their young. A popular car sticker around the turn of the century bore the gloating slogan 'Spending the kids' inheritance'. They sneer about their student children's penury. 'He [or she] has come home for another handout,' they say with theatrical weariness, yet the only reason their children have to come cap in hand for money is that the baby boomers climbed the ladder provided by the welfare state, then pulled it up after them.

At some level we baby boomers know we have squandered the inheritance our parents worked so hard to give us. It is as though the sixties generation decided that the freedom from worry which they had enjoyed was too good for their children, so they kicked away their children's legs, and now they sneer at them for being lame.

I see that, without noticing, I have started using 'we' instead of 'they'. I was one of the blessed: born in 1945, four days after VE Day and a month before Clement Attlee became Prime Minister. I recovered from polio in an NHS hospital; my tonsils lie, carefully preserved no doubt, in another one; and my parents did not have to live in terror of the hospital bill, as their parents would have done. I went to a new state grammar school at the age of eleven, and to a new university in the sixties, both of them monuments to the Attlee settlement.

As a student, my grant gave me enough to live on and I did not have to work in termtime, or beg from older relatives, or build up a mountain of debt, as my children have to do. I had small seminar groups, and tutors who encouraged my intellectual curiosity, since they were under no pressure to sell me another 'product' in the form of a useless but expensive further degree. I did not have to deal with the rapacious landlords my children meet today, who have grown to regard students as easy pickings. And I and my friends studied what we enjoyed, instead of doing what our children are told to do, which is to take whatever Gradgrind course will commend itself to employers.

It was the baby boomers who, in the sixties and the seventies, fought for greater intellectual freedom for students, and freedom from financial worry, which meant higher grants. (We took it for granted that we did not have to worry about paying for our tuition.) They were led by baby boomers like Jack Straw, who became president of the National Union of Students in 1969, and Charles Clarke, who got the same job in 1975. It was the baby boomers in government who took away these freedoms; and Clarke, as Education Secretary, who removed all grants and imposed tuition fees. The freedoms the baby boomers fought for, they deny to their children.

Schools, after a quick burst of sixties freedom, are being sent back to the fifties as fast as possible. The sixties generation in government has brought back the school uniforms it once rejected, the religious control of schools it rejected, and the rote learning it rejected, in the form of a rigid national curriculum and a punishing regime of testing.

Schools have been turned into education factories, forcing grounds in which a set of predetermined information is crammed into young heads, and in which there is no place for flights of fantasy or inspirational teaching. And the penalties for truanting are growing, with police now routinely frogmarching truants to their school. One of the arguments used in favour of school uniforms is that they help the police to recognise those who ought to be at school. We are forcing our children into prison uniform so they will be instantly recognisable when they scale their prison walls.

It is as though the children of the sixties decided that the freedom they enjoyed was too good for their children. Unlike the baby boomers, their children leave university burdened with debt. The sixties generation reinstalled the deference it rejected. Now they are in charge, politicians of the sixties generation realise that deference can be helpful to governments. So they are trying to revive it – only they call it 'respect', just as their parents did.

They decline to treat the young with the respect they themselves successfully demanded when they were young. Here's a straw in the wind. In the early days of University Challenge, at the end of the sixties, presenter Bamber Gascoigne gave his young teams respect, kindness and understanding. In the revived University Challenge, Jeremy Paxman sneers at them, bullies them, and holds them up to ridicule. It would not have been accepted when the baby boomer Paxman was a student, but the young are much less powerful now.

There is a generation war emerging. Wealth is being sucked up the age ladder, and the young have to struggle harder than they did before. Opinion polls show that the now elderly baby boomers will use their increasing voting power – for they constitute a growing segment of the electorate – to ensure a comfortable old age for themselves. When the baby boomers were young, they believed society could afford student grants; now they are old, they think it can afford pensions. There is nothing like impending and perhaps impoverished old age to remind a person that there is, after all, such a thing as society. They risk trampling on the impoverished generations that come after, and there is plenty of evidence that those generations resent it.

Almost none of the baby boomers learned to value the extraordinary legacy they had, and today most of them sneer at it. The right say that it was irresponsible of our postwar leaders to put the nation to the expense of educating, housing, employing and feeding the poor, the old and the young, for the nation could not afford it. The left say that Attlee betrayed the working class by not going further. Neither of them care about what was achieved. The right does not want to defend it, and the left cannot be bothered.

In place of the great ideals of the Attlee government, the baby boomers idealised youth and modernity. They created a society where the ultimate good lay in being new, and young, and modern, and new, especially new, which ironically is why there will be no more baby boomer Prime Ministers after Gordon Brown. The two Prime Ministers from the generation of 1918 who changed the world – Clement Attlee, who created the welfare state, and Harold Macmillan, who dismantled the British Empire – were both aged sixty-two when they got the job. The children of the sixties produced just two Prime Ministers, Tony Blair and Gordon Brown. Blair's predecessor John Major is two years too old to be a baby boomer, and all Prime Ministers after Brown will certainly be too young, for today everyone seems sure that sixty-two is far too old. The fact that the baby boomers are now all too old ever again to be trusted with the nation's affairs is entirely their fault. When they were young, they created a cult of youth, and now they are old they would like to undo it, but they can't.

The baby boomers had everything. We thought the world could only get better. Our parents watched us and shook their heads, saying, 'It will end in tears.' And it has.

1. How the baby boomers got their freedom: 1945–51

No generation has ever been as free as the baby boomers. They were freer than any of their ancestors, not just from oppression, but from poverty and ignorance, fear and illness. They were free because in 1942 Lord Beveridge called for a serious assault on 'the five giants', and in 1945 Clement Attlee's government launched that assault.

The year of the Beveridge Report also saw the first rise in the birthrate since 1880. Three years earlier, when the Second World War began in 1939, it had gone down to sixteen births per thousand of the population. A small increase in 1942 presaged the real baby boom, which began in 1945 and peaked in 1947 with a birthrate of 20.7 per 1,000.[1] It was an indication of optimism. In 1942 people were daring to hope, and in 1945 were starting to believe, that we were going to create a world fit for our children to live in: a world free, not just of the Nazis, but of the poverty that disfigured thirties Britain.

We have all seen those newsreel shots of wildly optimistic celebrations on Victory in Europe day – VE Day, 8 May 1945: people dancing in the London streets, climbing lamp-posts, singing. They were the parents of the baby boomers. And we know something that Prime Minister Winston Churchill and King George VI, watching benevolently from a balcony high above, did not know: that our parents were not just celebrating the end of Nazism, and of fear of invasion; they were also celebrating what they were about to do with their votes. Churchill's status as a national hero would not stop them voting him out of office. In the general election that was to follow, they were going to issue the sharpest call for a new and fairer society that Britain had ever heard.

Even Labour leader Clement Attlee was not expecting outright victory, and Winston Churchill never understood what had happened. When Clementine Churchill tried to console him by suggesting his defeat might be a blessing in disguise, he replied that it was 'a remarkably effective disguise'. Three years later, he wrote bitterly of how, with 'all our enemies having surrendered unconditionally or being about to do so, I was immediately dismissed by the British electorate from all further conduct of their affairs.'[2] But they were not dismissing Churchill so much as the Tories who had given them starvation and injustice in the thirties; and they were demanding a better world for their children by giving Attlee a landslide parliamentary majority of 146 seats. Attlee was to deliver their legacy to the baby boomers.

For the first (and last) time, two Communists were elected to Parliament, and Communist leader Harry Pollitt came within 972 votes of winning a third seat in Rhondda East. If Britain had had a system of proportional representation in 1945, the Communist Party's 100,000 votes would have given it enough seats to be a real power-broker, quite apart from the fact that several of Labour's new MPs were close to the Communist Party.

The Communist Party's brief popularity in 1945 was not just the result of Britain fighting the Second World War alongside the Red Army. The Communists had disavowed violent revolution in a new manifesto, *The British Road to Socialism*, and its popularity was a powerful sign that people had radical hopes of their new government. Great expectations were riding on Attlee's narrow shoulders.

Such expectations are often disappointed. People had radical expectations of Ramsay MacDonald in 1929, and of Tony Blair in 1997, and learned quickly not to hold their breath. But in 1945 the Labour Party was led by Britain's quietest and steeliest Prime Minister, and he had around him a small group of remarkable politicians, determined to seize the once-in-a-generation chance to change the world.

On 26 July 1945 Violet Attlee drove her husband to Buckingham Palace in the small family Hillman Minx and waited outside, just as Churchill's chauffeur had waited outside in the Rolls half an hour before when he resigned his office. Attlee and King George VI were both shy, awkward and understated men. 'I've won the election,' said Attlee, and the King replied, 'I know, I heard it on the six o'clock news.' It did not sound like the tumbrils, but it was.

Attlee came to power at the worst possible time to start spending great sums of money on improving the lives of the people. Britain had a war-devastated economy. Bombing had made thousands of people homeless. Daily life reflected the nation's poverty, even for those who were relatively well off. 'I travelled last Sunday to Newcastle upon Tyne,' wrote a prosperous journalist, J. L. Hodson, in 1945.

The journey which in peacetime took four hours now took eight and a quarter. No food on the train. No cup of tea to be got at the stops because the queues . . . were impossibly long. At Newcastle . . . no taxi to be got. My hotel towel is about the size of a pocket handkerchief, the soap tablet is worn to the thinness of paper, my bed sheets are torn.[3]

Things we take for granted were very hard to obtain. 'Her mother used to cut up newspapers into squares to hang on a piece of string in the outside privy,' reports the writer Julie Summers of a woman who was young in 1945. 'Her aunt, however, who was a little grander, used to use pinking shears to give her squares a more pleasing outline.'[4]

And in August 1945, just one week after Japan surrendered, the Americans dealt a final, crippling economic blow. They ended Lend-lease, the arrangement under which the USA supplied materials to Britain for which Britain was unable to pay. No one had imagined that it would be withdrawn so abruptly. Without Lend-lease Britain could not feed its people or pay its debts. It would, eventually, starve.

Lord Maynard Keynes, Britain's leading economist, was sent to Washington to negotiate a loan, and returned, not with the £5 billion loan he had hoped for, but £3.75 billion, on very harsh terms indeed. Britain had to agree to make sterling convertible to dollars on demand, which was likely to lead to a run on the pound and a financial crisis – as it did, three years later.

A lesser government would have taken the withdrawal of Lend-lease as an excuse to postpone or water down the great reforms that Labour had been elected to carry out, but Attlee knew that he had to seize the mood and slay the five giants, and he set himself a deadline of 5 July 1948.

He gave the task of slaying Want to Social Security Minister Jim Griffiths. Before 1945 there was an element of punishment about such relief as was available. If a father was out of work, his children might be saved from absolute starvation, but not from the many diseases, like rickets, resulting from undernourishment; and not from misery and humiliation. Griffiths's task was to ensure that benefits were universal, and that when people fell on hard times, they should not be driven to despair. His 1946 National Insurance Act for the first time insured every person in the land against sickness, unemployment and retirement, as well as providing widows' benefits, maternity benefits and death grants, with allowances for dependants. It embraced every person in the country who was over school age, but under pensionable age. A further piece of legislation, the National Assistance Act, was designed to catch those who, for whatever reason, fell through the system. The intention was that no one would ever again fall below a basic subsistence level, and it removed the fear of starvation from most of the baby boomer generation for the whole of their lives.

Ellen Wilkinson, Minister of Education, was given the task of slaying Ignorance. Wilkinson set to work to implement the 1944 Education Act, ignoring all the many voices that counselled delay in the light of the economic circumstances. The Act specified that education should be free and universal, and she raised the school leaving age to fifteen. It all required a huge school building programme and the training of 35,000 new teachers in a hurry. She also needed a rapid expansion of university places, which increased from 50,246 in 1938/9 to 76,764 in 1947/8.

She introduced free school milk. By October 1946 more than 90 per cent of all school children were getting their third of a pint of free milk, in those funny little bottles that became a part of the childhood memories of all baby boomers. 'Free milk will be provided in Hoxton and Shoreditch, in Eton and Harrow. What more social equality can you have than that?' she told the 1946 Labour Party conference, but of course free school milk undeniably made more difference in Hoxton and Shoreditch than it did in Eton and Harrow. In places where children did not get an adequate diet, or left home without breakfast, it contributed greatly to the defeat of childhood illnesses. Generations of poor children grew up stronger and healthier because of this one small and not very expensive measure. Before the war, private-school children were noticeably taller, healthier and stronger than the poorest state-school children, because they were properly fed. In the fifties this was so no longer, and the reason was free school meals and school milk.

Wilkinson's principle that everyone, rich and poor, should have it was what underlay the welfare state as the Attlee government envisaged it. The millionaire is entitled to his state old age pension, because he is a citizen. The only alternative to universal benefits was the means test, which caused great hardship and bitterness. This principle of universality was the first to be abandoned by the baby boomer generation in government, half a century later. And free school milk was the first of the Attlee government's measures to be clawed back by Margaret Thatcher, who abolished it when she was Education Secretary in Edward Heath's 1970–74 government.

Ellen Wilkinson avoided the extra battle necessary to implement the 1942 Labour Party conference resolution in favour of what we now call comprehensive schools. Instead the government created a three-tier system of grammar schools, technical schools and secondary modern schools, and the Eleven plus examination would decide which of the three each child should attend.

Wilkinson didn't like the system she created, but calculated that a comprehensive system was a political battle too far. She was appalled by the idea of dividing children at eleven into successes and failures, saying privately, 'The stigma of lower IQs should not attach itself to any particular institution.' She worried that history might not be taught outside grammar schools, caricaturing it as: 'Don't worry how we got India, let's go and do some nice work at the forge.'[5] But she saw the three-tier system as a necessary compromise if she was to get the rest of her package through.

Disease was to be confronted by Nye Bevan. Bevan nationalised hospitals, saying that if the nation did not own them, the Minister could not provide a National Health Service – he could only exhort others to do so – and he could not guarantee the right of a sick person to a hospital bed. Already between 80 and 90 per cent of voluntary sector hospitals' money came from public funds, so why should they not be accountable? In the teeth of furious opposition from the Conservatives and the British Medical Association, and despite its massive expense, his Bill received the Royal Assent on 6 November 1946, to come into operation on 5 July 1948.

The NHS was instantly so popular that both the BMA and the Conservative Party were soon claiming that they had been in favour of it all along. The infant baby boomers were taken to the doctor for cuts and bruises, coughs and colds, and were treated. Very quickly, people old enough to remember the thirties knew they would never permit a government to take them back to a time before the National Health Service.

Baby boomers still expect treatment when we feel we need it. We were the first generation to expect this; and if it is left to us, we might be the last. Most of the baby boomers were born in the NHS, so you would expect it to be safe in their hands. Yet since 1979 it has been tinkered with in ways that would horrify Bevan; and recently an influential thinktank, the Social Market Foundation, proposed a £20 fee for each visit to the doctor.

Bevan was also responsible for the assault on Squalor, providing housing in a country where thousands of homes had been destroyed in all major cities; where thousands of people still lived in slums; where a market-led housing boom in the thirties had produced hundreds of thousands of middle-class homes for sale, but nowhere for slum-dwellers to move to; where there was a chronic shortage of building materials; and where the baby boom was just starting. He made local authorities the engine of his housing policy. The postwar council estates are still the best social housing Britain ever produced, because Bevan insisted on higher standards than his successors thought affordable. The mean little houses and flats in tower blocks which now often pass for social housing were a long way in the future.

Squalor, like Ignorance, was not slain, but it was wounded. Many of the baby boomers grew up on Bevan's council estates. If they had been born a generation earlier, they would have been children in grim urban slums; and if a generation later, in terrifying tower blocks. They were indeed a blessed generation.

On 5 July 1948, five new acts became operational: Bevan's NHS Act and Town and Country Planning Act, Griffiths's National Insurance and National Assistance Acts, and the Children Act, providing for children cared for by the state. Clement Attlee broadcast to the nation on the radio:

> Tomorrow there will come into operation the most comprehensive system
> of social security ever introduced into any country . . . When I first went
> to work in East London, apart from what was done by voluntary organisa-
> tions and by private charities . . . the only provision for the citizen unable

to work through sickness, unemployment or old age was that given by the Poor Law . . . The Poor Law was designed to be, and indeed it was, the last refuge of the destitute.

The new Acts were based, he said, on a new principle: that 'we must combine together to meet contingencies with which we cannot cope as individual citizens.' They were 'part of a general plan and they fit in with each other . . . They are comprehensive and available to every citizen. They give security to all members of the family.' The NHS 'gives a complete cover for health by pooling the nation's resources and paying the bill collectively.' The words read strangely today, because we do not remember what life was like when the only relief available was provided by voluntary organisations and private charities.

The fifth giant, Idleness, or unemployment as it is more commonly known, had been slain for the duration of the war, but would demobilisation bring it back? After the First World War the streets had been full of former soldiers who had given their health for their country, and whose country could not even offer them the chance to work and feed their families. It did not happen after the Second World War. The government got about ten million people out of wartime jobs without unemployment ever going above 3 per cent.

In October 1945 Chancellor Hugh Dalton's first budget reduced the very high wartime level of taxation, but the tax cuts were strongly in favour of the worst off. Dalton took two and a half million people in the lower income groups out of tax altogether, and substantially increased tax for the wealthiest – at its highest level, income tax reached 19s 6d (97½p) in the pound. He introduced a profits tax and raised death duties. A second budget, in April 1946, increased substantially the sum spent on education, began the payment of family allowances and put £10 million into Development Areas that suffered from high levels of unemployment. Under Attlee and Dalton, the state played Robin Hood, robbing the rich to give to the poor. It had never done so before. It has never done so since.

*

Part of the reason it has never done so since is the relationship with the USA after the withdrawal of Lend-lease and the American loan.

American disapproval of Britain's welfare state mattered from the start. In the 1945 postwar settlement, the USA, the Soviet Union and Britain were referred to as 'the big three' but it was mere politeness: 'the big two and a quarter' would be more accurate.

The decision to withdraw Lend-lease and force Britain to pay on the nail for everything supplied by the USA was taken so quickly and unexpectedly that two ships about to leave New York had to turn round and go home. During the loan negotiations, senators grumbled that Washington might be subsidising socialism in Britain, while American newspapers jeered at the threadbare Brits and their begging bowl, presenting them as sponging socialists crawling to Uncle Sam so that they could feather-bed their people. Foreign Secretary Ernest Bevin had to stifle his fury at headlines in the American press calling Britain a nation of 'cry-babies', while Attlee told Parliament with characteristic understatement but uncharacteristic bitterness: 'If the role assigned to us [during the war] had been to expand our exports, we should, of course, be in an immeasurably stronger position than we are today.' The USA, he reminded MPs, had expanded its exports during the war.

The Americans made clear to the British negotiators that a nation deeply in debt to the USA should not oppose Washington in important foreign policy matters. The US Secretary of State, James Byrnes, presented Ernest Bevin with a list of places around the world where the US would like to have bases, implying that the loan depended on Britain's agreement. Thus Britain's financial problems merged with its foreign policy, and the two have remained in unholy alliance ever since.

Thus was set the tone of the special relationship, which was always akin to the relationship between a football and a boot; or, perhaps more accurately, to what a writer of the time, E. V. Rieu, described as the relationship between the lynx and the lion:

> So when the Lion steals his food
> Or kicks him from behind,
> He smiles, of course – but oh, the rude
> Remarks that cross his mind!

The British followed their government. Men who were young and fancy-free during the Second World War still smarted from the way that richer, more sophisticated and better-fed GIs tended to get their pick of the girls, and liked to think of America as a dangerously powerful child. 'The trouble with Americans is that they're overfed, oversexed and over here,' they said, and they quoted Oscar Wilde's line that the USA had gone 'from barbarism to decadence without going through the intermediate stage of civilisation.'

This indicates envy and just a little fear, but also a certain defiance and a sense of innate superiority. The generation that fought the war still thought it had something to teach the Americans. And even after the American loan, Attlee and his ministers were trying to maintain an independent line, though with considerable difficulty.

That was what lay at the heart of the government's decision to pursue an independent atomic weapon. Ernest Bevin put the argument with his usual bluntness and disregard for syntax at a cabinet committee in 1946:

> We've got to have this. I don't mind for myself, but I don't want any other Foreign Secretary of this country to be talked at, or to, by the Secretary of State in the United States, as I have just had in my discussions with Mr Byrnes. We've got to have this thing over here, whatever it costs. We've got to have a bloody union jack flying on top of it.[6]

The British sense of innate superiority was enhanced in 1950, when Attlee may have prevented President Harry Truman from making a dangerous ass of himself. Truman had made a statement that sounded as though he was giving General MacArthur, the outspoken American general who led the international force fighting against the Communist North Korea, permission to use the atom bomb there. Attlee instantly flew to Washington, where he and Truman engaged in a lot of superficial banter about their shared experience of fighting in the trenches during the First World War, with Major Attlee and Captain Truman singing First World War songs together after dinner at the British embassy, including a chorus of 'It's a Long Way to Tipperary'. That may have been the wily Attlee's way of getting what he wanted from Truman. The bomb was not used; the Americans neither withdrew from Korea nor broadened the conflict into a global war with China; and eventually Truman fired MacArthur. Those were the three things Attlee wanted. It was probably the last time a British Prime Minister had a decisive influence in Washington.

Things are very different now. Baby boomers in government since 1997 seem to have decided that when Washington says jump, they can only ask how high; while baby boomers in general are divided between those who admire America and those who despise it. The faint, very British feeling of genteel, threadbare superiority has quite disappeared. And this is odd, because the last instalment of the loan has been paid off, and in 2003 Britain was living in good economic times, but that year a baby boomer Prime Minister, Tony Blair, went to war in Iraq at the behest of Washington and against the wishes of his own people.

*

In the eighties, as the baby boomers were becoming fat and powerful and middle-aged, it became fashionable to see the Attlee years in the same light as the press at the time saw them. The new analysis was that Britain's own economic policy failures led to Keynes being sent to Washington to 'cadge' American 'handouts'. The phrase comes from the New Right historian Correlli Barnett, who cannot keep the sneer out of his prose when he writes of the NHS. 'It resembled a military plan for, say, the Normandy invasion which simply left out such calculations as the number of divisions needed to overcome the enemy defences, the number of vessels needed,' he writes, and he asks if Aneurin Bevan, 'being a true romantic, simply shut his eyes to the Cruel Real World in pursuit of his vision of the Brave New World?'

Bevan's colleagues, says Barnett, shared his 'innocent faith in socialism' and even the Conservatives had become 'pallidly pink New Jerusalemers themselves'. Bevan was 'convinced like a Nietzschean superman that his personal powers placed him among a natural elite' and the NHS was 'a plan of military organisation produced by a general staff for a great offensive, commencing with the role of the supreme commander: "General responsibility for the service will rest with the Minister of Health."'[7]

This sort of rubbish was talked by the baby boomers in the eighties. Bevan and Attlee had their answer when people talked of the cost of the welfare state, and Attlee gave it during the parliamentary debate on the National Insurance Bill:

The question is asked: can we afford it? Supposing the answer is no, what does that really mean? It really means that the sum total of the goods produced and the services rendered by the people of this country is not sufficient to provide for all our people at all times, the very modest standard of life that is represented by the sums of money set out in the Second Schedule to this Bill. I cannot believe that our national productivity is so low, that our willingness to work is so feeble, or that we can submit to the world that the masses of our people must be condemned to penury.

It was a good argument: very nearly good enough to win Attlee a full second term in the teeth of the sort of media criticism that makes Correlli Barnett look reasonable. Attlee won the general election narrowly in 1950 but without a big enough majority to survive, called a second election in 1951 and polled more votes than the Conservatives. But the distribution of his votes was wrong for the British electoral system: he piled up votes in safe Labour seats, and Churchill came back to Downing Street with a majority of twenty-five.

These two general elections showed the biggest voter turnout Britain has seen since 1945 – an almost incredible 83.9 per cent in 1950 and 82.6 per cent in 1951. The turnout at the 1950 election, the first time the people had had the chance to cast a verdict on the welfare state, was 7.5 per cent higher than at any of the elections between the wars, and 10.5 per cent more than in 1945. (The 1945 figure was depressed because the register was not very accurate – the real increase is probably more like 5 per cent.)[8] After 1950 the turnout started decreasing, and it dropped like a stone after 1997 when the baby boomers took control. Turnout was 59.4 per cent in 2001.

People voted to give their verdict on the Attlee settlement because it was clear that the votes counted. The welfare state helped make people aware of politics, because it was a direct political solution to an obvious problem. And it had been a bumpy ride. There has never been a government like Attlee's. In places where the status quo reigned, it was a hated and reviled government. Most Americans loathed what Attlee had done. The well-known American journalist Emily Hahn wrote in the *Evening Standard* during the 1950 election a veiled warning that the USA might not wish to tolerate it: 'I wonder whether it has occurred to Mr Attlee that this is a rough and naughty world, and that quite a lot of it is outside England. He talked as though England could decide to be a socialist state all by itself . . .'[9]

Many of the wealthiest in the land hated it, even most of those who pretended to be rebels. Attlee-style social democracy, wrote Harold Nicolson, was 'the only possible antidote to communism' but he added, in a passage that sounds today as though it comes from the sixties: 'I do not like the Labour Party. I am a mixture of an aristocrat and a Bohemian. The bedintness [this was an expression from his wife's relatives the Sackvilles, denoting the attitudes and manners of the lower middle class] of the Labour people is as repugnant to me as is their gentility.'[10]

West End theatre audiences craved the restoration of what they saw as a proper balance between the classes, and were rewarded in 1948 with William Douglas Home's *The Chiltern Hundreds*, a vacuous comedy that showed an uppity socialist defeated in an election by a Conservative butler. (Message: real working-class people, the salt of the earth, respect nobility and know their place.) No one could ever have imagined that within a decade, London theatre would be the place for literary innovation.

The Attlee settlement left no one neutral, and that is part of the reason why people turned out en masse to vote for or against it. Poverty and its antidote, the welfare state, had helped politicise the nation.

So did the direct, passionate political literature of the time. 'There can be no greater contrast,' wrote left-wing author Andrew Davies in 1984,

> between books such as *Why You Should Be a Socialist*, *Guilty Men*, *Your MP*, *The Trial of Mussolini*, *Why Not Trust the Tories?* and others published by Gollancz and Penguin Specials in the 1930s and the 1940s, and many of the 'left' books of today which use specialised and elitist language.[11]

Despite everything that anyone could throw at it during the lifetime of the Attlee government, the welfare state became so popular among people who remembered the hungry thirties that no politician dared confront it. The Conservatives ruled for thirteen years after 1951 and made no attempt to destroy the welfare state, though they tinkered with it in ways that enraged Aneurin Bevan. But now, as the baby boomers relinquish power, the welfare state is in greater danger than it has known before. If you want to see how bad things are, try reading with modern eyes what Beveridge told a meeting in Caxton Hall in 1943, and see how dreadfully dated it looks – and how utterly civilised it is:

> My Report as a whole is intended to give effect to what I regard as a peculiarly British idea: the idea of a national minimum wage, which we learnt from the trade unions and have embodied in the Trade Board acts, is necessary but isn't sufficient. There is wanted also a minimum income for subsistence when wages fail for any reason: a minimum of provision for children; a minimum of health, of housing, or education.[12]

Beveridge spoke to a nation that remembered what poverty and starvation were like. The baby boomers did not remember, and did not trouble to find out. If we know no history, we may be fated to force our children to relive it.

2. When we were very young: 1950–56

Decades have their own characters. We know what we mean when we talk of the Roaring Twenties or the Swinging Sixties, however simplistic these descriptions are. And anyone who was there knows what I mean by the frustrated fifties.

Until the start of the fifties, the immediate excitement of the postwar years, the victory over the Nazis and the sheer boldness and effrontery of what Clement Attlee's government did between 1945 and 1951, made a reasonable substitute for the things that were prohibited by postwar austerity: choice, colour and the instincts of youth. But after Attlee fell in 1951, Britain had the austerity without the excitement.

The excitement and radicalism that carried Attlee to power in 1945 were spent. The Communist Party of Great Britain, whose two seats in the 1945 election were such a powerful signal of the desire for change, was decisively swept out of Parliament in 1950. The fifties, at least until 1956, were buttoned-down and conformist. The baby boomers' earliest years were lived in an atmosphere of repression that made a lasting effect on them, even when, years later, they thought they had shaken it off. Those who are too young to remember them find it hard to imagine a world in which it was illegal to buy *Lady Chatterley's Lover*, to get an abortion, to have a homosexual relationship, or to stage a play without first obtaining permission from the Lord Chamberlain. It had, said Dennis Potter, who grew up in the fifties, a 'great greyness', a 'feeling of the flatness and bleakness of everyday England'.

Patriotism enjoyed an Indian summer between 1951 and 1956, for it had been in slow decline during the twenties and thirties. The first six years of the decade were the last years in which people used terms like 'patriotism' and 'proud to be British'. Britain's empire was a source of pride. Even though India had been given her independence in 1947, fifties schoolchildren could still be shown a map of the world with the Empire coloured in red, making red the dominant colour. It was still the empire upon which the sun never set. Rudyard Kipling's poetry enjoyed a modest revival – he was seen as the poet of empire, and his later, darker work tended to be ignored. I remember an English master reading Gunga Din to my class in a great vibrant voice:

Of all them blackfaced crew
The finest man I knew
Was our regimental bhisti, Gunga Din . . .

It was just before mass immigration redefined Britishness: the country was still overwhelmingly white, and the black and brown people who populated the Empire were still, as Kipling called them, 'the White Man's burden':

Your new-caught sullen people
Half devil and half child.

It seemed natural to Britons in the first half of the fifties that their country should decide who was, and who was not, fitted to govern far-flung parts of the world of which we knew little. The 1953 coup in Iran, which overthrew the democratically elected Prime Minister Mohammed Mossadeq and replaced him with the cruel and tyrannical Shah, was engineered by Britain and the USA; it has, of course, brought nothing but trouble to the baby boomer generation in government in the twenty-first century, for it led to the rise of militant Islam and the present clerical regime.

With patriotism went respect and deference. Ordinary people may have thought their country powerful, but they did not expect to share in that power. You didn't argue with what were, without any irony, called your 'elders and betters'. 'Things aren't that bad, and even if they are, there's nothing we can do about it,' says a young man about to go and fight in Suez, in John Osborne's 1957 play The Entertainer. And of course they were that bad: the young man was killed in a useless, immoral war which he and his friends would not have dreamed of questioning. His elders and betters condemned him to a pointless death. No wonder Osborne, in Look Back in Anger, called it a world in which 'nobody thinks, nobody cares.' And if they did think and care, they were sure they were wasting their time, because ordinary people could not change anything.

The death of King George VI in 1953 was greeted in humble homes with the sort of grief that even the death of his father George V in 1936 had not occasioned. Greg Dyke, who was brought up in Hayes, in west London, wrote fifty years later:

> For my parents the King represented something special because of the symbolic role he played in the East End of London during the Second World War. On the day of the King's funeral they both went to stand by the railway bridge in nearby Southall as the train carrying his body to Windsor passed by. They thought it important that they pay their respects and I can remember to this day my dad leaving in his best suit and trilby hat and my mother in her best dress. They were dressed to the nines just to stand by a railway bridge. This was still the age of respect.[1]

The humble Dyke family of Hayes were not alone. Prime Minister Winston Churchill and Opposition Leader Clement Attlee both wept tears of real grief when they heard about the death of their sovereign. But while the highest in the land may have shared the Dykes' grief, they did not share their deference. Class and money bought exemption from the most repressive features of the decade. Members of the upper classes in the fifties could get a safe abortion, although the poor and the middle-class had to take their chances among the illegal backstreet abortionists. The upper classes could carry on affairs, both heterosexual and homosexual, but the middle and working classes could not. The rich could get a copy of *Lady Chatterley's Lover*, or a rapid divorce. The point of the ban on Lawrence's book really was, as the crown lawyer in the *Lady Chatterley* case put it, that it was not a book you might wish your wife or servant to read.

For the fifties were remarkably tolerant about the peccadilloes of the celebrity, political and upper classes, so long as these were conducted discreetly. It was well known in political circles that Harold Macmillan's wife, Lady Dorothy Macmillan, the daughter of a duke, had for years had an extra-marital affair with Macmillan's fellow Conservative MP Robert Boothby, and the fourth and youngest of the Macmillan children, Sarah, born in 1930, was biologically Boothby's child. In a middle-class family, this would have been an intolerable embarrassment. But in the circles in which they moved, it does not seem to have affected the way in which Macmillan, Boothby or Lady Dorothy were regarded, and was no obstacle to Macmillan becoming Prime Minister as 1957 opened.

Britain's most respected actor, Laurence Olivier, was probably conducting affairs with both Noel Coward and Danny Kaye, and, although they were not reported in newspapers, they were widely rumoured. The Labour MP Tom Driberg's many homosexual affairs were the subject of tolerant jokes among his parliamentary colleagues, none of whom seems to have thought of using them against him. Yet among the middle classes it was an age of extraordinary reticence about sex. The sixties did not invent liberalism, but they did democratise it.

The early fifties were a time, I suspect – there is no way this can be proved – when more people married as virgins than at almost any other time, before or since, for its prudery was new. Compared with the fifties, the two decades between the world wars had been years of joyful sexual liberation. Prudery came with austerity, and rationing, and bad cooking. The wedding-night meal for Ian McEwan's newlyweds in his 2007 novel *On Chesil Beach*, set in the early fifties, begins with 'a slice of melon decorated by a single glazed cherry' while 'in the corridor, in silver dishes on candle-heated plate warmers, waited slices of long-ago roasted beef in a thickened gravy, soft boiled vegetables, and potatoes of a bluish hue.' With a flourish, Edward gives Florence his sticky cherry, and she eats it flirtatiously. 'If only eating a sticky cherry was all that was required.' For the real dread is not the meal, bad as it is, but the nameless horror that she knows is supposed to follow it.

Edward and Florence were 'young, educated, and both virgins on this, their wedding night, and they lived in a time when a conversation about sexual difficulties was plainly impossible.' Of course the subsequent coupling is so complete a disaster that it taints their love and destroys their lives.

My mother, who was twenty in 1929, used to say that the sixties generation acted as though it had invented sex. Her scabrous thirties jokes were far too improper for the buttoned-down fifties, and it was only she, who was capable of being a very genteelly improper lady, who still told them – which is why almost nobody apart from me now knows the Little Audrey jokes, whose punchline always began: 'Little Audrey laughed and laughed.' Here's a sample:

The newly married couple in the hotel didn't come down to breakfast and people nudged each other. They didn't come down to lunch and people started to look puzzled. They didn't come down to supper and people started to worry. But little Audrey laughed and laughed. She knew who'd put glue in the Vaseline.

The reason the sixties thought it had invented sex was that in the fifties nobody spoke about it.

*

The class system, like deference and prudery, had an Indian summer in the early fifties. In September 1955 Nancy Mitford, in an article for *Encounter* magazine, defined 'U' and 'non-U', asserting the distinction between the upper and upper middle classes on the one hand, and the middle classes on the other. It was the same snobbish distinction that Harold Nicolson voiced when he talked about his horror of lower middle-class gentility, of 'bedintness'. John Betjeman, very much a man of the upper middle class, joined in the mockery of lower middle-class gentility in his 1954 poem 'How To Get On In Society':

> Are the requisites all in the toilet?
> The frills round the cutlets can wait
> Till the girl has replenished the cruets
> And switched on the logs in the grate.

Requisites (such a prudish lower middle-class euphemism), cruets, cutlets with frills on, a fake open fire – it was enough to send Mitford or Nicolson rushing for sanctuary to the ancestral home of an aristocratic friend.

The much-mocked middle class felt impelled to try to keep up appearances. 'I definitely think of myself as middle class,' a woman civil servant told Mass Observation at the start of the decade.

> I had a typical middle-class education (small private school and secondary school). I have a middle-class job and I live in a middle-class district. But none of these things would make me middle-class in themselves. If I had

been clever enough to get a higher post or profession, or rebellious enough to choose a more attractive manual job, I should not thereby have changed my class . . . Income has something to do with it but it is not the deciding factor.[2]

Class, she seems to be saying, is indefinable, but absolute. You know what class you are, and that's all there is to it. Other Mass Observation quotes from the period, from people of all classes, confirm this. Middle-class men and women talked openly of 'servants' and even the phrase 'below stairs' still meant something. They did not keep servants, as they might have done between the wars, but they still talked as though one day, when the war had been forgotten and the welfare state had withered away, they might have them once again.

The class system was back with a vengeance, and the baby boomers were never able to defeat it. Most of them, whether from a right-wing standpoint or a left-wing one, claimed they were building a classless society, but they were doing nothing of the kind. They all knew what class they were born into, and what class they became, and whether they were moving up or down in the class system, and they still do. In the sixties, it became a little easier to move between the classes, and people no longer talked openly about it. The middle classes (though not the upper classes) became ashamed of it. Class was open in the early fifties. Since then, it has become a dirty little secret. Nice people, who in the fifties would have put requisites in their toilets and frills on their cutlets, in the sixties started to avoid all mention of class.

People even dressed according to their class. Dress in the early fifties was dull and grey: partly because of the war and austerity, partly because there were few consumer choices, and partly because of the spirit of the times. 'Short back and sides,' a man would say as he walked into the barber, and it would have been unmanly to say anything else. If he was middle-class he wore a grey suit, baggy trousers with turnups, white shirt and a tie, Brylcreemed his hair and thought himself lucky to have the chance. There was a fashion rebellion of sorts: the first recorded use of the phrase 'Teddy boy' was in March 1954. But Teddy Boys were in and of the working class, and demonised by the press in much the same way that 'hoodie' is now.[3] In public schools and universities, tweed jackets and grey flannel trousers adorned even the most radical male torso.

Wartime food rationing persisted until 1954. Few people went hungry but there was not a lot of food about, and most of it was of poor quality and badly cooked. The baby boomers' childhood diet was adequate, but uninteresting. The only take-aways were fish and chips. Sweets were on ration. 'Waste not want not,' the grownups would say as they tried to coax the last little bit of soggy cabbage into us. Like most of my generation, I knew nothing different, and I was never hungry, though I grew very bored with food. The big treat of my early childhood – and everyone who was a child in the early fifties remembers it with pleasure – was a packet of crisps with a little blue bag of salt in it. You dug around for your salt bag, which was simply a piece of blue paper twisted shut; you untwisted it, and sprayed it on the crisps. Ready salted crisps never matched it.

We grew to like the food we were served, because there was nothing better. To this day I will guiltily buy a loaf of white processed bread or a pork pie, and try to hide the contraband comestible from my disapproving family. Grownup baby boomers, with sophisticated culinary tastes, are still secretly children of the bland and boring fifties.

The spirit of the times was spirit. Alcohol was the drug of choice, and it was drunk discreetly, as befits a buttoned-down generation, but deeply, as befits a frustrated one. Alcohol consumption was much greater in the fifties than it has been for most of the postwar period. 'Pink gin' (gin with a few drops of angostura bitters shaken into it) was really a way of gentrifying neat gin – 'mother's ruin' – and respectable ladies guzzled it daintily. Winston Churchill, who became Prime Minister for the second time in 1951 at the age of seventy-seven, was still regularly consuming a bottle of white wine with breakfast, followed by a flow of wine, whisky and brandy throughout the day. Hitler had called him a depraved drunk. Today he would be called an alcoholic, and he would be drummed out of public life long before he rose to be Prime Minister.

Descriptions of mammoth drinking sessions figure large in fifties literature, two of the most memorable being in Kingsley Amis's *Lucky Jim* and John Braine's *Room at the Top*. It mirrored their authors: Amis, John Osborne and many others drank what today would seem prodigious amounts, and a typical entry in Evelyn Waugh's diary reads: 'Tuesday, a drunken day; lunched at Beefsteak . . . Drinking in White's most of the afternoon. Then to Beefsteak where I got drunk . . . Then to St James's for another bottle of champagne.'[4]

Northerners spent their holidays in Blackpool, and southerners spread themselves along the Essex coast, or, for a special adventure, went to the West Country. My family usually went to the Essex sailing town of Burnham-on-Crouch. My parents could not sail, but they would have liked to, so I mostly watched the estuary, and badgered to be taken yet again to nearby Maldon, where there was a pond with paddle boats, and a swimming lake, and a stall selling candy floss. Foreign travel was out for all but the rich, because of currency restrictions.

Partly for that reason, it was a society that today would seem incredibly inward-looking. People had travelled, if at all, within the Empire, not to Europe or America. Peter Hitchens, the son of a naval commander who had been posted all over the world, puts it this way:

> They understood the world in a different way from us. They were far less continental. My father, who spoke Spanish, travelled widely in South America, visited Murmansk and Archangel, lived in Ceylon, Malta and the now-forgotten Chinese treaty port of Wei Hai Wei, rarely set foot upon the European continent, never went to the USA and never visited Germany . . . In the same way as many Americans never leave the territory of their nation, which is also an empire, prewar Britons lived within the pink bits.[5]

The baby boomers, who think of themselves as international and cosmopolitan, grew up in a world that was just the reverse, and that rather distrusted Johnny Foreigner. They were at once in awe of internationalism and afraid of it. The very word 'cosmopolitan' conjured up images of greasy Mediterranean folk who were not to be trusted. Just a decade earlier, at the start of the war, the word 'cosmopolitan' had been annexed by anti-Semites as a euphemism for 'Jew'. We baby boomers like to think of ourselves as a cosmopolitan generation, and we pretend that when we describe a place as 'horribly white' we mean it as an insult, but we are closer to our parents than we think.

*

Intolerant as they were, the fifties were very tolerant of sadistic and sexually abusive teachers, and this remained true well into the sixties. People knew what was going on in some of the dreadful religious establishments of the period (more of this in Chapter Five) but it never seemed to occur to anyone that anything should be done about it.

They were also tolerant of violence against both women and children, and of bullying and abusive sexual relationships. The cinema image of a dominant male, pulling a struggling woman towards him and stifling her protests with a long, hard kiss until she melted in his arms, was a staple of the time. One of the first West End shows I ever saw was a massively successful musical called *Salad Days*, which opened in 1954, in which the boyfriend puts his disobedient girlfriend across his knee and spanks her, and we are invited to laugh at her humiliation and discomfiture. She, after a little sulking and pouting, realises that she deserved her punishment, and (naturally) melts into his forgiving arms.

The fifties were tolerant of racism, too. It was a world where I heard my father (who had been one of Britain's top fascists in the thirties), in a roomful of some of the most respectable people in Hertfordshire, talk of seeing a 'big buck nigger' in the street. No one in the room protested. But they would have been horrified if he had said 'fuck'.

His audience would have been members of the small Roman Catholic community in and around Rickmansworth in Hertfordshire. They were decent, pious, lower middle-class fifties folk, kind but easily shocked. They were not people in front of whom you could express doubts about God or His Holy Catholic Church. To them, the Pope and the Cardinal Archbishop of Westminster could do no wrong, and neither could Father Brendan Fox, our parish priest.

A cheerful Galway man, Father Brendan had been educated by the Irish Jesuits and trained for the priesthood in Normandy, where he had acquired a taste for fine red wine and calvados, tastes that could not be easily satisfied in Rickmansworth in the early fifties. Father Brendan dutifully visited all his flock and drank the endless cups of tea they made for him, but he visited us more often than most because my father gave him wine instead.

I saw his flock mostly at Mass on Sunday, the men in grey suits with baggy trousers, spotlessly clean white shirts, and ties, the women in flowered dresses and hats (a woman was not supposed to enter the

church with her hair uncovered). Among them were the Creeks, who lived near us: we were at one end of Croxley Green, half a mile or so out of the small town of Rickmansworth, and they were at the other end. They had two daughters. The older one went to school with me. Her slightly younger sister, Hilary Creek, went to Watford Grammar School, a couple of miles away, and in the early seventies served a long prison sentence as a member of the Angry Brigade, which had carried out a series of bombings. Given the state of the fifties in which she and I grew up, perhaps it is understandable that the baby boomers grew to despise anyone older than they were, and that folk like Hilary Creek, from comfortable but limited middle-class homes, might have been filled with inchoate rage about the things the fifties cheerfully tolerated, and the things they would not tolerate.

*

Fifty years after the start of the fifties, in 2000, the New Statesman ran an editorial headlined 'Lest we forget: 1950s were awful', which listed the miseries of the decade and expressed wonder that baby boomers in the political and intellectual elites seem to want to return there. How is it that the baby boomers rejected everything that was mean and dictatorial and warlike and pious and God-bothering about the fifties; rejected the idea that those in charge must know best; rejected the assumption that age knew best; rejected hierarchical schooling, uniforms, the class system and the supremacy of wealth; and, years later, sought to recreate them for their children?

Partly, of course, it is because we became middle-aged and complacent. But it is also because we made a dreadful mistake. We thought the fifties were repressive because they were the domain of earlier generations. So as we became middle-aged, the one idea we clung to was the nonsense that if something is new, it must necessarily be better, more humane and more progressive than that which is old.

It was all rubbish. The fifties were repressive because they were the fifties. They were repressive because the postwar years were an age of austerity. Until 1951, that austerity had at least been relieved by a political adventure, the adventure of the Attlee settlement; but that adventure was over.

The fifties were repressive because people were clinging to crumbling certainties – that Britain was a great nation and its empire a great civilising force in the world; that the British class system was ordained by nature and both right and indestructible; that God, King and Country deserved respect and loyalty; that the white man had a mission to civilise the world.

Had the baby boomers looked about them in the fifties, they might have seen the generation born just before them – let us call them the war babies, born during and just before the war – battling quietly for a more tolerant world; and they might have realised that they had not invented tolerance and liberalism. The war babies had already done so.

Unlike the baby boomers, most of the war babies had to do national service. Despite – or in some cases, because of – this crash course in conformism, it became a freethinking generation which paved the way for the freedoms of the sixties. It showed a sense of liberation in a buttoned-down decade.

National service was itself radicalising, for it meant that the war babies knew what they were fighting. 'Frightened and humiliated by systematic bullying, we cut strange figures in those days, with our shorn hair and baggy uniforms,' wrote John Turner, who started his national service in 1956 (and spent much of his subsequent career in the army's public relations department).

> The day began with reveille at 6 a.m. to the accompaniment of shouted obscenities from the NCOs . . . We were marched everywhere 'at the double'. Going to meals with our drinking mugs containing our knife, fork and spoon in one hand behind our back was always good for a laugh for our tormentors, as someone always dropped a cutlery item and was roundly abused . . .[6]

It was the war babies who knew that this was not good enough, and they showed a spark of healthy rebelliousness. In 1953 the famous actor John Gielgud was arrested for importuning young men in a public lavatory. Terrified and suicidal, he wanted to pull out of N. C. Hunter's play *A Day by the Sea*, which was due to open a few days later. Gielgud was persuaded by his friends to go ahead with the play, but on the first night at London's Haymarket Theatre, when his cue came, he stood in the wings, paralysed with fear, until his co-star Sybil Thorndike came to get him, and led him on stage. And then the audience stood and applauded for several minutes in an impromptu show of solidarity.

Yet just a few days later, Malcolm Sargent came backstage to see Sybil Thorndike, and declined to meet Gielgud, saying: 'I don't think I can; you see, I mix with royalty.'[7]

It was the war baby generation that caused the first rumblings of rebellion against the racism and homophobia that had until then been casual, unquestioned presences in British national life, as the *Empire Windrush* generation of black people began to settle and look for work. Those who were middle-aged in the fifties never saw the need to rename Agatha Christie's book *Ten Little Niggers* as *Ten Little Indians*, nor understood what the fuss was about when the Black and White Minstrels first hit television screens, and black people objected to white men in blackface singing in the way that black men were commonly (and erroneously) supposed to sing. The fuss made my father apoplectic; he loved the Black and White Minstrels just as they were. I cannot remember exactly what he said, but if I shut my eyes I hear him growling, 'Political correctness gone mad.' Of course he cannot have said anything of the kind – that idiotic phrase was not current until decades after his death – but that was the spirit of it.

His generation did not understand. But the war baby generation – they understood. The war baby generation went to the theatre and saw that it would not do. Fifties London theatre offered mostly innocuous light comedies, and elegant, beautifully crafted plays from the likes of Terence Rattigan. In August 1954, when *Salad Days* opened in the West End, the *Evening Standard* drama critic Milton Shulman wrote that it would be enjoyed by 'an aunt, an uncle and some fond relatives of the cast'. Nonetheless, it became one of the most successful British musicals ever.

It was during the early fifties that theatre ceased to be the preserve of the middle-aged and the upper classes, a revolution that paved the way for John Osborne and Arnold Wesker. That revolution began with the unlikely figure of actor Brian Rix, an impresario of farces, who worked out that there was a new kind of audience to be won: the coach trade – local clubs or pubs putting together sufficient people to earn a discount at the box office. In 1950 he produced, at the Whitehall Theatre, the first Whitehall farce, naturally about the war. It was called

Reluctant Heroes, and showed the downtrodden proletarian private soldier giving the officer class its comeuppance – exactly the opposite message from *The Chiltern Hundreds*, which had been so popular in 1948. The formula sustained Rix and his theatre for years. The same trade as the one Rix relied on also sustained Agatha Christie's *The Mousetrap*, which opened in 1952. It is still running.

The baby boomers were too young to go to the theatre, or care about a great actor hounded almost to suicide for his sexual preferences, or about a notice on a flat for rent that said, 'No coloureds, no Irish'. But the war baby generation – they cared. It was the war baby generation, not the baby boomer generation, who built the culture of rebellion. Bob Dylan, that sixties icon, always disliked being called a child of the sixties, for it was not accurate: the fifties made him, he said, not the sixties. It was true. He was a war baby.

*

The war babies envied Americans. In the grey gloom of the fifties, they consoled themselves with pale imitations of the delights they saw on the big screen. Life for young Americans seemed so much better than theirs. It was all driving Chevys, wearing smart clothes, having fun and spending money.

But the war babies, like their parents, still thought that the British were superior: uncritical admiration of the USA is a baby boomer phenomenon. Everyone knew, when British heavyweight boxing champion Don Cockell flew to San Francisco to fight world champion Rocky Marciano, the first Briton to challenge for the title for seventeen years, that our boy didn't have a chance, but we all hoped against hope that the arrogant, uppity Yanks might get theirs. It looks as though poor Cockell shared this sad delusion, because on 16 May 1955 he fought on when every rational argument was for getting out before he was permanently damaged. Marciano won by a technical knockout fifty-four seconds into round nine, after Cockell had been knocked down twice, for counts of eight and seven.

We comforted ourselves: what American would have shown Cockell's grit? Peter Wilson wrote in the *Daily Mirror* that Cockell had fought with 'the kind of courage which refuses to bandage in front of the firing squad. The driving urge which made men die rather than surrender to Everest... The sun had set on the arena, but it had never set on the heavyweight champion of the Empire.' British newspapers complained of the baiting and bullying doled out to Cockell by the American press, which homed in on his shape, calling him 'fatso', 'the waist of time', 'the Battersea butterball' and other opprobrious epithets. They said that Marciano fought dirty. He probably did, but Cockell never complained. Cockell also never recovered; he lost his next two fights to opponents he might have beaten before the dreadful battering he received in San Francisco, and then retired.

Newspapers fed national pride with the discovery of things a Briton could do that no American could do. On 29 May 1953, Edmund Hillary reached the top of Mount Everest, the first man to do so. On 6 May 1954, Roger Bannister ran a mile in less than four minutes. 'English victory beats the world,' roared the *Daily Express*. Years later Bannister told Peter Hennessy that fifties patriotism was a part of it all, but he did so in a curiously understated fifties way:

> It was a lot of fun to be an athlete in those days. We were poor. The only way to travel round the world was to represent your country so we also had a curious kind of loyalty to country and even patriotism. The war was over. Everest had been climbed. And we were part of this scene. And I was going to have to do my national service anyway. So that again linked you to the country.[8]

Patriotism is not a particularly elevated or useful quality – it is too close to nationalism and racism, and too irrational – but it kept the war babies free of the delusion that the USA had all the answers: a delusion that, in the end, overcame and sank the baby boomers.

*

One last thing needs to be said about the fifties. Fifties parents loved their children with an all-consuming uncynical love that has somehow been lost. If they sent them to dreadful, abusive schools – and they did – their motive was love; they thought they were doing the best thing for them. It was often over-protective, possessive, even manipulative love, but it was love. 'I want him [and, just occasionally, her] to have the chances I didn't have,' they would say, and put aside all the money they could afford 'for a rainy day'.

A 1951 survey confirms what everyone who was a child in the fifties knows. A young mother is quoted as saying: 'When I was a kid Dad always had the best of everything. Now it's the children who get the best of it. If there's one pork chop left, the kiddie gets it.' I know, as I write, a very elderly lady whose children were born in the forties and fifties and have been earning their own livings for years, and who is still saving out of her meagre pension so that she can help them if they need it. John Lennon was thinking of the aunt who brought him up in the fifties when he inserted into a song of Paul McCartney's, 'She's Leaving Home', words that millions of children of the fifties understood at once, words that explained to us why the parental love of the fifties had to be rejected, or we would never be free. We, the parents, it said, 'sacrificed most of our lives' for our daughter, we 'gave her everything money could buy.' So why should she want to leave home?

The baby boomers were warmed by their parents' love, but they were also scalded by it. 'We rejected our parents, but our kids aren't rejecting us,' Greg Dyke told me with a kind of wonder, and he is right. The baby boomers, the recipients of this unprecedented, unselfish and stifling love, were the first and last generation to grow up with a grim determination to reject their parents.

3. The cradle of the sixties: 1956

The sixties started in 1956 when Lonnie Donegan's 'Rock Island Line' hit the charts, though few people noticed until the Beatles released 'Love Me Do' in 1962.

The things that made the sixties happened in 1956. John Osborne's *Look Back in Anger* opened at the Royal Court, 4 miles and several light years away from Shaftesbury Avenue, and his anti-hero Jimmy Porter told the world: 'There are no good, brave causes left.' The British and Soviet governments instantly set out to prove him right: Britain invaded Suez and the Soviet Union invaded Hungary; the recently dead Stalin was revealed to have been a murdering, torturing tyrant; and suddenly there really were no good, brave causes left. The British government's foolishness and pride destroyed the old, brave, patriotic causes, the idea that Britain was a civilising force for good in the world; and the Soviet government's cynical brutality destroyed the brave, egalitarian cause of Communism.

The year 1956 was the hinge of the twentieth century, the moment when the old Britain died and a new one was born. The baby boomers were to grow up into a nation where nothing was certain any more. Jimmy Porter's father, terribly injured fighting for the Republicans in the Spanish Civil War in the thirties, had used up the last good, brave cause. The stage was set for a generation that had the instinctive radicalism of the young, the freedom to express it that had been denied to its predecessors – and nothing in particular to do with it.

So 1956 was the bridge across which Britain walked from 1948 to 1968: from the year of the Attlee revolution, the National Health Service, universal unemployment pay, universal sickness benefit, the things we have taken for granted ever since, to 1968, year of the Paris *événements*, the student sit-ins, demonstrations against the Vietnam war. It was the year when the young rebelled against the austerity and grey conformity of the immediate postwar years, and when everything

Britons had known turned to ashes. It was the nursery of the sixties, and the seeds of all that was good and all that was bad in the sixties are to be found in it.

It was the year when the old assumptions were shattered. The assumptions that Britain was a great power; that being British was something special; that politics and political dogmas and doctrines could make the world a better place; that the British Empire was strong and benevolent and for ever; that British theatre mirrored the unchanging values of the British upper and middle classes; that British music was gentle and tuneful, unlike the raucous rock 'n' roll that seemed to have gripped the USA.

Yet no one could have predicted on 1 January that 1956 was going to be anything special. The year before, the new Prime Minister, Sir Anthony Eden, had won a handsome general election victory, and if ever a Prime Minister looked like a safe pair of hands, it was Eden. He was one of the country's most experienced and respected politicians, and his long-expected arrival at 10 Downing Street did not look like the end of a political era. If you had said in almost any company that within a decade the British Empire would cease to exist, you would have been laughed at or patriotically punched.

But as early as March, there was a dim realisation of the terrible truth, for March 1956 saw the desperate measure of deporting Archbishop Makarios from Cyprus, and the suppression of the Mau Mau in Kenya.

In July, President Nasser of Egypt announced his intention to nationalise the Suez Canal. Egypt had been a British possession in all but name until the early fifties, and British troops had protected the British interest in the vital Suez Canal. By 1956, the Middle East was providing 70 per cent of the West's oil, and half of Europe's supply came through the Suez Canal. The imagined innate superiority of the British character and culture, which most British people still took for granted, allowed the troops in Egypt to behave with an imperial arrogance that naturally infuriated the locals.

British soldiers never referred to Egyptians; they were always 'the Wogs'. An officer once found on his desk a driver's report of a traffic accident between a British army vehicle and a Rolls-Royce which read: 'Two Wogs were inside, and their names were King Farouk and Ali Ismail.' The officer told the driver to rewrite it: he could not refer to the King of Egypt as a Wog. The report came back: 'I asked them their names . . . they were King Farouk and another Wog called Ali Ismail.'[1]

It would never have occurred to the British that they might not be welcome. But they were not; and in 1951 the Egyptian Prime Minister demanded that British troops should leave. There were gun battles and riots, and in 1952 the Egyptian king was deposed. The country's new leader was General Neguib, who was himself ousted two years later by the charismatic, confident Colonel Gamal Abdel Nasser, only thirty-four when he came to power, and determined to get rid of the British.

A deal was done in 1954 for the eventual British departure, and the next year Eden, then Foreign Secretary, visited Nasser to get him to sign up to the Baghdad Pact, an anti-Communist alliance. Nasser thought the pact was a ruse to enable Britain to continue to control the Middle East. He failed to take a shine to Sir Anthony. 'What elegance!' he said to a confidante. 'It was made to look as if we were beggars and they were princes.'[2]

Egypt refused to sign up to the Baghdad Pact, so Eden refused to sell Nasser armaments, and Nasser therefore began buying his arms from Czechoslovakia. So Eden decided Nasser must be a Communist stooge, and Britain and the USA withdrew their offer of $100 million to build a dam at Aswan. Nasser's response was to nationalise the Suez Canal, calculating that he could get the revenue he needed for the dam from the canal.

During a broadcast speech, he secretly arranged a code for his army. The moment they heard the name of Ferdinand de Lesseps, architect of the Canal, they moved swiftly into the offices and installations of the Canal, and took it over.

This seemed to the British press – and to Eden, now Prime Minister – to be very alarming indeed. Harold Macmillan, Chancellor of the Exchequer, wrote in his diary: 'If we lose out in the M. East, we lose the oil. If we lose the oil, we cannot live.'

But at that stage Macmillan's countrymen had more important things to think about. In the month of Nasser's invasion, at Old Trafford, one of the greatest spin bowlers who has ever lived, Jim Laker, took nineteen Australian wickets for just ninety runs, a feat that has never been achieved by anyone else, before or since, and probably never will be. It sealed a victory by an innings and 170 runs. It also triggered a wave of pure patriotic pride which ensured that, when it came to it, Britons were determined not to be pushed about by some damned Egyptian generalissimo.

Britain, France and Israel reached a secret deal. Israel would attack Egypt across the Sinai. Britain and France would call on both sides to withdraw from the Canal. Nasser was sure to refuse, and this would enable Britain and France to place their armies, supposedly as a peace-making force, between the Egyptian and Israeli forces – and they would take control of the Canal and humiliate Nasser.

Israel attacked, and Britain and France issued their ultimatum to Israel and Egypt. Israel accepted it, but advanced nonetheless. An eager young colonel called Ariel Sharon, who was to become Prime Minister, exceeded his orders, taking all his objectives at once. No one had explained to Colonel Sharon that he was depriving Britain and France of their flimsy excuse to invade, by completing his mission and ensuring there was no further fighting that the European powers could step in and put a stop to.

On 31 October Britain and France started bombing Egyptian airfields and defence installations, and a fleet sailed from Malta. In the House of Commons, Foreign Secretary Selwyn Lloyd denied any prior agreement with Israel. He lied. So did Eden. Amazingly, the British government seems to have thought that the American government would go along with whatever the British decided to do. In the USA it was six days to polling day in the presidential election and, without telling him, President Eisenhower's old wartime friends in Britain, Anthony Eden and Harold Macmillan, had thrown sand in his face. It was now clear to the President that they had been lying to him for weeks. His wrath was terrible. For the first time ever, the USA combined with the Soviet Union at the United Nations, to condemn Britain and France.

The British landings went ahead on 5 November. But when, the next day, Eisenhower won his expected landslide electoral victory, Macmillan had to report to the cabinet a serious run on the pound, orchestrated deliberately in Washington. Britain's gold reserves had fallen by an eighth, and only a ceasefire by midnight would bring American support for an IMF loan to prop up the pound. Britain had to withdraw, the Chancellor told his colleagues. At midnight on 6 November Britain was forced to accept a ceasefire or face bankruptcy as a result of American displeasure.

The humiliation was felt most severely in the army, the prop of

Britain's imperial pretensions. The soldiers, sailors and airmen felt demoralised, even betrayed. They had done the work that was asked of them, faultlessly; now they were effectively told that it was all a mistake. People die in war, and men had died in this one. But generally, in the past, their grieving families were able to cling to the idea that the sacrifice was in a noble cause – the defeat of the Nazis in Europe, the defeat of Communism in Korea. This time, no one could pretend that the sacrifice achieved anything. Such a dreadful thing was not to happen again until Tony Blair invaded Iraq.

So instead of pride there was bitterness and cynicism, made worse in the army because the post-Suez cuts in army expenditure bit deeply. That cynicism is the legacy of Suez to the baby boomers. It affected them in different ways, propelling some to the far left and some to the far right, and some to each of these extremes in turn.

By 1956, Britain had not been a world power for at least a decade; but neither the people nor the government had fully accepted this. After 1956, no amount of self-deception could hide it. A curt instruction from Eisenhower to give up the invasion or be ruined forced Britain to face the finality of the postwar settlement, in which it was financially and militarily a vassal to the USA. Every Prime Minister since Eden has remembered that lesson. Only Harold Wilson dared a serious rebellion, and only Edward Heath questioned the idea that British foreign policy should revolve around our 'special relationship' with the USA.

Heath's thinking was influenced by having watched that terrible moment in November 1956. He – unlike Eden – understood that while British politicians were thinking of nothing but Suez and Washington, the European Economic Community was taking shape. On the very day in November 1956 that Eden telephoned French Premier Guy Mollet to say that a withdrawal from Suez was unavoidable, Mollet and German Chancellor Konrad Adenauer were meeting to eliminate the last obstacles to European integration; Mollet left the meeting with great reluctance to take Eden's call. Roy Hattersley writes: 'As the old order was crumbling on one side of the channel, a new order was being created on the other.'[3] The Treaty of Rome was signed in March 1957 by Italy, France, Germany, Belgium, Holland and Luxembourg.

*

The baby boomers watched from their prams and their primary schools, and for the rest of their lives they never knew whether they were Europeans or Atlanticists, or whether they regarded both America and Europe with dark suspicion. The unbeatable power of the USA was the first lesson the baby boomers learned as they began to be conscious of world affairs, and they seem never to have forgotten it, expecting their leaders to behave like musical doormats that play 'See the conquering hero comes' every time the US president of the day wipes his feet on it. The first baby boomer Prime Minister, Tony Blair, was the most slavishly obedient Atlanticist British politics has ever seen. That's the long-term legacy of Suez.

Those with some connection to the military were probably even more closely affected by it than their contemporaries. One of the career soldiers to be forced unwillingly out of the service in the aftermath of Suez was Commander Eric Hitchens, whose younger son Peter, then a child of four, says his father would far rather have stayed with the navy he loved. It left Commander Hitchens with some anger and bitterness, which Peter imbibed, and this was, perhaps, the start of the strange political journey of Peter Hitchens, baby boomer and child of the sixties, from far right to far left and back again.

*

Suez should have been the moment the Communists had waited for, ever since the foundation of the Communist Party of Great Britain in 1920. For thirty-six years, Communism had been the hope of radical, egalitarian reformers. Suddenly, in 1956, it ceased to be so. It left a vacuum so vast that in the half-century that has elapsed, no one has yet found a way of filling it. Its collapse was at the heart of the emptiness of the sixties.

In June Britain heard about Nikita Khrushchev's 'secret speech' in which he denounced, in compelling and horrific detail, the crimes of Stalin: the regime of torture and mass murder which Stalin had run throughout the thirties and right up to his death in 1953. It was delivered to the Congress of the Communist Party of the Soviet Union at the beginning of the year, but kept secret from the world until June. It was not until The Observer obtained a copy of the speech, with its revelations not just of torture and mass murder but of anti-Semitic purges too, that Britain learned of it.

Some of the British Communist Party's own most dedicated members had been tortured and killed in the Soviet Union. Phil Piratin, who had been the Communist MP for Mile End from 1945 until 1950, and in 1956 was a member of the party's Political Committee, told me shortly before his death in the 1990s:

> Sometimes at our political committee meetings after Stalin's death, Harry Pollitt [the party's general secretary] would take from his pocket a piece of paper, and say that the Czech Ambassador or someone had given him the following names of people who had been – what was the word they used? Terrible word. Horrible word. Rehabilitated, that's it. A terrible word, because if you had to be rehabilitated, you had been killed.[4]

Yet even years after that speech, there were those who clung to the old certainties and claimed Stalin never really tortured and murdered people. The baby boomers never forgot how to practise this sort of self-deception. Fifty years after 1956, some baby boomers could be found claiming against all the evidence that Britain was not collaborating in the torture of suspected terrorists, and that waterboarding was not really torture.

Four months later, Soviet tanks rolled into Hungary, and put an end once and for all to the idea of Communism as a generous and idealistic movement. The suppression of the Hungarian uprising was swift, ruthless and brutal. As Hungary's prisons opened, hundreds of gaunt men and women crawled out, seeing the sun for the first time for years, with dreadful tales of torture and ill-treatment to tell. The *Daily Worker* reporter Peter Fryer came back to London, tore up his Communist Party card, and wrote, very fast, a harrowing book called *A Hungarian Tragedy*, published the same year. 'I saw a crowd of demonstrators,' he wrote, 'and the police just mowed them down with machine guns, including women carrying their children.'[5]

Fryer had seen evidence of crimes committed throughout the time the Communists had controlled Hungary. He had met Edith Bone, an English writer and translator who had disappeared in Hungary seven years previously. During the riots, she crawled out of her prison cell

– a cell where one wall was solid ice, where her guts had been ravaged by the dreadful food, where she had been kept for seven years in solitary confinement, and where she had been tormented by arthritis for which her captors gave her neither treatment nor painkillers. He found out that former Prime Minister László Rajk had been forced to confess in return for a quiet life in which he and his wife and child would be looked after in the Soviet Union. Then his wife was forced to watch his execution.[6]

Before 1956, young idealists impatient with the caution and reformism of the British Labour Party could find a home in the Communist Party. It had worked ruthlessly and successfully for two decades to make itself the only party on the left. The Independent Labour Party, a force in the land in 1931, was reduced to virtually nothing by 1945, because Communists were told to join the ILP, get themselves elected to important positions in their branch, and then expel all the other members for deviating from the line.[7] The party had managed to keep its enemies on the Trotskyist left confined to tiny, warring, discontented factions.

But the left could no longer fool itself about the Soviet Union. The world in which radical idealists had lived for three decades was suddenly uninhabitable. Radical youth was finally decoupled from Communism. In 1956 the British Communist Party lost a third of its members. The crucial commercial branch of the party, which had supplied a large part of its money, ceased to exist, for the commercial branch was made up largely of Jewish business people, who gave generously because they saw the party as a bulwark against fascism and anti-Semitism, but now knew that Stalin persecuted Jews. Even the staff of its own paper, the *Daily Worker*, started to peel off. They agreed a resolution saying that what had happened in Hungary, so far from being the suppression of an anti-socialist conspiracy as their paper had claimed, was in fact 'a national uprising against an infamous police dictatorship'.[8]

The party's new leader, John Gollan, was forced to beg Moscow for money, explaining to Khrushchev that if it was to carry on any real level of activity, Khrushchev had to reinstate the Moscow subsidy which the party had had in the thirties, but which had not been needed since the outbreak of the Second World War. From 1957 on, Britain's

Communists secretly received about £100,000 a year in cash from the Soviet embassy, handed over in cash and in great secrecy to a senior party official. The amounts gradually decreased until they stopped in about 1979. Only four top Communists knew about it.[9] Seven thousand people left the party.

The Communist Party had provided a home for young radicals of the twenties, thirties, forties and fifties, but their sons and daughters, their younger brothers and sisters, the baby boomers, had to look elsewhere for hope and for inspiration. Communism suddenly looked like yet another oppressor. Its headlong decline left a gaping hole. Just as there was radicalism to be harnessed, there was no credible party to harness it. This left many homeless idealists, ripe for the shibboleths of the sixties. The sons and daughters of young idealists who had turned to Communism in the thirties and forties had to look elsewhere for hope and inspiration.

*

As old gods decayed, new ones rose up. Television became a power in the land very quickly in 1956.

Television as a mass medium was uncharted territory. As 1956 began, no one knew where it would take Britain. By the time the year was over, everyone had a pretty good idea, and few people found the prospect comforting.

For 1956 was the first full year of independent television, which began broadcasting on 22 September 1955. That first night, advertising on television was a great shock. It seemed like sacrilege to bring the sleazy world of advertising into the sanctum of the home, like pole dancing in a cathedral. When our parents saw the first advertisement, it seemed something dreadful, a precursor of a world we were not sure we wanted to live in. Viewers saw a tube of toothpaste embedded in a block of ice and a woman brushing her teeth in the approved manner, 'up and down and round the gums'. The slogan was: 'It's tingling fresh. It's fresh as ice. It's Gibbs SR toothpaste.'

Quite soon children and teenagers were going round singing jingles from the advertisements, and most of them can still sing them: 'You'll wonder where the yellow went/When you brush your teeth with

Pepsodent' or 'Murray Mints, Murray Mints/The too-good-to-hurry mints'. Advertising had already entered deeper into the lives of the baby boomers than into those of any earlier generation.

Jokes began to centre on advertising slogans. Here's one, told over pink gins in my parents' Hertfordshire home. A man is walking through the desert with a camel and a native bearer when he hears a quiet, insistent sound: 'One, two, three . . .' He tells the bearer, 'If you don't stop that, I'll shoot you.' But the monotonous, maddening sound continues: 'Twelve, thirteen, fourteen . . .' He shoots the bearer, but still it goes on: 'Fifty-seven, fifty-eight, fifty-nine . . .' So he shoots the camel. All alone, he hears it go on: '145, 146, 147 . . .' In despair he sits on a rock and takes out his matches and his packet of Players cigarettes. Then he remembers. It's the tobacco that counts.

Television enabled the whole nation to watch, with horror and disbelief, as their proud and powerful British Empire made a prat of itself at Suez. The whole world saw. Enemies laughed. Friends looked the other way, embarrassed, but with a little secret smile too, as though they had watched a pompous senior colleague about to deliver a reproving homily when his trousers fell down.

And it was in 1956 that television stepped into the centre of political affairs, when the government was forced to abandon a rule preventing television discussion of anything that Parliament was to discuss within the next fourteen days.

Churchill and Attlee had been the first political leaders to learn to master radio. Their successors had to learn to master television. The new Labour leader, Hugh Gaitskell, elected the previous year, was the first top politician of the television age, and in 1957 Harold Macmillan became the first Prime Minister to make himself into a first-class TV performer.

*

ITV conditioned the childhoods of the baby boomers, making them fundamentally different from any earlier generation.

Nine-year-old Greg Dyke lived in 1956 in his parents' small suburban house in Hayes where the television could receive only BBC. 'My dad was always of the view that the BBC was "proper" television and that advertiser funded television was inevitably inferior.' Dyke felt terribly left out in the playground while the others were all talking about *The Invisible Man, Robin Hood, Take Your Pick* and *Double Your Money*.

He was lucky to have anything, though. His had been one of the first houses in the street with a television – one of the houses which all the other children crowded into at strategic moments – though the machine ceased to work after they had owned it for a week. 'My dad called out the TV repair man who came and plugged it back in. My dad was never a practical man.'[10]

Three decades on, Greg Dyke was to be the leading voice in defining independent television for the baby boomer generation.

One of the first ITV programmes was *The Adventures of Robin Hood*, with a theme song which today many baby boomers can still sing:

Robin Hood, Robin Hood, riding through the glen.
Robin Hood, Robin Hood, with his band of men
Feared by the bad, loved by the good –
Robin Hood, Robin Hood, Robin Hood.

But who were the bad, and who were the good? *Robin Hood* scripts, although they were providing work for American writers banned by Senator Joe McCarthy's House Un-American Activities Committee, were nonetheless careful to dilute the dangerously socialist message of the original Robin Hood myth: that taking money from the rich and giving it to the poor – or redistributing it, as Clement Attlee would have put it – was a good thing to do. The baby boomers were not to be offered an ideology to harness to their impatience for change.

So the show redefined the Robin Hood myth, put scent behind its ears and made it innocuous. Before the programme, I remember reading and loving a book about a rough, hairy outlaw who robbed the rich to give to the poor. But the glossy television Robin Hood eclipsed that image in my impressionable young mind. Television offered the baby boomers the matinee idol Richard Greene as a dimpled, clean-shaven and prettified version of the famous outlaw, and storylines that presented the tax collector as the enemy instead of the rich. In 1956, it was just six years since the state had ceased to be Robin Hood, and the original pre-television Robin Hood message had a distinctly socialist feel to it. It would not do at all.

In two-channel London households, *Robin Hood* was Number 1 for January 1956 with a staggering 78 per cent audience share. That year, we rushed home from school to watch it, or went to the home of a friend with a television. The luckiest of us were allowed to sit up until 10 p.m. and see *Sunday Night at the London Palladium*, which also began in 1955. We went to school the next day and regaled our less fortunate classmates with the jokes told by regular compere Tommy Trinder. He said how lucky it was that his fellow comedian Bob Monkhouse could take a joke, 'and he doesn't mind whose jokes he takes.' He added: 'I put him on a plane with Shakespeare – no one knows who wrote his stuff either.'[11]

Trinder was chairman of Fulham Football Club, where he made Johnny Haynes the first footballer to earn £100 a week. He once told Field Marshal Montgomery what a great player Haynes was – 'He'll be captain of England one day, though he's only eighteen.' 'Eighteen?' said the old soldier. 'What about his national service?' 'Ah,' said Trinder, quick as a flash. 'That's the only sad thing about the lad – he's a cripple.'[12]

But we did not get to stay up so late that we heard that wonderful old professional come on after the show had been delayed by an hour and a half because of a technical fault. He had kept the audience in the theatre entertained all that time with his ad-libbing, and when the cameras were finally on him, and he was live, he strode to the front of the stage and said 'Welcome to Monday morning at the London Palladium.'[13]

Sunday Night at the London Palladium was, though it never knew it and neither did we, part of the world that was dying. After a year, Trinder was fired in favour of the less irreverent Bruce Forsyth. It lost such edgy modernism as it had possessed, and its suited comedians and sequinned crooners started to look fatally dated after Lonnie Donegan's 'Rock Island Line', Britain's first skiffle hit, entered the charts on 6 January 1956.

A few days later, fifteen-year-old John Lennon walked into a Liverpool record shop and bought the record – a precious 78rpm disc, the first he had ever bought, which he took home with infinite care and ceremony. After he had listened to it over and over again, he begged and pleaded for a guitar. 'Rock Island Line' became the first song he learned to play, which makes it as good a symbol as you will find of how 1956 fathered the sixties.[14]

It is not that skiffle was new. Black musicians had been using the term for impromptu music-making since the twenties, and 'Rock Island

Line' was a song first performed by the black American folksinger Lead Belly in the thirties. The point was not newness, but a new spirit of irreverence. British musicians had been, or had appeared to be, content with the sort of well-behaved feelgood music that had adorned musicals like *Salad Days*: light melodies, sweet lyrics, innocent and inoffensive songs that rhyme moon with June, sung by wholesome singers like Pat Boone, Dickie Valentine and Rosemary Clooney.

The new, raucous music was coming from America, and until 'Rock Island Line' most of the rock melodies in the British charts were American imports, so British youth culture spoke with a transatlantic accent. From a nation still marked by shortages and austerity, young people gazed enviously at their richer and freer US counterparts. They watched American youth films hungrily, for there they saw elegantly casual teenagers leaning nonchalantly against mammoth but sporty convertible motor cars with rows of gleaming teeth where the radiators ought to have been. The very word 'teenager' was an American import, and it conferred a sort of status on the latter end of childhood that older words like 'adolescent' lacked.

The British music industry relied for the new music on American imports like 'Rock Around the Clock', recorded in 1954 by Bill Haley & The Comets but not heard in Britain until 1955. It wasn't quite the first rock 'n' roll record, but it was the first one most people in Britain heard, and it put rock 'n' roll on the map.

'Rock around the Clock' was utterly different from what young people had been dancing to, and it was inherently subversive: the word 'rock' originally had a sexual meaning, and 'rock around the clock' was a boast of sexual prowess. To the horror of an older generation, it swiftly replaced the gentler music they had courted to. It was the fearsome approach of music that sounded, to men and women brought up on crooners, like a declaration of war.

So 1956 marks the moment when the young started to demand music that, however incoherently, spoke of rebellion. Or perhaps it marks the moment when record companies caught up with what was going on among the young.

Despite 'Rock Island Line', even after January 1956 most of the Top Ten were still American. Elvis Presley made his first appearances in the British charts with 'Heartbreak Hotel' in January 1956 and 'Love Me

Tender' in September. But Britain's own rock stars were waiting in the wings: Lonnie Donegan, Tommy Steele and many more.

A lot of complacent middle-aged arbiters of British good taste were made to look very foolish, very fast. 'I don't think the rock 'n' roll craze will come to Britain. It is primarily for the coloured population. I can't see it ever becoming a real craze,' said bandleader Ted Heath early in 1956. But in September there were disturbances at packed British cinemas when *The Blackboard Jungle* was shown and cinema seats were torn up. The blame was laid at the door of 'Rock Around the Clock', which was heard over the opening credits, though it may also have had something to do with the subject matter – the film was about a teacher at a tough high school, where the teenagers make the rules and the staff meekly accept the fact that they've lost control.

In fact, no one knew why they were doing it, and that was what puzzled people. Riots with an end in view, people knew. Even riots against something, with no clear idea of the end, they knew. But riots for the sake of them, because the film conjured up an inchoate conviction that the world was amiss and ought to be put right – these were new, and no one understood them, least of all the people taking part in them.

When Haley came to Britain later in the year, a stoutish, conventionally dressed man in his thirties, he was not what British youth had hoped for. He had the guitar, the symbol of the revolution, but ought not someone younger be offering to carry it for him?

It was that moment, perhaps, that crystallised the new spirit. The rebellion centred on being young, not on being right or radical. And that was the spirit that 1956 bequeathed to the sixties, the spirit that turned the worship of youth into a religion – the only religion. It had been spookily foreshadowed the previous year by that sixties hero in the making, James Dean. In the 1955 film *Rebel without a Cause* he had been perhaps the first to articulate the philosophy of the sixties. What, he was asked, are you rebelling against? 'What've you got?' he replied.

*

If Ted Heath (the bandleader, not the politician) was swiftly to be made to look foolish by the fast-emerging spirit of the sixties, how much crueller was the fate of the theatrical establishment. The idea that the theatre existed for the cosy middle class, whose tastes must predominate, had been firmly established in the postwar years. The playwright Terence Rattigan, whose first successes had been in the thirties and who was forty-five in 1956, had once described the audience member whom, he thought, no playwright dared upset: 'That nice, respectable, middle-class, middle-aged lady.' Most people confidently assumed that this philosophy would survive the challenge being mounted from the east of London by Joan Littlewood at the Theatre Royal Stratford East and from the west by George Devine at the Royal Court in Chelsea. Most people were wrong.

At the Royal Court, Devine began in 1956 to offer a new kind of play. John Osborne's Look Back in Anger had its premiere there on 8 May, and changed the world that British theatre reflected. It announced the end of what critic Kenneth Tynan, who was to be a sixties icon, once called the 'dododramas', set in Colonel Bulstrode's library somewhere in Hampshire.

Look Back in Anger was Osborne's second go at this idea. His first, in many ways a better play, was Epitaph for George Dillon, which showed more starkly the conflict between the generation that had grown up after the war and the one that knew the thirties. A middle-aged man could still say, as a character does in Epitaph for George Dillon: 'Hitler had the right idea. 'Course, he went too far.' 'You think so?' asks the young hero, a prototype of Jimmy Porter, with a heavy irony that is entirely lost on his companion, who replies, 'Definitely.'

Look Back in Anger was a good play, but not, despite its fearsome reputation, a particularly radical or left-wing one. But it did puzzle and irritate the middle-aged. Milton Shulman told Evening Standard readers: 'It aims at being a despairing cry but achieves only the stature of a self-pitying snivel.' When Laurence Olivier went to see the play, when he heard Jimmy Porter shout, 'There are no good, brave causes left' – the cry of a generation that could not go and fight for socialism and democracy in Spain, as Jimmy Porter's father had done, or fight Hitler in Europe – Olivier did not know what the man was talking about. He just thought it was a rotten play. He had no idea of the flowering of brave causes this presaged, from the Campaign for Nuclear Disarmament to Anti-Apartheid – and would not have thought much of them if he had.

But the *enfant terrible* among the theatre critics, Kenneth Tynan, wrote in *The Observer*: 'I doubt if I could love anyone who did not wish to see *Look Back in Anger*.'[15] He added, 'I agree that *Look Back in Anger* is likely to remain a minority taste. What matters is the size of the minority. I estimate it at roughly 6,733,000, which is the number of people in this country between twenty and thirty.'[16] This was, of course, fatuous, and wrong in pretty well every respect – many young people hated the play, and many more were indifferent to it or had never heard of it. Tynan had been an exceptionally clever undergraduate, which is what he remained all his life, really. But it was only in the prologue to the sixties that an exceptionally clever undergraduate could make so foolish and arrogant a statement and be taken seriously. The spirit of the sixties is one in which youth believed it was right because it was young; and its legacy is the cult of youth that the baby boomers now complain of, in which politicians and business leaders have only to speak the words 'new' or 'modern' or 'modernise' in order to be automatically right; in which the most damaging thing you can say is: 'You're against modernisation, then?'

Osborne was bracketed with writers like Kingsley Amis as one of the 'angry young men'. Just as ownership of 'young' was to become a battleground for decades, so was ownership of anger, claimed by Osborne in 1956 and in the seventies by the Angry Brigade.

But Tynan was right in this sense: whether you liked or disliked *Look Back in Anger* did depend partly on your age. Terence Rattigan, until 1956 the king of London's West End, almost walked out of the Royal Court on the first night, and emerged at the end to tell waiting journalists that the play should really have been called *Look Ma, I'm Not Terence Rattigan*. Four years later, in 1960, Rattigan was still saying of what by then was known as kitchen sink drama, 'I'm pretty sure it won't survive. I'm prejudiced because if it does survive, I know I won't.'

The new work did survive, and Rattigan's went into a lengthy eclipse, helped on its way by unremitting hostility from Tynan: an eclipse from which it is only now, over half a century later, beginning to emerge. Yet as the twenty-first century opens and Rattigan's plays are benefiting from a modest revival, theatregoers are finding, rather to their surprise, that his message is generally a good deal more radical than Osborne's.

For Osborne's play, and Osborne himself, were not at all clear what it was about the old order that they disliked and despised, or what their new order might consist of. By contrast, in the thirties, radical works of literature were normally the work of socialists, angry at extremes of wealth and poverty – think of *How Green Was My Valley*. Rebellion against the old order simply because it was old was something new. Osborne was a rebel without a cause.

But that was the mood of the time, one quickly grasped by Laurence Olivier, whose political antennae were much more sensitive than Rattigan's. When Olivier's friend, the great American playwright Arthur Miller, came to London and said he would like to see the new play that the *New York Times* claimed had 'wiped the smugness off the frivolous face of English theatre', Olivier agreed to give it a second try. After the first act Miller said, 'God, Larry, you're wrong, this is great stuff.' The great actor suddenly felt old, stuffy, establishment; and he also started to see merit in the play. So when he met John Osborne, he asked the young writer if he might think about writing a play with him in mind. Osborne was delighted, and within what seemed to Olivier to be an amazingly short time, the first act of *The Entertainer* arrived.

Nine days after *Look Back in Anger*, Peter Ustinov's *Romanoff and Juliet* opened at the Piccadilly Theatre, foreshadowing the Suez crisis and offering a new irreverence towards British imperial ambitions. 'You have only to strike oil,' says the Prime Minister of Ustinov's fictitious European country, 'to be invaded tomorrow. The English have been here often on the grounds that we were not fit to govern ourselves.'

Arnold Wesker's angry plays about social injustice were the most radical of the post-1956 theatre, and it was Wesker, not Osborne, who caught the hopelessness of a generation whose good, brave cause had been taken away from it. Wesker came from a family of East End Jewish Communists. His aunt Sara Wesker was one of Britain's most important Communists in the thirties and a member of the party's national executive, and his mother was also a Communist activist. His trilogy of plays, first performed between 1958 and 1960 – *Roots*, *I'm Talking About Jerusalem* and *Chicken Soup with Barley* – follow the life of an East End Communist Jewish family from hope in 1936, with the Spanish Civil War, to despair in 1956.

As Michael Billington writes, reviewing the 2005 revival of *Chicken Soup with Barley*, 'Wesker's great strength is that he allows the politics to emerge through the interstices of domestic life.' Wesker 'shows the Kahn family, dominated by the matriarchal communist Sarah, exuberantly celebrating the defeat of Mosley's fascists in Cable Street in 1936. Ten years later, during the Attlee government, the family is already splintering, with daughter Ada abandoning the urban jungle for rural Norfolk.'[17]

And ten years later still, as the cold winds of 1956 blow over Sarah's faith in Communism, she becomes the spokeswoman for a generation that had seen too much to change, a generation that was the despair of the baby boomers. As her son says, 'You're a pathological case, mother, do you know that? You're still a Communist!' Yes, she says, she is still a Communist: 'All my life I worked with a party that meant glory and freedom and brotherhood. You want me to give it up now? You want me to move to Hendon and forget who I am?'

Wesker told me in a sentence the trauma of 1956 for a woman like Sarah: 'You can admit the error of an idea but not the conduct of a whole life.' It was something the sixties generation never understood: the comfort and clarity of having one clear political idea that was to make a better world, to the achievement of which men and women gave their lives. A good, brave cause.

4. The baby boomers go to school

The baby boomer generation grew up into the sixties, and had little idea what use to make of the unprecedented freedoms that decade offered them. How could they? They were not educated for the free, colourful sixties, but for the grey, monochrome fifties.

To understand why the baby boomers so badly mishandled the freedom they were offered at the end of the sixties, you have to look at the schools they went to.

There were two things wrong with them. First, the school system enshrined and perpetuated the class system. Secondly, fifties schools were designed for an age of conformity, and used beating and bullying to enforce conventional thought and behaviour.

As mentioned in Chapter 1, Attlee's first Education Secretary, Ellen Wilkinson, had been forced to abandon her desire for a comprehensive system, and accept three different sorts of state schools: grammar schools, technical schools and secondary modern schools. The technical schools never really took off, and in most areas there was a stark division between those who succeeded and went to the grammar school and those who failed and went to the secondary modern. The division between grammar and secondary modern schools was very stark, and reinforced class divisions.

So Ellen Wilkinson's compromise meant that, at the age of eleven, the baby boomers were told what their station in life was to be. The vast majority who could not afford fee-charging schools sat the Eleven plus examination. If they passed, they went to the grammar school, and if they failed, they went to the secondary modern. Of course the words 'pass' and 'fail' were officially banned: the official line was that Eleven plus failures were 'selected for a different sort of education'. But no one was fooled, and the pretence simply engendered cynicism about government which eventually helped undermine the spirit of deference.

Greg Dyke, born in 1947, is one of many who remembers the horror of results day:

> These were the days when the Eleven plus dominated all for parents in streets like ours. If you were one of the 20 per cent who passed you went to the grammar school, if you didn't you went to the secondary modern and educationally you were effectively written off. No one we knew went to private school. I don't think anyone considered it an option, it wasn't on their radar screen even if they could have afforded it, which they couldn't.
>
> One of the most traumatic memories I have of my childhood was when my eldest brother Ian failed the Eleven plus. It was a family tragedy and my parents were distraught. I took the exam six years later when there were four or five boys from our street taking it. Only one failed and his parents were broken-hearted. My hatred of the Eleven plus, and the whole concept of selection at the age of eleven, is rooted in those experiences and it was one of the main reasons why later in life I joined the Labour Party and Sue and I sent all our kids to comprehensive schools.[1]

Neil Kinnock, born in 1942 and therefore a war baby and not a baby boomer, made the same point in the House of Commons when he was Labour's education spokesman: 'Nobody who has observed a community that operates a selective Eleven plus system can doubt that on the morning of the results there are . . . floods of tears in many homes. The guilt for those tears will remain on the backs of the [Conservative] government.'

Grammar schools were quickly annexed by the middle class, and started taking disproportionately middle-class children, from homes where they were prepared (and often coached) for the Eleven plus. The secondary moderns educated the poorest.

Throw the private fee-charging schools into the mix, and you have the school system of the fifties: a system that, while preaching equality of opportunity, actually set the class system in concrete. There were, in practice, three sorts of secondary school: private fee-charging schools for those who were going to run the country; grammar schools for those destined to be the middle managers; and secondary moderns, to give a bare minimum of schooling to those who would become manual workers. Your station in life was clearly marked from the start. In

Church of England churches they still sang that verse from 'All Things Bright and Beautiful' which is now banned:

The rich man in his castle
The poor man at his gate
God made them, high and lowly,
And ordered their estate.

If you doubt me, think about your friends. If you are a baby boomer and went to a grammar school or a fee-charging school, how many people of your age do you know who went to a secondary modern? The answer, in most cases, is none, or just one or two who managed to defy the system and pull themselves up in later life.

It was not just a rigidly class-based school system, but a dark, regimented one, in which – in most schools, and especially the old-established grammar schools and fee-charging schools – children were expected to keep quiet and do as they were told.

It was not an education that equipped people to walk out into the sixties and make good use of more freedom than any generation before them had ever known. Some sixties icons subconsciously spent their lives fighting their public or grammar schools, in their old, old buildings, with their dark oak corridors and heavy doors and Latin mottoes and chalky pedagogues in academic gowns.

The more these schools tried to hold the tide against the army of the unknown and unwashed, the more their pupils yearned for the bright and the brash, the expresso bar and the juke box.

The public schools – the poshest of the fee-charging schools – were still educating the sons and daughters of the rich, and still glorifying in their regime of beating, bullying, bigotry and frequently buggery. Fee-charging schools did not, of course, have these things entirely to themselves, though they tended to be more systematic about it than state schools. Boys in most fifties schools expected to be caned. In many boys' schools, beatings, sometimes judicial and sometimes savage, were a regular, daily part of life. It started early. Like many others, I was first beaten at school when I was seven, required to hold out my hand for the teacher to hit me with a ruler, and bend over a chair for him to hit me with a gym shoe.

Easily the most extreme were the schools run by the Catholic order of the Christian Brothers, which were famous for sustained brutality. There, the teachers, most if not all of them in holy orders, regularly beat pupils to a pulp with their fists or any weapon that came to hand. We still do not know the full extent of child sexual abuse in these schools, for new cases are coming to light every day, and it looks as though, when the full story is out, we will find that priests were abusing children in Britain on the same industrial scale as we now know they were abusing children in the USA, Canada and Ireland.

Thousands of baby boomers still bear the scars of sustained pious brutality, and many more the even darker scars of sexual abuse. Everyone knew what was going on in these dreadful places. I remember my father saying he would never send me to the Christian Brothers because of their brutality, and being quite worried when, at twelve, I told him that a priest I did not know had befriended me in the street. Yet no one seemed to think anything should be done about it.

Fifties schools were not all dreadful. The very best of its grammar schools were like Rickmansworth Grammar School, which I attended briefly: purpose-built at the start of the fifties to cater for the new customers created by the Attlee government's swift implementation of the 1944 Education Act and the raising of the school leaving age, with young and idealistic teachers and no 'traditions' with which to oppress their pupils. But they were the exception.

The more well-heeled baby boomers did not have to wait until they were eleven or thirteen for a regime of beating and bullying. They could go and board at one of the dreadful prep schools that thrived well into the sixties, rather like Evelyn Waugh's Llanabba Castle in *Decline and Fall*, where beating and flogging children were considered almost saintly. These were dark, frightening places in which to place a seven-year-old child, generally situated in old manor houses, with eccentric, autocratic and frequently violent headmasters and unpredictable teachers, many with a kind of crazed temper, and ever-present instruments of chastisement – the cane, the gym shoe, the ruler. They provided the earliest memories for many of the men who were to hold the highest positions in the land, in every walk of life, as the twentieth century drew to its close.

'At my prep school,' one baby boomer told me with relish,

we were all scared of being beaten. Almost all the masters had military rank. One of them used to smoke cigarettes all through his lessons, and cough his lungs out as he taught. Another disappeared one day, and the local paper later carried the story of his court appearance for interfering with three boys. Normally the local paper was laid out for us all to see, but not that week. The man was bound over. The boys were not named, but everyone at the school knew exactly who they were.

When the deputy head of another prep school, Lindfield School in Sussex, resigned in protest at the use of a cricket bat to beat boys, the *Daily Express* approvingly quoted the cricket captain at the school, David Chapman. Apparently young Master Chapman 'produced a well worn bat from the games room and . . . said with a little smile: "This is our local instrument of execution."' Mr Hart said: 'I believe a few off-cuts administered with the flat of the bat stings more than a caning . . . I administer the beatings before the whole school and staff.' The departing deputy head, George Dennis, claimed Mr Hart attacked him when he left, punched him sixteen times and broke his nose.[2]

Formally beating and flogging young children seems so deeply shocking today that it is odd to recall how fee-charging schools in 1960 still did it routinely, and it had to be extreme before it became newsworthy. There was even a lobby for extending beating of children to everyday life. On 27 January 1960 *The Times* carried an article headlined 'Is flogging a remedy?' under the mysterious byline 'A Medical Correspondent'.

Many of the leading sixties figures were shaped by this violent, abusive, regimented school system. That helps explain why baby boomers were a muddled generation, and why baby boomer Prime Ministers Tony Blair (educated at a fee-charging school to run the country) and Gordon Brown (educated at a grammar school to be a middle manager) lacked the clarity of purpose that Attlee and his ministers displayed.

Dimly seeing what the sixties might bring, many of the old public schools embarked on a last effort to tell the new wave to go away. They relied on the tried and trusted methods of repression and cruel, meaningless ritual, which had never before failed to produce men who could govern an empire.

In 1958, one of them, Fettes, near Edinburgh, appointed a new headmaster called Ian McIntosh, who was pledged to repel the new spirit, and to strengthen and buttress the old fortress walls. According to the official school historian, McIntosh's 'instinct was to batten down the hatches and ride out the storm,' assisted by liberal use of the cane.[3] Tony Blair was to enter the school eight years later, and he and McIntosh took an instant dislike to each other. It shaped Blair's life and thought, as it did for many of his generation. The mixture of renewed repression and the spirit of the sixties was to prove, in the long term, toxic.

Thirteen-year-old Blair had to fag for a senior boy called Michael Gascoigne. Fags had to wait on an older boy, making him toast, polishing his shoes, breaking up coal for his fire, cleaning and folding his mud-caked rugby kit, polishing the studs on his rugby boots. Older boys could cane their fags whenever they liked, and Gascoigne did; he is said to have demanded that his toast be done just so – too light or too dark earned a beating. Some senior boys took a runup with the cane to make it hurt more, though we do not know if Gascoigne did this.

When it was time to go back for his second year, Blair tried to run away, attempting to board a plane at Newcastle Airport for some exotic foreign location. Later, he spent much of his time trying to hang on to his long, flowing hair but being regularly escorted to the barber by his housemaster. He shared a love of Lindsay Anderson's If . . . with his roommate at the time, Gordon Dowell, who has said that Blair was a typical 1968 product: he was 'an ersatz rebel, more concerned with the style than the substance of revolt. He had a talent for sailing close to the wind without badly capsizing, relying on his charm to get him out of trouble.' He was a fan of Mick Jagger, that equally muddled sixties icon.

Blair was last caned at the age of seventeen, which was unusual even in these places, where they tended to stop beating boys around the age of fifteen.[4]

*

Fettes called itself The Scottish Eton, and Beaumont College, a Jesuit-run school near Windsor, called itself The Catholic Eton. Its first head boy, in the days of Queen Victoria – or so the snobbish old story went – wrote to his counterpart at Eton suggesting a sports fixture, and the Etonian replied, 'Harrow we know, Winchester we know, but what is

Beaumont?' To which our hero sent back the message: 'Beaumont is what Eton was: a school for the sons of Catholic gentlemen.'

The year that Ian McIntosh arrived at Fettes, my father decided that he could, after all, afford his dream of sending me to this expensive boarding school. I spent the four most miserable years of my life at Beaumont, being force-fed with snobbery and religious bigotry by the time-honoured methods of beating and bullying, while the sixties were beginning beyond the gates of my prison.

Four decades later, I visited Fettes while writing a biography of Tony Blair, and was struck by how much it felt like Beaumont. They were both nineteenth-century foundations, rather than ancient ones like Eton, and had created their own traditions, hoping perhaps to make up in brutality what they lacked in antiquity. These traditions were reinforced as the sixties approached, in shivering anticipation of what might be going on beyond the school walls. Both schools saw the sixties coming and pulled up the drawbridge.

At Beaumont, there was a corridor, the 'Higher Line gallery', that led to the library. If you were not in the sixth form you had to march down it – straight down the middle, looking neither to the right nor to the left – with your jacket buttoned neatly, until you could make a smart right-turn to enter the library. Older boys with nothing better to do would lounge along the sides, watching languidly, and, if your marching was not good enough, drawl, 'Boy, go back and start again,' or send you to be caned by the head boy.

Beaumont's Jesuit priests patrolled its corridors and classrooms in their full-length black robes, embellished with 'wings' – ribbons of black cloth hanging from each shoulder. The College Cadet Force was compulsory, one afternoon a week. Mass was compulsory, every morning, as was High Mass on Sunday, Benediction two or three evenings a week, and evening prayers in the chapel conducted by a sepulchral old priest and including some cheery meditations on death such as: 'Your best friends will desert you, leaving you nothing but a winding sheet' and 'If you die ill, the loss is irreparable.' Believing not only in God but also in the Holy Catholic Church was compulsory. In fact, everything that was not forbidden was compulsory, and vice versa.

There was no sex education – not a scrap – just a looming certainty, never discussed, that sex destroyed the soul, and a chorus of squeaking bedsprings after lights out, as the tiny cubicles in which we slept sprang to life.

Beatings were regular and formalised. The head boy caned on the posterior, but teachers ordered you to be beaten on the hand with the ferula (an instrument made of whalebone and rubber) during morning break by one Father Brogan. Failure to learn the requisite three questions and answers from the Catechism each morning was one of the crimes that earned a painful visit to Father Brogan, presumably to teach us the love of God. But the terror was a panning, Beaumont's version of the formal flogging. The condemned boy was collected at night from his dormitory to be ceremonially beaten on his pyjama'd posterior. I believe someone said a prayer. The mere thought of it gave me sleepless nights for a week.

*

Two years after I went to Beaumont, eleven-year-old Paul Mackney, later to become a revolutionary socialist and later still one of the most significant trade union leaders of the nineties, arrived at a boarding school called Christ's Hospital School. It was a charitable foundation of the sort that New Labour wanted to bring back – half the boys had their fees paid by some wealthy businessman, the other half went there because they had done exceptionally well in the Eleven plus exam.

So gratitude to the wealthy sponsors was compulsory. 'Blessed Lord, we yield thee hearty praise and thanksgiving for our founders and benefactors, through whose charitable benevolence thou hast refreshed our bodies at this time' was the grace they said before meals. When Mackney later joined the International Socialists, he had not forgotten that God and the rich were bracketed together as his benefactors.

Nor, when he was told in later years that capitalism delivered diversity, did he forget that they were all forced to wear a uniform of knee-length breeches, long yellow woollen socks, a dark-blue serge coat drawn in at the waist by a leather strap, and a coarse white shirt with bands at the throat; and that they marched everywhere, like columns of soldiers, often beneath an archway that barked: 'Fear God! Honour the King!'

Bullying, as in many fifties schools, was not just tolerated; it was institutionalised. If one of the younger boys who laid the tables gave an older boy a bent knife, the older boy was entitled, under the rules, to say, 'See me afterwards' and hit the younger boy as hard and as often as he wanted. If an older boy required a menial task to be performed, such as cleaning his shoes, he would shout to a younger one, 'Boy!', and the younger one must come running, if he did not want a beating. Older boys were allowed to punish younger ones more or less at will, for more or less anything.

Even today Mackney cannot bear people to hover behind him, because there was one older boy who made it his self-appointed (but officially sanctioned) task to stand behind younger boys and randomly hit some of them over the head with a huge book.

The boy with the book is now a judge. Mackney has seen his picture in the newspapers, and says he hasn't changed at all.

In 1966, fourteen-year-old Graham Wilmer started at the Salesian College in Chertsey, run by the Salesians, a Roman Catholic order. 'Minor misdemeanours were punished by beatings of one sort or another, by hand, fist, belt or cane,' he writes. On his first day, a priest suddenly hit him hard in the face for whispering to the boy next to him. But he and his best friend Martin Allen enjoyed themselves, made light of the constant beatings, and vied to come top of the class. In the summer, he fell in love with Martin's sister Nicky, and she with him.

One day Nicky realised that he had gone cold on her. It was to be more than thirty years before she learned the terrible secret that made Graham suddenly feel too dirty and ashamed to touch her. His school work went to pieces. He sank to the bottom of the class.

For at the end of that summer of 1966, a young science teacher called Hugh Madley befriended him, taking him for rides in his car and coming to his home to give him extra maths lessons. It was the start of two years of regular sexual abuse.

In 1968, Martin Allen was injured playing rugby, and died two days later. Martin's father asked Graham to be an altar boy at Martin's requiem mass. This created a dreadful dilemma. If Graham served at the requiem mass, he would be expected to receive holy communion. But every Catholic knew that it was a terrible thing to receive communion while in a state of mortal sin. So, at last, he went to confession, and told one of the Salesian priests his story. The priest asked him to repeat it outside the seal of the confessional, so that he could take the matter further. Graham agreed. He was interrogated by three priests: the head-master, the rector, and a third who, though he did not know it, was the head of the Salesian order in Britain, Father Williams, who told Graham to mention the matter to no one, not even his parents.

Father Williams then took two swift and extraordinary decisions. He gave Madley a job in another school, the Salesian school in Battersea, south London, where he taught until he took early retirement; and when Graham failed most of his O-Levels in summer 1968, Father Williams refused to let him come back and retake them. He left school, deprived of self-respect and hope and a future, and embarked on a miserable series of dead-end jobs.

Exactly thirty years later, in 1998, he suffered a serious nervous breakdown. Since then, his life has been devoted to tracking Madley down, trying to get the Salesians to admit what they did, and setting up a charity, The Lantern Project, to help adults who were abused as children.[5]

He tells me that the Lantern Project has been flooded with messages. 'Father B put his hand on my knee and began to stroke inside my short trousers.' 'Mr C put his hands up my trousers.' 'Father D told me to take my trousers down.' I asked the order's current head, Father Michael Winstanley, if Hugh Madley was the only child abuser employed in Salesian schools. There was a long pause before he replied, 'He is the only abuser who has confessed.'

Graham Wilmer today is a tall, heavily built man with a neat mous-tache. He worked much of his life as a commercial writer who mixes largely with soldiers and businessmen, and he is bluff and entertaining, with a gift for mimicry. His frequently politically incorrect language fits well with that, and rather oddly with a member of the caring profes-sions, which is what he is today. But when he talks of Hugh Madley, the events of 1968 and the Salesians, his voice becomes lower, his sentences longer, and his devotion to the detail, his ability to quote verbatim from a mountain of letters and documents, signal an obsession coming from a very dark place deep inside him.

We talked of Madley in Graham's small sitting room, surrounded by the many documents he had laid out for my inspection. To talk about the rest of his life, we went to his cosy local pub, where they keep the draught ale nicely and serve good fish and chips, overlooking the Mersey, which Graham loves to sail on. As we finished our second pint, I said I needed to leave to catch my train. 'Time to Foxtrot Oscar,' said Graham, and for a moment I felt I was in the company of a bluff but raffish army officer, until I mentioned the Salesians and the darkness of the sixties descended again.

One of Paul Mackney's later comrades in the International Socialists was Peter Hitchens, whom we shall meet again demonstrating in Grosvenor Square in 1968 before moving fast and far to the right and becoming a *Daily Mail* columnist. If Mackney's rebellion was nurtured at Christ's Hospital School, Hitchens's stemmed from his years at The Leys in Cambridge, where 'they were obsessed with the length of our hair.'

Outside, he says, there was pirate radio and the Rolling Stones, but inside there were petty rules and a crabby atmosphere. 'The world outside seemed so alluring and the school so drab and narrow.' He managed to avoid being beaten there: having been to prep school, he knew how to stay underneath everyone's radar.

Minor breaches of the rules at The Leys were punished by making the miscreant write out twenty times: 'Few things are more distressing to the well regulated mind than to see a boy who ought to know better disporting himself at improper moments.' Hitchens must have had plenty of time to absorb the complacent inanity of the sentiment he was obliged to reproduce, over and over again.

*

In Kirkcaldy at the start of the sixties, the crème de la crème – the cleverest of those who were clever enough to go to grammar school, judged on the old method of IQ – were fast-tracked a year early, and at the age of ten were put into a special intensively taught class of eleven boys and twenty-five girls.

So Gordon Brown was marked down as one of the cleverest as early as ten. But he thought it was all a very bad idea. In May 1967, aged fifteen, he typed out an essay saying exactly what he thought of it.

> I watched as each year one or two of my friends would fail under the strain.
> I saw one girl who every now and then would disappear for a while with

a nervous breakdown. I stood by as a friend of mine, who I knew was intelligent enough, left school in despair after five years of strain with no university or higher qualifications. I thought continually of how it could have been for these young guinea pigs, how the strain of work, the ignominy and rejection of failure could have been avoided. All this, I thought I saw better than any educationalist in his ivory tower.

*

People came out of places like Beaumont, Fettes, The Leys, the Salesian College and Christ's Hospital School, after teenage years filled with a crash course in conformism and religious bigotry, into the sixties. It's hardly surprising that their new freedoms went to their heads, and they failed to make constructive use of them.

As these schools tried to fight off the sixties, they made them inevitable. But they also helped make them turn to pointless rebellion, full of undirected anger. Years later, the sixties generation were still fighting their reactionary schoolmasters when they should have been fighting exploitation and injustice. The sixties sounded inclusive, but they were not. They were for the middle classes. When you think of children of the sixties, you seldom think of a former secondary modern pupil.

And even among those they were aimed at, the middle and upper classes, they were not inclusive. You could miss the sixties. I knew someone who did. Here's his story.

In June 1962, I escaped from boarding school to find the sixties waiting for me, freer, fresher, fairer and infinitely more fun. I drank in my new freedom, fell in love with satisfying regularity, and discovered after a few false starts that you didn't have to be alone to have sex. I had no A-Levels, but I knew that everything would be all right, for the sun that shone on the early sixties was at last also shining on me.

I studied for A-Levels at the City of Westminster College, a grubby old building near Victoria Station which, I now know, represented what education ought to be. The deal, once you understood it, was so clear and beautiful that a young man straight out of boarding school could hardly believe it. They offered wonderful teaching. If you took advantage of it, that was fine by them, and if you didn't, it was your funeral.

They could not get away with it today. In government, the baby boomer generation has made it impossible for a school or college to operate in this freewheeling way. English was taught by N. F. Simpson, who was just emerging as one of the most significant of the new wave of sixties playwrights, a sort of terribly English Ionesco. His work was liberating in a very sixties way: it exploded the myth that things have to make sense. His first play, *A Resounding Tinkle* in 1958, was about a suburban couple who had been delivered the wrong size elephant. 'If it goes berserk in the night I'm not getting up for it,' says the husband. The next, *One Way Pendulum*, offered a suburban man training 500 Speak Your Weight machines to sing the 'Hallelujah Chorus'.

And as I was drinking in the early sixties, I met a boy I had known at Beaumont. Michael had been one of Beaumont's outcasts, so the sixties cast him out too. His father was a Pole who had come to England in the thirties, made an immense amount of money and drove a pink Bentley Continental. So everyone muttered 'nouveau riche' meaningfully whenever Michael was near.

He had been to Beaumont's prep school as well, so he'd been beaten and brutalised in a boarding school since he was seven, and the little boy's life was irremediably destroyed there one dreadful day when the other boys discovered the shaming information that his mother's first name was Pixie. He was tormented with this every day of his life until he left Beaumont at the age of seventeen, and the Jesuits could think of nothing to do with him but have him regularly beaten for fighting and not working.

From that fateful day, I do not believe Michael had a happy hour. By the time I knew him, when we were both thirteen, the pattern was set. Each day, sometimes each hour, he would have to walk past groups of boys all hissing 'Pixie, Pixie'. Sometimes he tried to pretend he did not notice, other times he piled into the centre of the group in a fury, both fists flying, perhaps inflicting a bruise or two, often receiving bruises. He was always fighting, always hurting or getting hurt, never for an hour at peace.

My reunion with Michael came about because my mother had taken a job as secretary to an eminent Harley Street psychiatrist, William Sargant, and told me she had met there the mother of a Beaumont friend – Pixie. It was the first time I had heard the name used without a cruel sneer. Pixie had come to Harley Street because her husband had by then decamped to South America, leaving her to handle the baffling problem of Michael's misery. One day Michael suddenly hit her, hard, full in the face, with his fist. Beaumont had poisoned everything for Michael, including his love of his mother, which was stronger in him than he knew how to cope with.

It was possible to live through the sixties and not be part of them, and Michael's ten years in the hands of the Jesuits gave him a personality from which laid-back sixties folk recoiled.

My mother persuaded me to take Michael on one of my evenings out with my friends, but I did it only once. Michael was still trying to earn the respect of Beaumont. He wore a tweed jacket, white shirt and Beaumont old boys' tie, and muttered a few reactionary prejudices that he thought Beaumont would have expected of him. My friends knew instinctively that they were being asked to shoulder a burden, and it was not theirs to shoulder.

I understand he died in his fifties, having done nothing with his life or his intelligence, and apparently by his own hand. Not all the baby boomers were children of the sixties.

But my friend Eric was. He seemed to personify everything that was free and fun and life-enhancing about the sixties. He was living alone in London and blossoming into the sort of young Italian whom girls at the start of the sixties dreamed about. I understood, with admiration and envy, that it was his stream of conquests that caused Holland Park Comprehensive to cast him adrift after he had completed his O-Levels.

He arrived at the City of Westminster College with a dark beard over his tanned and handsome face, black clothes, and dark glasses behind which – so I was frequently informed, until I grew rather tired of hearing it – lurked eyes so big and dark and sensual that girls could often not stop looking into them. We hunted together, and I was glad to gather the scraps from his groaning table.

The sun that shone on the sixties shone with intoxicating brilliance on me and Eric.

5. What if Mr Macmillan's out? 1957–63

People think of Harold Macmillan, who entered 10 Downing Street at the start of 1957, as the last Prime Minister of the fifties, brought low in 1963 by his failure to understand the new world of the young. But he was really the first Prime Minister of the sixties.

He did the unthinkable and wound up the British Empire. He was the first Prime Minister consciously to adapt his style for television, which helped him to sell his policies to the nation, but did not help at all with his party. He was the first Prime Minister to see the key importance of the new European Economic Community in Britain's destiny, and his decision to seek entry, though unsuccessful, paved the way for Britain's eventual membership. And it fell to him to build our new, subservient, post-Suez relationship with the USA. Macmillan recognised the shaming truth that, even if Eden's health had not collapsed, he would have had to go in any case, because the Americans had lost faith in him. No British Prime Minister could last without support in Washington, and no one in Washington was willing any longer to keep up the polite fiction that the relationship with Britain was something like a relationship of equals. Without US patronage, there was nowhere in the world to hide, because under Attlee, Churchill and Eden Britain had stayed aloof from the discussions that were soon to lead to the creation of a European common market.

So the baby boomers, as they grew up, absorbed through their pores not only the message that the USA was a magical place, full of free, rich people, but also that its word was law, which explains a good deal about what happened when at last, in 1997, the baby boomer generation took charge of Britain's affairs.

Post-Suez, Britons were facing the fact that so far from ruling the waves, they did not even rule their own back yard. Their country no longer counted for much in the world, and the jingoism on which they had lived for the first half of the century was now a shallow farce. Even today, a person's attitude to patriotism and Britishness is partly dictated by whether they reached adulthood before Suez or after it. I was eleven in 1956 and cannot say the word 'patriotism' with a straight face (nor do I want to.) But a person only five years older than me can use the word entirely naturally.

It fell to Macmillan to make the best he could of these harsh realities. No more unlikely figure could be found to usher in the sixties than this wealthy 63-year-old Edwardian gentleman, a product of Eton, Oxford and the Grenadiers, with a Duke for a father-in-law and a liking for grouse moors, whose awkward, shambling gait was the result of dreadful First World War injuries. Yet many traditional Tories, both the old and the young reactionaries, grew to think of him as the sort of traitor who should be horsewhipped in the street.

The old Conservative reactionaries were personified by the Tory grandee Lord Salisbury, scion of key advisers and Prime Ministers since the first Elizabeth reigned, an ageing peer who had patronised Macmillan as a parvenu, both at Eton and in the Conservative Party. Salisbury rightly suspected that Macmillan harboured treasonable thoughts about the sanctity of the British Empire.

At the other end of the age spectrum, Macmillan's right-wing enemies included the young financial secretary to the treasury, Enoch Powell. Powell had an almost religious devotion to the free market, and turned his boss, Chancellor of the Exchequer Peter Thorneycroft, into what we would now call a monetarist, in favour of limiting the money supply and against public expenditure, especially on such matters as welfare.

Monetarism went against all the Prime Minister's instincts, and he asked for a second opinion from his own favourite economist, Roy Harrod, the biographer of John Maynard Keynes, who told him, 'The idea that you can reduce prices by limiting the quantity of money is pre-Keynesian. Hardly any economist under the age of fifty subscribes to it.'[1] Macmillan eventually divested himself of the services of both Thorneycroft and Powell, but what they represented was to appear again in the seventies, their banner by then in the hands of Margaret Thatcher.

Within weeks of becoming Prime Minister, Macmillan was on a plane to Bermuda to meet President Eisenhower. Personally, it was all friendly enough, but Britain's status as supplicant was never in doubt. Macmillan carried it off with as much dignity as possible, managing to appear like an English gentleman, in reduced circumstances but with his dignity intact. Eisenhower offered to supply Britain with an American ballistic missile, equipped with nuclear warheads. To be any use against the Soviet Union, this would have to be based in Britain, so the offer was not exactly disinterested. Macmillan agreed, and managed to sound grateful.

Macmillan appealed for Eisenhower's help in getting a face-saving agreement with Nasser which 'we can claim as reasonable, if not quite what we would like . . . I hope you will denounce Nasser and all his works . . .'[2] But he found the President unsympathetic, and eventually he quietly settled the canal dispute entirely on Nasser's terms.

Macmillan did not focus much on the Britons whom the government had placed in danger but whom he could not defend. In 1956 my friend Eric Camilleri's family had been living in Cairo, where his father Walter, an Anglo-Italian with a British passport, ran a successful business. After 1956 they were thrown out of the country, along with the rest of the British business community, and everything they had was confiscated; they came to Britain penniless. It was one of the results of Suez that few people in Britain knew about, for the British did not compound their humiliation by advertising the fact that there was nothing at all they could do about this treatment of British citizens.

In late September Macmillan had to swallow his pride yet again, in order to meet and greet Nasser at the United Nations in New York. Yet Macmillan managed to make this visit one that, so far from reminding his people of their humiliation, gave them the feeling that they were still a great nation. He did this with one of those instinctively lordly gestures that were such an enormous asset to him as he set about rebuilding Britain's faith in its leaders. As Macmillan was addressing the UN assembly, Soviet leader Nikita Khrushchev heckled him furiously, banging his shoe on the table in front of him. I can still remember watching on television as Macmillan looked up from his notes, waited politely until the rude, fat foreigner had finished, and then said, with an air of Old Etonian detachment, 'Could we have a translation of that, please?' People talked about it for days afterwards. It may have been the last time Britain collectively felt that sort of patriotic glow, all the better for being understated. The raucous, manufactured tabloid patriotism of later generations never matched it.

Macmillan quickly grasped a great truth about Britain's post-imperial politics, the truth summed up years later by Bill Clinton: 'It's the economy, stupid.' 'I am always hearing about the Middle Classes,' Macmillan wrote to the head of the Conservative research department. 'What is it they really want? Can you put it down on a sheet of notepaper, and I will see if we can give it to them?'[3]

That is pure Macmillan: the self-mocking lordliness, the apparently effortless superiority, combined with ruthless appreciation of the political reality that to win an election, he needed the middle classes.

In the 1959 general election he produced the phrase universally associated with him, and with the start of the sixties: 'Most people in this country have never had it so good.' It was true, though it was cheeky of Macmillan to claim the credit, which belonged to the Attlee settlement and the receding impact of the war. In 1959 no politician dared attack the welfare state. People were better off than they could remember having been. In 1950, 300,000 Britons had owned a television; in 1960 it was ten and a half million. In 1961 four million went on foreign holidays, unknown a decade earlier. Teenagers, especially those at work, had disposable income for the first time. Young people became serious consumers, able to make choices and support those choices with cash. The young rather despised the past, a small faraway country of which they knew little. Things were done differently there.

Most of the baby boomers who were starting to be aware of the world during Macmillan's premiership hardly realised the privations of their parents, or the struggle that had taken place to ensure that they were not equally deprived. All previous generations thought of free health care as nothing short of miraculous, but the baby boomers casually assumed that it was the ordained order of things. To the baby boomers, the welfare state had become boring. They no longer valued the Attlee settlement. It was many years before it became clear that, because they did not value it, it was not safe in their hands.

The battlements of the fifties collapsed as the sixties generation approached them, without having to be stormed. National service ended in 1961. The contraceptive pill arrived. There was an economic boom and something like full employment.[4] Many people who were young in the sixties felt able to answer their bosses back in a way that would have been inconceivable just a few years earlier. And because people were less frightened of their bosses, they were more likely to join and support trade unions. Macmillan grasped another truth about the start of the sixties: that in the world in which he now lived, trade unions were a force in the land. The choice was to confront them, as Margaret Thatcher eventually did, or to propitiate them. Macmillan chose the latter, not just because he thought it advisable, but also because he thought it was right. A union was the collective voice of the workers, and, in his patrician way, Macmillan thought it ought to be heard.

Unions were flexing their muscles, in search of better wages, better conditions, greater security, a fairer share of economic prosperity. There were strikes or threatened strikes of engineering workers, tugmen, railway workers, even British School of Motoring driving instructors. The right-wing *Daily Express* seemed to be all in favour of the rail strikers' demands being met, and contemptuous of the argument that the railways were losing money. A Cummings cartoon showed a plutocrat in a car that carried a coffin, with the caption: 'But the motor car is economic – THAT only loses lives.' There was no question of Macmillan's government turning on the unions.

Macmillan's policies on trade unions and workers' rights were so radical that Tony Blair would have considered his cabinet a dangerous nest of ultra-leftists. But at the time, the baby boomers who made New Labour thought Macmillan was an elderly reactionary. They did not value the powers that their trade unions had. The benefits of strong trade unions were something the baby boomers took for granted, and eventually, in the seventies and eighties, they negligently threw them away.

The baby boomers looked at Macmillan and knew that he was of the past, and therefore valueless. They were wrong. Macmillan was the bridge along which we walked from Edwardian England to Thatcher's Britain: the Edwardian toff who looked at the new egalitarian world and saw that, whether it was good or not, it was the world in which he had to operate.

The baby boomers looked at the new political order of the fifties, which was called Butskellism – from the names of the Conservatives' Rab Butler and Labour's Hugh Gaitskell – and despised it instinctively as the compromise of hopelessly timid elderly folk. Yet it represented something revolutionary: the new political fact that civilised, egalitarian ideas like the welfare state, which sounded like red revolution in the hungry thirties, were now part of a consensus, accepted by Conservatives as well as the Labour Party. The young radicals who despised Butskellism eventually made possible the altogether harsher settlement after 1979, that of Thatcher and Blair. For many in his own party, Macmillan moved too far, too fast, but for the baby boomers, he was too old, too cautious, too cunning. They wanted a revolution, they said.

The economy won a stunning election victory for Macmillan in October 1959 – a victory that would have been thought inconceivable just two years earlier. The Conservatives had 365 seats against Labour's 258. 'We were defeated by prosperity; that was without doubt the predominant factor' was the internal Labour Party assessment. Eight out of ten working-class voters now owned a television; three in ten owned a washing machine.[5] But they were also defeated because Macmillan's government was not a threat to the achievements of Labour – rather the opposite, as a top Conservative cabinet minister, Iain Macleod, made clear at his party's conference in 1962:

> The people of this country think that the society which we have created is not sufficiently just . . . They are puzzled by the fact that still in this twentieth century the child of a skilled manual labourer has only one chance in a hundred of going to university, while the child of a professional man has thirty-four chances. They are puzzled that 42 per cent of the people in this country still earn £10 a week or less . . . You cannot ask men to stand on their own two feet if you give them no ground to stand on.'[6]

The election done with, Macmillan set about dismantling the British Empire. The distress of Lord Salisbury and Enoch Powell was as nothing compared with that of Sir Roy Welensky, Prime Minister of the Central African Federation, which comprised Nyasaland and Northern and Southern Rhodesia. A former heavyweight boxing champion of Rhodesia and railway driver, with a Polish Jewish father and an Afrikaner mother, Welensky's answer to a British television interviewer who asked if he understood the African mind was: 'Considering that when I was a lad I swam bare-arsed in the Makabusi with the piccanins, I think I can say I know something about Africans.'[7]

Almost as soon as the election was over, Macmillan set off to tour Africa. He began in newly independent Ghana and Nigeria, where he gave everyone the impression he was ready to see majority rule throughout Britain's African empire, then made his way to Salisbury, the capital of Welensky's Federation, where he managed to give exactly the opposite impression; and thence to South Africa, where he was to address both Houses of Parliament. And there he laid out the future for all to see. He said:

> The most striking of all the impressions I have formed since I left London a month ago is of the strength of this African national consciousness. In different places it may take different forms, but it is happening everywhere. The wind of change is blowing through this continent . . . As a fellow member of the Commonwealth, it is our earnest desire to give South Africa our support and encouragement, but I hope you won't mind my saying frankly that there are some aspects of your policies which make it impossible for us to do this without being false to our own deep convictions about the political destinies of free men . . .

To men like Salisbury and Powell, Macmillan's treachery knew no bounds. It became slowly clear to them that, not content with dismantling the empire, he wanted to throw in Britain's lot with the Europeans. Macmillan saw that it was the only alternative to being an attentive and permanent supplicant on Washington's doorstep.

He raised the question of membership of the European Economic Community when he visited the new American president, John F. Kennedy. Kennedy was unexpectedly positive about the idea, seeing the chance that Britain might influence the rather less pro-American governments of France and Germany. Armed with permission from Kennedy, Macmillan authorised Edward Heath to apply for membership. Meanwhile, in December 1962, US Secretary of State Dean Rusk showed clearly that there was nowhere for Britain to go apart from Europe, in a speech so brutally honest that he has never been forgiven for it:

> Great Britain has lost an empire and has not yet found a role. The attempt to play a separate power role – that is, a role apart from Europe, a role based on a 'special relationship' with the United States, a role based on being the head of a 'Commonwealth' which has no political structure, unity or strength and enjoys a fragile and precarious economic relationship by

means of the sterling area and preferences in the British market – this role is absolutely played out.[8]

More than three decades later, an aide to President Bill Clinton reminded him, as he was about to meet the British press, to mention the special relationship. 'Oh, yes,' said Clinton. 'How could I forget? The special relationship.' And he laughed.[9] Britain in the twenty-first century is still not ready to throw off its comfort blanket.

Five weeks after Rusk's speech, on 14 January 1963, Macmillan's old wartime friend General de Gaulle vetoed British membership of the European Economic Community. De Gaulle could not, he said, believe that Britain was ready to put its European friends before its commonwealth, its American friends, and its European Free Trade Area partners. He had a point.

The winter of 1962 was one of the longest and coldest anyone could remember, and Labour's lead in the Gallup poll was the highest for seventeen years. Macmillan's Tory enemies were circling, and the young – the war babies and the baby boomers – appeared to have nothing but scorn for him. Things were looking black for his premiership even before the Profumo affair burst over his head in 1963.

Rumours that Defence Minister John Profumo was having an affair with Christine Keeler, a 'call girl' who had also been sleeping with a Soviet embassy official, had been circulating for months. When the Labour opposition raised them in the House of Commons, Profumo denied it. In June, he was forced to admit that he had lied to the House. He had to go.

Macmillan was puzzled, at one stage muttering that he did not 'live much among young people' – among whom he apparently counted the 48-year-old Profumo. The young thought the Prime Minister was ludicrous and out of touch, and he could hear their raucous and rather cruel laughter.

The young did not know that there were much more reactionary people than Macmillan around, and it was their spirit, not Macmillan's, that was to rule in the eighties and nineties, and into the twenty-first century. The editor of The Times, for one, thought this display of sexual self-indulgence was all the fault of the 'never had it so good' society the Prime Minister had encouraged – presumably believing that things were better when the poor were in daily fear of near starvation. Bernard Levin identified 'armies of Pharisees marching in their holy wrath; and of these the commander in chief, beyond a doubt, was [Conservative Party chairman] Lord Hailsham . . . He called Mr Profumo a liar seven times in ninety words.' Levin added that in his final sentence – 'A great party is not to be brought down because of a scandal by a woman of easy virtue and a proved liar' – Hailsham said the word 'liar' 'with such manic violence that those watching might have thought that he was about to go completely berserk.' Hailsham received, and probably deserved, one of the cruellest rebukes ever offered to a politician, from Reginald Paget MP, who said, 'When self-indulgence has reduced a man to the shape of Lord Hailsham, sexual continence involves no more than a sense of the ridiculous.'[10]

The spirit of the world in which the baby boomers were to be middle-aged was presaged by a series of financial scandals. At the start of the sixties, Emil Savundra enriched himself by defrauding the policyholders of his insurance company, and John Bloom, a millionaire at twenty-eight, was held up as an example of what the enterprise culture could do, until his company collapsed and he was prosecuted. 'Here,' said the *New Statesman*, 'was an ambitious young man who grew up in the opportunity state and absorbed its atmosphere of unrestrained commercialism almost in the schoolroom . . . He has been taught to believe that the best employment for agile brains was to make a million before you were thirty . . . and he did it.'[11]

Like most lessons learned at the start of the sixties, the baby boomers forgot this one, and we have had to go over the same ground over and over again as we grow older; we fawn over those who make themselves very rich, and are surprised when they turn out to be very corrupt and very destructive. If the young could have torn their attention away from Macmillan, they would have found that there were far worse things in the world, and they would prove so durable that they would help blight the lives of the children and grandchildren of the baby boomers.

*

Whether the old master could have turned it round one last time in 1964, we will never know. An inflamed prostate, coming on top of all his political troubles, persuaded him to resign on 8 October 1963. The announcement was followed by a rather messy Tory Party conference in which his would-be successors paraded their wares, and the next week saw a procession of senior figures to his hospital bedside. Then he told the Queen his recommendation. It was a very surprising one: the patrician peer who was Macmillan's Foreign Secretary, Lord Home of The Hirsel.

An early draft of the memorandum Macmillan wrote for the Queen contained truly revealing passages which were expunged from the later, official, draft the queen actually received, and it is pure Macmillan – at the same time thoughtful, snobbish and patrician:

> Lord Home is clearly a man who represents the old, governing class at its best and those who take a reasonably impartial view of English history know how good that can be . . . It is interesting that he has proved himself so much liked by men like President Kennedy and Mr Rusk and Mr Gromyko. This is exactly the quality that the class to which he belongs have at their best because they think about the question under discussion and not about themselves. It is thinking about themselves that is really the curse of the younger generation – they appear to have no other subject which interests them at all and all their books, poems, dramas and all the rest of it are almost entirely confined to this curious, introspective attitude towards life . . . [12]

It seemed as though the old gentleman, in defiantly proposing an Etonian peer almost as old as himself to succeed him, was making one last effort to hold back the tide.

*

The draft memorandum reads like a sketch from *Beyond the Fringe*, the revue that started out as an Edinburgh Festival fringe show and was a surprise hit in 1961 at the Fortune Theatre in London's West End, where it made the reputations of the four young Oxbridge graduates who wrote and performed it: Alan Bennett, Peter Cook, Jonathan Miller and Dudley Moore.

Cook's famous imitation of the Prime Minister would seem today relatively mild, but at the time it was ground-breaking in its disrespect:

I then went on to America, and there I had talks with the young, vigorous president [here Cook would sound dreadfully old and weary] and danced with his very lovely lady wife. We talked of many things, including Great Britain's position in the world as some kind of honest broker. I agreed with him, when he said that no nation could be more honest; and he agreed with me, when I chaffed him and said that no nation could be broker . . .

Cook had Macmillan opening a letter from 'an old age pensioner in Fife', reading it, and saying, 'Let me tell you, Mrs MacFarlane, as one Scottish old age pensioner to another . . .' It was in the spirit of the sixties that what counted against Macmillan, more than anything, was his age.

Macmillan went to see the show, a smile nailed to his face, and Cook, seeing him in the audience, added a few gratuitous insults to the Macmillan sketch.

'Why wasn't Macmillan told about Cuba?' asked the new satirical magazine *Private Eye*, launched on the back of the success of *Beyond the Fringe*, when Kennedy and Khrushchev had a standoff over the delivery of weapons for Cuba and for a few days it looked as though the two superpowers might destroy the world in a nuclear war. The magazine gave its answer in tiny type at the foot of the page: 'He was, but he forgot.'

While Macmillan was building the political furniture of the sixties, he found that those who were to live in it thought him ludicrous.

I saw *Beyond the Fringe* in the summer of 1961, after a friend telephoned me in great excitement to tell me to go, post haste, to the Fortune. I set out not quite knowing what to expect, but somehow certain that I was about to receive permission at last to do what I had done guiltily all through my teenage years: to question authority, to think for myself, to live in the world of my own generation, and to laugh helplessly at things at which one was not supposed to laugh. It gave me all that. Not just Peter Cook sending up the Prime Minister, though that was liberating enough, but – oh, ecstasy – Alan Bennett making fun of the clergy, with no one to have him caned for disrespect.

Another sketch had a civil defence official explaining that, before they let off a nuclear missile, the Americans had to ask Mr Macmillan's permission. But what if Mr Macmillan was out? 'Common sense really. They'd ask Lady Dorothy.'

The idea that the Americans might ask a British Prime Minister's permission to do anything often got the loudest laugh of the evening. The days when Clement Attlee could visit Washington and stop President Truman using his atomic weapon were long gone.

Even in irreverence, the Americans had got there first. Before Peter Cook there were the great American satirists of the late fifties and early sixties – Mort Sahl, Shelley Berman and the wonderfully subversive Tom Lehrer, who made fun of many sacred subjects. At last, to my joy, he turned on the Catholic Church. Hearing his 'Vatican Rag' was, for this Catholic-educated boy, one of the great liberating moments for which people remember the sixties:

> First you get down on your knees
> Fiddle with your rosaries
> Bow your head with great respect
> And genuflect, genuflect, genuflect . . .

But it was in the Fortune Theatre that I heard the sixties message most clearly. It sounded revelatory at the time, though now I think it was probably rather banal, boiling down to this: 'The fifties are over. Man.'

In 1962, late on a Saturday night, the BBC confirmed the message, when it began to screen *That Was the Week That Was*, which was rude about everybody and everything. This was the BBC saying that it did not care what the government of the day thought, and, as I now realise is usual with the BBC, it took fright pretty soon and stopped saying it: despite its huge popularity, *TW3* (as everyone called it) was taken off the next year and never came back. It was replaced by far tamer stuff. But it was not forgotten. We thought it was the future. We were wrong.

*

A remarkable new wave of playwrights from the war baby generation was providing a critique of the old world and a blueprint for a new one. For literary innovation in the early Macmillan years, says Arthur Marwick, you had to go to the theatre.[13]

After *Look Back in Anger* John Osborne looked back at the old British music hall. *The Entertainer* opened in 1957 with the grandest of the old theatrical knights, Laurence Olivier, in the lead part. He played Archie Rice, a washed-up stand-up comic in the dusty, depressing dying days of music hall, tap-dancing in three-quarters-empty theatres perilously perched on windswept piers – getting his laughs at his own predicament, as he looks sadly skywards after a thin audience reaction and says, 'Don't laugh too loud, it's a very old building.'

The Entertainer, set in 1956 during the Suez crisis, is a more political play than Look Back in Anger. It is not just about the death of music hall, but the death of the England in which music hall had flourished: an England in which Archie Rice's father, Billy Rice, could carry audiences with him while he sang songs pleading with the government to keep up a strong navy; an England where authority was unquestioned; not the England of the sixties.

After Arnold Wesker's trilogy, whose story ended in 1956, Wesker became more, not less, political. The Kitchen in 1959 and Chips with Everything in 1962 were angry socialist statements about working-class life, turned into urgent theatre. So was Shelagh Delaney's A Taste of Honey (1958). Even the less obviously political of the new-wave playwrights, like Harold Pinter (The Birthday Party, 1958) and John Mortimer (What Shall We Tell Caroline, 1958) had a clear view of an unjust society, and a prescription for putting it right.

Chips with Everything was probably the last important play to focus on national service, so big a part of the war baby experience and unknown to the baby boomers. 'We'll break you,' says the corporal, 'because it's our job.' Harold Hobson in the Sunday Times called it 'the left wing drama's first real breakthrough, the first anti-establishment play of which the establishment has cause to be afraid,' and Alan Brien in the Sunday Telegraph thought it was 'the most outspoken and explicit challenge so far from a young left wing playwright to our assumptions about social progress'.

Nearly half a century on, we wonder what happened to all that radicalism, and why the establishment has hardly felt afraid since then.

It's because the sixties and the baby boomers doused it in pretend radicalism; because the baby boomers are now the establishment; and because the baby boomers had no national service to radicalise them.

National service, designed to produce respect and fear, had by 1962 produced mostly disrespect and anger: the Whitehall farces, Chips with Everything. From 1957 on, Brian Rix's subversive idea of mocking the officer class reached a wider television audience with *The Army Game*, in which working-class soldiers made fools of their officers weekly. The heroes were the other ranks in Hut 29, Surplus Ordnance Depot, Nether Hopping, Staffordshire: Michael Medwin as an East End wide boy, Alfie Bass as 'Bootsie', so named because he was permanently excused boots on some scam or another, Norman Rossington as 'Cupcake' Cook, Charles Hawtrey as the brainy and effete one, and Bernard Bresslaw as the brainless but brawny one who said, 'Well, I only arst' – perhaps the first television catchline to catch on in playgrounds throughout the land. The sergeant major tries to bully them, and the officers, public-school twits to a man, are transparently out of their depth.

Nineteen-year-old Greg Dyke realised the difference national service made, one day in 1966 when he got his first job, on his local newspaper the *Hillingdon Mirror*. His editor was in his mid to late twenties. Dyke told me, 'He said to me, "You're the first person I've met who makes me feel old." That was because we were the first generation who didn't do national service.'

*

Deferential England was dying. But it still had its champions, whose spokesman, more often than not, was Lord Beaverbrook's *Daily Express*. One of its concerns seems to have been to stifle at birth the idea of sexual equality. A page lead on 29 January 1960 told *Express* readers that women would rather not be told what their husband earned. The Gambols – a popular daily strip cartoon in the *Express* – was about a young husband and wife; the husband worked in the week and watched sport at weekends, and the wife was only interested in clothes and her looks. The Gambols strip that day began in a shop, with the husband saying, 'Hats, hats, all you think of is hats.' In the second and third frames, walking home, he says, 'You need a psychiatrist,' then 'Don't worry dear, the cure's probably very simple.' In the fourth frame we see the cure: he has her over his knee, smacking her, and she is crying.

A week later the front page carried a big picture of a young and attractive newly elected woman MP. 'She is thirty-four and the mother of six-year-old twins,' the *Express* reported, and she had just triumphed with her maiden speech, after which, it being mid-afternoon, she apparently said, 'All I would rather like now – I have had nothing since breakfast – is a quiet cup of tea.'

The *Express* gushed, 'She is tall, willowy, handsome, with auburn hair.' After describing her clothes, it added, 'And what woman would want a higher tribute than the final appeal that came from her leading opponent, 32-year-old Mr Gerald Reynolds? He said with a smile of concealed despair: "Don't be swayed by Mrs Thatcher's charm."'[14]

It was not just Margaret Thatcher who was encouraged to think first and foremost about her looks and her grooming, and leave silly old politics to men. In April 1960 John Elliott, Chief Education Officer for Manchester, told the annual conference of the National Union of Women Teachers at Buxton that he wondered whether women teachers had yet accepted the fact that clothes are of great interest to girls. Women teachers, he suggested, should give girls more advice on grooming and clothes. He was saddened to see the new school-leaver, the shorthand typist and the office girl with 'the handbag too big, the heels too high, the hair not quite right and the make-up all wrong'. For this the *Express* called him 'the most courageous man in Britain'.[15]

Susan, the eighteen-year-old daughter of Victor Goodhew, Tory MP for St Albans, was wheeled on to rubbish the idea of lowering the voting age to eighteen. 'She does not seem very interested in politics,' said forty-year-old Mr Goodhew, opposing a Labour move to lower the voting age. 'It may be she goes to a Young Conservatives dance from time to time, but I suspect she is more interested whether there is a super band that plays the cha cha divinely.'

Susan was not, of course, consulted about what her father had told the newspaper, but when asked, she loyally supported him: 'I agree with Daddy. I think young people of eighteen don't know their own minds, and are a little too young to vote.' Daddy refused to let her wear black stockings, she said sadly. 'But in spite of that Daddy and I are on the best of terms.'[16]

Despite Susan Goodhew's loyal best efforts, the voting age was lowered to eighteen that very year, appropriately the first year of the sixties. The same year, *Lady Chatterley's Lover* was declared fit for publication by an Old Bailey jury and, when it came out eight days later, sold out its whole 200,000 print run in one day.

*

The sixties, then, were well under way by 1963 – indeed, I maintain they had been going for a full eight years. So why do most people follow Philip Larkin and date the start of the sixties (or the discovery of sex, which is more or less the same thing) to 1963?

> Sexual intercourse began in 1963
> Which was rather late for me
> Between the end of the Chatterley ban
> And the Beatles' first LP.

Chatterley and the Beatles have something to do with it. And of course some people did discover sex in 1963. Seventeen-year-old Marianne Faithfull, not yet the famous singer, actress and consort of Mick Jagger that she was to become, was one, and she discovered it in the simple but fashion-conscious way that the sixties generation took their sex. A nice and rather clever Home Counties convent girl of the Catholic middle classes, the daughter of a British army major (who was also a spy) and an Austro-Hungarian baroness, she turned up that year at Lord's cricket ground on the arm of one of my school friends for the annual cricket match against our 'traditional' rival, the Oratory. She must have abandoned him quite quickly, because later in the year she went to a Cambridge ball with another boy, and abandoned him in his turn when she met John Dunbar.

'He wasn't actually at the ball, he was much too cool for that. He would never have been caught dead at a bourgeois event such as a ball. But there was a party on the staircase at Churchill College.' On his door was a poster of the Da Vinci drawing 'The Measure of Man'. Marianne asked, 'Who lives there?' and John Dunbar came through the door. 'John had a beautiful, sensitive face and he was the very model of hipness, circa 1963. He was wearing pressed jeans and a jacket and little horn-rimmed glasses . . . I got rid of the boy I had come with and spent the evening with John.' We think the sixties was about being free, but from a very early age its icons knew it was about being cool.

Nineteen sixty-three was also the year of Dr Strangelove, in which Peter Sellers played several parts, including a mad American general determined to nuke the Commies. We knew America had all the power, but we could still stick our tongues out and make fun of them behind their backs. Watching *Dr Strangelove* in 1963 felt strangely like doing my celebrated impersonation of my old form master Father Bamber as his short, stout form disappeared down the corridor.

That same year, 70,000 CND demonstrators marched on London, and Harold Wilson took over as Labour leader after the untimely death of Hugh Gaitskell, presenting himself at his party's October conference as the politician who understood 'the white heat of technology'. It was the first year in which, in the cities, many women had access to oral contraceptives – the first oral contraceptive tablet, Conovid, came on the market two years earlier. It was the year the Beatles had three Number 1 hit singles: 'She Loves You', 'From Me to You' and 'I Want to Hold Your Hand'. And it was the year the Establishment held up its hands in defeat and invited the Beatles to perform at the stuffiest Establishment event there was, the Royal Variety Performance at the Prince of Wales Theatre, in front of the Queen. John Lennon displayed the best of sixties irreverence, suggesting from the stage that those in the cheap seats should clap and those in the expensive ones should rattle their jewellery.

Already, in 1963, not only were the sixties well under way, but the fifties had begun to fight back; and the fightback continued for the next two decades. Letting the Beatles on stage during the Royal Variety Performance was a tactical retreat, not (as some at the time thought) unconditional surrender. The BBC went into headlong retreat over *TW3*. The Beeching Report on the railways appeared on 27 March 1963, demanding that 2,000 stations should close, 70,000 jobs should be lost, and vast tracts of the countryside should in future be accessible only by motor car. Railways seemed of little interest to the baby boomers in 1963, but it signalled the beginning of the end of the egalitarianism inaugurated by the Attlee government. And on 22 November 1963, John F. Kennedy was assassinated. The glamorous and youthful President of the sixties generation was replaced by yet another middle-aged machine politician. It was a glimpse of what was to happen to the sixties.

6. The very model of a modern fluent technocrat: 1964–67

An age that sanctified youth and demonised age could not have chosen a more suitable Prime Minister than Harold Wilson. He was forty-eight when he took office in October 1964, the youngest Prime Minister since the Earl of Rosebery in 1894. Back in 1947, when he was appointed President of the Board of Trade at thirty-one, he had been the youngest cabinet minister since 1806. He was fluent in sixtiesspeak (though it fast mutated beyond him after he became Prime Minister). He was the very model of a modern fluent technocrat, establishing his credentials with his first speech as leader to Labour's conference the previous year, in which he talked of the scientific revolution, which

> cannot become a reality unless we are prepared to make far-reaching changes in economic and social attitudes which permeate our whole system of society. The Britain that is going to be forged in the white heat of this revolution will be no place for restrictive practices or for outdated methods on either side of industry . . .

He was photographed with the Beatles and arranged for them to be awarded MBEs 'for services to exports'. John Lennon stoked the indignation of what we would now call Middle England by claiming that they had smoked cannabis in Her Majesty's toilet on the day they were given their MBEs, which was what counted for rebellion in those days. The award distinguished Wilson from his predecessor as Prime Minister, the elderly aristocrat Sir Alec Douglas Home, whose speechwriters had inserted into a speech in Newcastle during the 1964 election the words 'I am too modest to claim that the country loves us, but you know that can't be bad' – the last six words being a line from the Beatles' hit 'She Loves You'. Showing he knew these words, they fondly hoped, would give the Prime Minister credibility with the young. Sadly, he did not know them, and, staring at the words on his script, he mumbled, 'You know, er, that can't be too bad.'[1]

Wilson's principal mentor in modernity was his Postmaster General, Anthony Wedgwood Benn, better known now as Tony Benn. Newspapers attacked Benn for being an over-zealous moderniser, but within twenty years they were attacking him for allegedly being out of date, and he had become a radical baby boomer icon. A former television producer, he was keen for Labour to adopt the most up-to-date advertising and public relations techniques, but after the mid-seventies was regularly accused of holding up Labour's march into the world of advertising and PR. His career holds within it all the ironies and oddities of the world the baby boomers made: a world that thought being modern was the ultimate good. 'Modern' is a wonderfully flexible word. It can mean anything at all. Once you have announced that something is 'modern' – say, for example, that cuts in welfare benefit are 'modern' – then anyone who opposes it is out of date.

The idea that modern was magic enjoyed a revival in Wilson's early years that it had not seen since the thirties, when it was annexed by Oswald Mosley's fascists, who called their organisation 'the modern movement'. In 1964 it was such a wonderfully resonant word that a national newspaper was founded specifically to promote it. The Sun was born out of the ashes of the Daily Herald, which had for years been the paper of the trade unions. That a national newspaper should exist in support of the unions seems a very strange idea to us, but for most of the fifties most people thought it entirely natural that the representatives of the workers – the forces of organised labour – should have a national newspaper to speak for them. After all, the employers – the forces of capital – had quite a lot of national newspapers to speak for them.

Here is how The Sun spelled out its purpose: 'It is an independent newspaper designed to serve and inform all those whose lives are changing, improving, expanding in these hurrying years. We welcome the age of automation, electronics, computers. We will campaign for the rapid modernisation of Britain.'[2]

People used to read the Daily Herald – so went the theory – because they were poor and therefore cared about their trade unions. Now they were part of the affluent society, and cared not a jot for their trade unions, and what they wanted instead was New, and Modern, and Young, and New, and Shiny, and New, especially New. New Labour was exactly thirty years in the future, but in the birth of *The Sun* the baby boomers were seeing the laying of the shallow foundations which were all that it required.

The theory was wrong, though that did not stop it from being the dominant theory of the next forty years. *The Sun* sold three million on its first day, but within four days the circulation was down to 1.75 million, and it carried on falling until it was selling fewer copies than the *Daily Herald* had in its last months. In 1969, having never turned a profit, *The Sun* was sold for a knockdown price to Australian newspaper proprietor Rupert Murdoch. The voice of the unions was swiftly replaced with vigorous union-bashing.

If modern was God, old things were valueless. Because it knew no history, and was sure it had little to learn from it, the sixties generation protested against everything except the destruction of their own history. It was left to thirties figures like John Betjeman to point out that the Doric arch at Euston Station, which came down in 1961, or the Coal Exchange in Lower Thames Street and Lewisham Town Hall, both of which came down in 1962, could never be replaced for future generations. Thousands of other Georgian and Victorian buildings were destroyed in that decade, and replaced by nondescript concrete lumps. Betjeman, full of unfashionable anger, wrote:

> And if some preservationist attempts to interfere
> A 'dangerous structure' notice from the borough engineer
> Will settle any buildings that are standing in our way –
> The modern style, sir, with respect, has really come to stay.[3]

The idolising of modernisation did at least give science its moment in the sun. For a little while, scientists were the favoured sons in universities and government departments, getting the best of everything: money, buildings, equipment, research grants.

*

Harold Wilson had the political brain to profit from the cult of the new and the glitzy, and the common sense not to be taken in by it, which makes him 50 per cent cleverer than his baby boomer successors. But his government had a wafer-thin parliamentary majority of just four seats, and was bound not to survive long. On their first day in office, Wilson and Chancellor James Callaghan learned that the annual trade deficit was £800 million, twice the figure they had been led to expect. Swiftly they decided against devaluation – which meant that for the next three years everything else had to take second place to the defence of the pound.

Yet he and Callaghan set out a radical and ambitious agenda: abolishing prescription charges, scrapping the Tories' Rent Act, allowing a free vote on hanging (which was abolished), nationalising the steel industry, improving pensions and benefits and increasing income tax to pay for them, introducing capital gains tax and corporation tax. Wilson established the Open University – a personal dream of his, and probably the single greatest contribution to universal education since the 1944 Education Act. When Wilson died, Tony Benn said, rightly, that if Wilson had done nothing else with his life, the Open University was still an achievement massively greater than most political lives could boast.

New universities were built, colleges of education were expanded, and the recommendations of two landmark 1963 reports advocating expansion of higher education, the Robbins and Newsome Reports, were energetically implemented.

But there was a run on the pound, and the governor of the Bank of England, Lord Cromer, demanded savage cuts in government spending. Wilson threatened to go to the country on a 'bankers versus democracy' ticket if the Bank did not back down, and he won, though it meant raising a $3,000 million loan to protect sterling. The contrast with Gordon Brown's cautious approach to the bankers in 2009–10 could hardly be more marked.

US President Lyndon Johnson pressed him to send troops to support the Americans in Vietnam, and Wilson refused. It was the first time since Suez that a British Prime Minister had stood up to an American President, and it was the last. Johnson did not like it at all, reminding Wilson on every possible occasion of Britain's poor financial standing and America's ability to cripple her financially. Wilson withstood this heavyweight bullying. Few British Prime Ministers in the last half-century would have done that. Without Wilson, the baby boomers might well have had to fight and die in Vietnam.

He settled a rail strike with a reasonable compromise, rather typically sending out for beer and sandwiches so that he and the rail union leaders could keep talking without going hungry, a sensible arrangement for which he has been sneered at by most of his successors. The sneer was supposedly for appeasing union leaders with beer and sandwiches, but there was an overlay of snobbery too. It would have been better if he had sent out for caviar and claret.

All of this would have been brave and radical from a Prime Minister with a large Parliamentary majority. From one with a majority of just four, it was extraordinary.

Wilson called a general election for 31 March 1966 and won an overall Commons majority of ninety-seven. But the radical edge seemed to go out of his government. He did not bring left-wingers like Michael Foot into the government, which his old friends on the left had hoped he would do once he had a comfortable majority. He allowed himself to be dissuaded by Richard Crossman, who had been his Housing Minister and was now Leader of the House of Commons, from announcing straightaway a renewed bid to negotiate entry to the EEC. He handled the seamen's strike much less sure-footedly than he had handled the rail strike, famously denouncing the National Union of Seamen leaders as 'a tightly knit group of politically motivated men' and accusing them of being pawns of Moscow. MI5 had told him that the NUS leaders were in clandestine contact with Bert Ramelson, industrial organiser of the Communist Party, which they were, but nonetheless the seamen had a good case and were united in pursuit of it.

Speculators moved against the pound, and Wilson introduced a statutory incomes policy. Callaghan and other ministers wanted to devalue the pound, but the Prime Minister vetoed that, instead cutting public spending and reining in the radicalism of his government. His dream of an expanding, science-led economy was no more.

Labour government no longer looked radical, or glitzy, or exciting, or new, or modern, and by 1967 the baby boomers had decisively turned against Harold Wilson. They saw him executing careful political balancing acts and thought him hypocritical. The two things wrong with Wilson, ran the joke at the time, were his face. And it was certainly true that Wilson was one of the great political high-wire acts. He kept his fractious party more or less united, postponing for a decade the factionalism that split and splintered Labour in the seventies and eighties. The baby boomers learned to despise him for trying to be all things to all men, for being a cautious, compromising, homely, pipe-smoking, petit-bourgeois politician. They despised him for paying lip-service to President Johnson's war in Vietnam, while they marched in the streets chanting, 'Hey, hey, LBJ, how many kids did you kill today?' One of the most hypnotically horrible cartoons ever published appeared on the front cover of *Private Eye* on 30 April 1965. It was by Gerald Scarfe, and showed a slavering Wilson kneeling behind LBJ and lowering the back of the President's trousers. 'VIETNAM – WILSON RIGHT BEHIND JOHNSON,' read the headline.

They did not realise that Britain could easily have had a Prime Minister, of either party, whom LBJ could have bullied; who would have lost his nerve in the face of the President's power to destroy Britain's economy. Then Britain would have been part of the war.

While the baby boomers were demanding more freedoms, Wilson was providing them. Nineteen sixty-seven was a remarkable year for liberal legislation. There was the Abortion Act, put forward by Liberal MP David Steel and supported by the government, which liberated working-class baby boomer women from the horrors of illegal back-street abortionists: it required only that two doctors be satisfied that an abortion was necessary on medical or psychological grounds. The National Health Service (Family Planning) Act made it possible for local authorities to provide contraceptives and contraceptive advice. And Labour MP Leo Abse piloted through the Sexual Offences Act, which at last made homosexuality legal. Two years later, in 1969, the Divorce Reform Act allowed divorce if a marriage had broken down irretrievably and the couple had lived apart for two years. For centuries, divorce had only been allowed if one party could prove the other was guilty of a 'matrimonial offence'. It was the most liberal package of legislation provided by any government, though Wilson got little thanks from its chief beneficiaries, the young.

It helped break the shackles of class for the baby boomer generation, who are far more socially mobile than their parents. For their parents, as Arthur Marwick puts it,

to be working class in the sixties, despite the occasional instance of rapid upward mobility, meant a life sentence of hard manual work where, by an implicit irony, the attainment of middle-class living standards was only possible through expending, on overtime, even more excessive amounts of energy in a traditionally working class way.

The upper class still had most of the positions of power. More than a third of Wilson's Labour cabinet were traditional upper-class figures, and six had attended the most exclusive of the public schools. Only two ministers had graduated from universities other than Oxford.[4] The Wilson government was not exceptional in this, and things have not improved since. Every one of the eleven Prime Ministers in the second half of the twentieth century who went to university had been to Oxford. (Three did not go to university at all: Winston Churchill, James Callaghan and John Major.) And Oxford University still takes about half its intake from the 7 per cent of the population who attended fee-charging schools.

The baby boomers despised Wilson for being lower middle-class instead of upper, but such was the spirit of the time that they had to pretend they were despising him for not being working-class. In truth, one of the most attractive things about Wilson and his wife Mary was that they were not ones for show, and never became rich or aspired to become rich. They lived very simply, in a bourgeois and rather old-fashioned way, much as Clement Attlee and his wife Vi had done. But Attlee had been to public school, so in him it was considered a lovable eccentricity. Wilson was a lower middle-class Yorkshireman, so he was sneered at by former public schoolboys, such as Winchester-educated Richard Crossman, who went to lunch in the Downing Street flat in which the Prime Minister of the day lives with his family, and reported afterwards with distaste: 'An Irish maid slammed down in front of me a plate with a piece of steak, two veg and a bit of cold salad. On the table were two tins of Skol beer, which I don't like.' I do not see what the rather snobbish Crossman was complaining about – it sounds like a perfectly good lunch to me, and the Prime Minister saw that his guest didn't take to the Skol and fetched him a glass of claret – but Crossman went on: 'Nothing could be more petit bourgeois than the way he lives in those crowded little servants' quarters up there.' Crossman at least recognised that this was a strength in Wilson – 'He doesn't respect the upper classes for having superior cultural tastes which he would like to share.'[5]

But that phrase of Crossman's – 'petit bourgeois' – was a very sixties insult. In the fifties it would have been 'bourgeois' with a Marxist significance. The addition of the word 'petit' enabled it to be both radical and snobbish at the same time. It allowed the children of the sixties to sneer at a man for having capitalist views, and at the same time to sneer at him for being lower, not upper, middle-class.

Thus *Private Eye*'s regular feature 'Mrs Wilson's Diary' had the Prime Minister's wife betraying her lower middle-class origins by talking about arranging her plaster ducks nicely in the lounge, offering her husband 'yellow cling peaches with banana-flavoured topping' for his lunch, putting HP Sauce on food and drinking Sanatogen Tonic Wine. Somehow all this made her at one and the same time reactionary and plebeian. It was a triumph of the early sixties to make snobbery look radical. This is what enabled children of the sixties, who were far less radical and left-wing than Wilson himself, to sneer at him and feel somehow that they were being progressive in doing so. They never realised – for they had not yet heard of Tony Blair – how lucky they were to have Wilson to despise.

They despised him for not implementing a red-blooded socialist agenda, but they would have denounced him for a Stalinist if he had. Most of all, they despised him for being middle-aged. The lure of the new, the worship of the young, from which Wilson had benefited in 1964, had become a stick to beat him with by 1967. He wasn't new and shiny any more. He was shop-worn and sly and over fifty.

*

For there had never been a time that was so unforgiving about age. Even Winston Churchill, whom an earlier generation considered beyond criticism and called the greatest living Englishman, was lampooned in *Private Eye* as he lay dying. The magazine called him the GDE, or Greatest Dying Englishman, and reminded the world that he had once turned the army on striking Welsh miners. Was nothing sacred? No: that was the whole point.

Churchill's state funeral on 30 January 1965 divided those who, however dimly, remembered the war from those who did not – the war babies from the baby boomers. The baby boomers had only the most approximate idea what it was all about. Churchill was neither the present, nor was he history, for the history we were taught in our schools was all about medieval monarchs. Those who were born before the war ended thinking respect is a virtue; those born afterwards think it a weakness.

Greg Dyke told me that his older brother, born just six years earlier in 1941, respects authority and always has done; but Dyke himself does not. It is not a difference in their character, he says, but their generations. Richard Crossman wrote in his diary after Churchill's funeral:

> But oh, what a faded, declining establishment surrounded me. Aged marshals, grey, dreary ladies, decadent Marlboroughs and Churchills. It was a dying congregation gathered there and I am afraid the Labour cabinet didn't look too distinguished either. It felt like the end of an epoch, possibly even the end of a nation.'[6]

Twenty-five million people watched the ceremony on television. Laurence Olivier spoke the commentary for the ITV coverage, which he considered a great honour. London pavements were crowded with silent people, most of them dressed in their best, as Greg Dyke's parents had dressed to see King George VI's coffin pass on the train. They watched the gun carriage bearing Churchill's coffin leave Westminster Hall at 9.45 on its way to St Paul's Cathedral for the funeral service. On the steps of the cathedral, Churchill's old comrade and opponent Clement Attlee, himself old and frail and with only another year to live, could suddenly no longer stand, and had to sit on the steps and recover himself. He had turned up at both the funeral and the rehearsal the previous day, against his doctor's advice: he was not going to make a mistake at Winston's funeral through missing the rehearsal. He was in a state of near-collapse when he got home.

After the service, the funeral cortege was accompanied by a nineteen-gun salute and an RAF flypast as the coffin was taken to the Thames and piped aboard a launch to go to Waterloo, where a train named *Winston Churchill* carried it to Oxford, to be taken to the Oxfordshire parish churchyard of Bladon, close to Blenheim Palace, where he had been born ninety years before.

Amid all the grief, no one stopped to ask: why Waterloo? If you want to go to Oxford, you leave from Paddington. The reason was that

Churchill had asked to go via Waterloo. The civil servant responsible for the arrangements said, 'Surely you mean Paddington, Sir Winston. You can't get to Oxfordshire from Waterloo.' Yes, you can, explained Churchill: there was a spur line. He was told it was much more complicated, so he agreed a compromise. If General de Gaulle died before he did, they could take him out through Paddington. But if De Gaulle were alive, and had to attend the funeral, Churchill insisted that it should pass through Waterloo.

For Peter Hitchens, Churchill's funeral was 'also the funeral of the British Empire, leaving all British people who witnessed it shaken, bereft and afraid for the future.'[7] Perhaps. I think I felt optimistic about the future. But it was certainly the funeral of respect and deference. It freed a new generation to do its own thing. Whatever that might turn out to be.

*

The cult of youth penetrated the arts too. Laurence Olivier, when he was appointed the first director of the National Theatre in 1962, felt so fearful of the charge of being stuffy and middle-aged that he appointed as his literary manager the young critic Kenneth Tynan, the man who had written of *Look Back in Anger* that it would be liked by everyone under thirty. Olivier was advised against the appointment, not least by John Osborne himself, who saw in Tynan simply a superficial sense of what was fashionable. Perhaps that was what Olivier wanted. He wanted the critic of the modern theatre, in Lyndon Johnson's famous phrase, inside the tent pissing out, not outside pissing in.

John Osborne was only one of those who thought the professional result disastrous, with several avant-garde productions of obscure plays generally championed by Tynan. The big row came in 1967 over a play by a German playwright, Rolf Hochhuth, called *The Soldiers* – an attack on the Allied bombing of Hamburg and Dresden during the war, and on Olivier's old hero Winston Churchill, the Prime Minister who ordered it. Olivier did not much like the play, but Tynan did, and Olivier did not want to appear out of touch. The board decided against the play, and the Lord Chamberlain ruled that it could not be seen without the permission of Churchill's family. The board wanted Tynan's scalp;

Olivier, who still thought he needed Tynan, managed to protect him. Tynan's judgement was starting to cause Olivier embarrassment, but he continued to defer to it, for he thought it was the voice of Youth.

But what did Youth actually think? Youth thought folksinger Bob Dylan was a revolutionary symbol, and Bob Dylan told them in 1964 that all that was needed was to get rid of the nitpicking of the middle-aged. 'The Times They Are A-Changing' told mothers and fathers not to criticise what they couldn't understand: 'Your sons and your daughters are beyond your command.' Parents should get out of the way of the young if they couldn't help to build the new world. But the song offers no hint about what the new world consists of.

Today, 'The Times They Are A-Changing' is on YouTube, and the comment from the person who put it there is: 'People, Obama isn't going to bring change. He's another puppet in the stage that is the New World Order. Broaden your perspective to beyond what CNN tells you, yeah?' The spirit of the sixties lives on, weary, negative, but unbowed.

Dylan, rightly, thought of himself as a child of the fifties, not the sixties, but his, more than almost anyone else's, was the voice that shaped the sixties, when he was the royalty of the young, and shaped the mindset of the baby boomers.

On 26 April 1965, wrote Marianne Faithfull, 'God himself checked into the Savoy Hotel; Bob Dylan came to town, wearing Phil Spector shades, an aureole of hair and seething irony. Dylan was, at that moment in time, nothing less than the hippest person on earth . . . I adored Dylan as a prince of poets, hoped he'd be nice to me and dig me (the only possible word, that year).'

She went to his hotel suite, and she sat on the floor with the rest of the Dylan court. She knew that 'the tribute traditionally laid at the feet of pop stars by their female fans was sex.' But when it came to be time to pay that tribute, she found herself dreadfully in awe of this god of the sixties and blurted out the truth: 'I'm pregnant and about to get married next week.' He threw a tantrum and threw her out.[8]

Dylan emerges from Marianne Faithfull's account of the meeting as a fraud, a ridiculous poseur, a misogynist and a shit. Nonetheless, Greg Dyke, who remains to this day an ardent Dylan fan, says, 'Bob Dylan represented something, as did the Beatles, as did Jagger.' But what on earth was it? 'He represented a rejection of society as it was organised.'

To this day there are men (and perhaps a few women) who think he represented the free spirit of the sixties. Perhaps he did.

That year, 1965, came The Who's 'My Generation', with Roger Daltrey's famous scream of generational intolerance: 'I hope I die before I get old.' He didn't; he is with us still, a comfortable, well-off man in his sixties. In 2006 he starred as the voice of Argon the Dragon Bus Driver in a children's DVD, for which he sang 'The Wheels on the Bus Go Round and Round'.

The Rolling Stones signed their first recording contract with Decca in 1963, and within a year they were very big, second only to the Beatles. The same year as The Who released 'My Generation', the Stones released 'Mother's Little Helper', in which Mick Jagger lamented, 'What a drag it is getting old!' They also produced a remarkable song (released as the B side of '(I Can't Get No) Satisfaction') called 'The Spider and the Fly'. The Stones seemed somehow more in tune with the mood of rebellion than the Beatles; the Beatles still looked smart, wore suits and sang about love, while the Stones looked and sounded edgy, a little dangerous, and Mick Jagger's good looks were raddled and youthfully careworn.

'The Spider and the Fly' was a wonderful, evocative song, sixties music-making at its best. It told of Jagger sitting in a bar after he had done his gig, and looking at the blonde beside him. She was 'common, flirty, she looked about thirty.' She was, for heaven's sake, a machine operator, and she told him she liked the way he held the microphone. All these warning signs! Listening to it, you could hear, feel and smell the noisy, grubby bar where it is set, the tobacco smoke and stale booze, the desperation of the girl whom Mick Jagger was about to go to bed with, for want of anything better to do.

Mick Jagger, a middle-class grammar-school boy from Kent, the son of a teacher, must surely have picked up the word 'common' from his parents or grandparents. It was an old-fashioned way of saying that someone came from too low a social class to be proper company for you. Machine operators, of course, would have come from such a class. Jagger's class antennae had been activated. On top of that, she was a full thirty years old, a sin in the youth culture of 1965. But the woman – too old, too poor, and so musically ignorant that all she noticed was the way he held the microphone – would do for a quick screw.

What 'The Spider and the Fly' told you about 1965 was that while rebellion was in the air, it wasn't rebellion for a better society, or a fairer society. It was a cruel, snobbish, cynical, misogynistic rebellion.

Marianne Faithfull writes of the ex-girlfriend of one of the Rolling Stones, Brian Jones, holding up a baby outside his flat, in 1965, the year of 'The Spider and The Fly'. 'It's your kid, Brian, you know it is. We're really in a bad way, we need some help.' Faithfull writes: 'Brian and Anita [Pallenberg, his then girlfriend] just peered down on them as if they were some inferior species. Foppish aristocrats in their finery jeering at the sans culottes below.'[9] The fantasy, said Mick Jagger about this time, 'is driving around in a big car, having all the chicks you want and being able to pay for it. It always has been, always will be.'[10]

Another 1965 Stones release spelled out clearly how the leaders of the new world thought their women should behave. He's told his girl friend over and over again what she's to do, but she persists in her faults: 'You don't try very hard to please me. / With what you know it should be easy.' In 1966, after Mick Jagger started his long and difficult relationship with Marianne Faithfull, he wrote 'Under My Thumb' about his previous girlfriend, Chrissie Shrimpton. The song is about the satisfaction of subduing a formerly dominant woman. No vision of a better and fairer world here. Nor in Manfred Mann's 'Kingpin' (1965), a contemptuous look at how working-class men were popularly supposed to handle unemployment and their women. I love you, it says, but don't forget that 'I'm your kingpin.' 'Kingpin' gives the orders, spends the dole, says where we're going to go. 'Kingpin', too, was beautiful, melodic, evocative. It was like watching a brilliant production of Shakespeare's *The Taming of the Shrew* – the performance, the words, the sounds, all wonderful, all to a dreadful, bullying, misogynistic purpose.

Nor could Harold Wilson look to the gilded young for support for even modest measures of redistribution of wealth. In the warm summer university term of 1966 The Kinks had a Number 1 hit with 'Sunny Afternoon', the lament of a rich man after a visit from the tax inspector: 'Tax man's taken all my dough . . .'

Marianne Faithfull walked in Kings Road, Chelsea, in 1966. There she saw 'shop windows filled with bright Smartie colours. Miniskirts, sequinned gowns, slinky thigh-high boots, brass earrings, boas. Everything sparkling, modern, dazzling.' She and her friends were, she says with disarming honesty, 'young, rich and beautiful, and the tide was turning in our favour. We were going to change everything, of course, but mostly we were going to change the rules. Unlike our parents, we would never have to renounce our youthful hedonism in favour of the insane world of adulthood.'[11]

The rebellion in that world was in being young, and new, and modern; and in nothing else at all. Even sex and drugs, supposedly emblematic of the sixties, were used largely as distinguishing marks by which a generation could separate itself from the generation ahead of it. Two of the Rolling Stones, Mick Jagger and Keith Richards, were prosecuted for possession of drugs in 1967. The police raid had been set up by the editor of the News of the World, who needed to stand up an incorrect story that Jagger had been seen taking amphetamines.[12] They were demonised by journalists and politicians, who, as Marianne Faithfull puts it, were 'no more capable than the most smitten rock fan of disentangling the two Micks, the dancing god on stage and record, and the mild-mannered, middle-class boy he actually was.'[13]

The playwright Tom Stoppard says:

> By the mid-1960s young people started off with more liberty than they knew what to do with, but confused it with sexual liberation and the freedom to get high so it all went to waste – wasted, that is, in a cultural revolution rather than social revolution . . . The idea that 'make love, not war' is a more practical slogan than 'workers of the world unite' is as airy-fairy as the I Ching.[14]

But even 'Make love, not war' had more meaning than much that passed for revolution in the sixties. Marianne Faithfull acquired a reputation among the young as a rebel, and a reputation among the middle-aged as a seriously dangerous revolutionary, for this sort of stuff, from a BBC interview in 1967:

> This studio, for instance, is fantastic! Light, Communism and electricity! Electricity is the answer! We live in light – light – fiat lux! Do you see? Marijuana's perfectly safe, it's an old scene, man. Drugs really are the doors of perception . . . Do you feel them closing in on you? I do. It could be Harold Wilson or MI5 or little men in offices . . .'[15]

Marianne Faithfull herself knows how absurd it all was. Sadly, she didn't in the sixties, and neither did journalists or politicians, who seem to have thought they were dealing with someone dangerous.

*

There had never been a time when young people in Britain took so much of their political lead from young people in the USA.

The counterculture, as it came to be called, was being carried to Britain from the USA, first by Bob Dylan and Joan Baez, then by young men who fled here to avoid the draft. These young men refused their parents the right to tell them what to do, on much the same grounds, had we but known it, as Rudyard Kipling adopted after his beloved son was killed in the First World War:

> If people question why we died
> Tell them, because our fathers lied.

Once in Britain, these young Americans sounded more schooled in radicalism than we did, because they had been through more; and because they knew more about drugs; and because their rhetoric outstripped their radicalism. I remember one tall, raddled young Californian telling me that he was guilty and would always be guilty, and would spend his life atoning. 'For what?' I asked, and he replied in a tormented voice, 'Because I'm white, man.'

We did not realise that, beneath its revolutionary rhetoric, the ideology of left-wing young people in the USA was only cautious liberalism. They lived in a country where socialism had been destroyed by decades of repression. I did not realise until I visited the USA in 1969 how far to the right of ours was their centre of political gravity in those days. (We have closed the gap since.) I, too, thought those young Americans in London spearheaded some sort of revolution. But they did not.

The American influence on British universities was greatest in what were then called the new universities. Today when we talk of new universities, we mean former polytechnics, but the phrase meant something very different in the sixties. New universities then meant the clutch of genuinely new institutions, some of them in 1965 still largely building sites – Keele, Sussex, York, Essex, Kent, Lancaster, Warwick – which had broken the artificial perimeter walls that surrounded different subjects. Like American universities, they had a campus, rather than a clutch of buildings in a city, and you could mix and match your courses, which made them a cut above the stuffy old-fashioned English universities where you went to study, say, history, and that is what you spent three years studying. These were the places where those most addicted to the sixties really wanted to go.

I felt the cult of the new as keenly as anyone, perhaps more than most. In the winter of 1964–5, I was at work and not enjoying it. I had done a series of jobs and reached the very sixties conclusion that working was a drag, man. I decided I would go to university after all, two years late.

But which? At Beaumont, university meant old ivy-covered institutions – Oxford, Cambridge, Trinity College Dublin. At other, less privileged schools, university meant what Beaumont would contemptuously have called redbrick – the great civic universities like Manchester and Leeds: old, without even the compensation of being posh. No: for me, university had to smell of the sixties.

I wanted to be housed in utilitarian concrete buildings with odd-shaped spaces and a whiff of New World excitement, where I could mix every day with the products of the sixties, without ever seeing the grey middle-aged folk who constituted most of my fellow citizens.

So in September 1965 I presented myself at Keele University in Staffordshire. Keele was the first of the new universities, founded as the University College of North Staffordshire in 1949 by A. D. Lindsay, former Master of Balliol and Vice Chancellor of Oxford, who had earned his footnote in the history books by standing for parliament in the 1938 Oxford City by-election as an independent candidate opposed to Neville Chamberlain's Munich settlement with Hitler. After the war, unnoticed by most history books, he had done something far more significant, and founded a university the like of which has never been seen in Britain, before or since.

Lindsay was at one with C. P. Snow – he too thought that Britain had too many illiterate scientists and innumerate writers. At his university you studied two main subjects, and two subsidiary subjects – and one of the four had to be a science, and one a humanities subject. It had a four-year course, the first being a foundation year in which you surveyed the whole spectrum of human knowledge. Like almost every Keele graduate of my generation, I regret not taking it seriously enough.

But how could I have done? Life was good. For me Keele became, in a real sense, a home. I was two years older than many of my contemporaries – I had more experience, and I had hung about the streets of Notting Hill, and smoked a lot of cannabis, which did not reach Keele until a year or two later. In my childhood I had lived in eight homes and attended seven schools, and had never rested anywhere long enough to feel at home.

Compared with the life students live now, my student days were idyllic. My by now widowed mother being demonstrably penniless, I had a full grant, which all local authorities had to provide to those students who needed it; and of course no one paid for tuition. The very thought would have horrified us. We did not stop to think that not so long ago, everyone paid. Keele had on-campus accommodation for all its students (no university has that today) so that I had not a care in the world. It was built around an eccentric but interesting seventeenth-century manor house, Keele Hall, which had a splendid lake, and beyond the lake was wild, wet woodland.

Everything else – lecture theatres, teaching spaces, halls of residence, the library, the students union – was simple, modern, built of concrete and glass, and convenient. The new students' union building, erected just before I arrived, stood in the centre of the campus, and in a sense in the centre of my life. It felt spacious, with a minimum of walls and a great, wide, sweeping staircase right up the centre. There was a big, square, domed ballroom for dances and debates and union meetings, and a bar with draught beer for one shilling and elevenpence halfpenny a pint.

Because it was a campus university, small and a little inward-looking, life was intense. Politics was taken seriously. In the early sixties, the university was known locally as The Kremlin on the Hill because it was left-wing, in a tweedy sort of way, but who knew what the mid-sixties were to bring? There was a hint of it just before I arrived – it happened in the previous summer term, but the whole campus was still talking about it. One Sunday morning, the BBC's *Songs of Praise* was being broadcast from the Keele chapel. The night before the broadcast, someone interfered with the electrics so that in the middle of the service, what was being heard in the chapel and broadcast to the nation suddenly was not some great, orotund hymn but the ferocious 1964 hit by the Shangri-Las, 'Leader of the Pack', which had been banned by the BBC, with its insistent motor-bike noises, its raucous music and lyrics, and its very sixties attack on the middle-aged.

As though he had anticipated the sixties spirit, A. D. Lindsay had thoughtfully provided a ludicrous rule requiring men to be out of women's blocks, and women out of men's blocks, by 11pm, and the university attempted to enforce it. It was something stupid that the sixties generation could kick down, which we set to work to do, and it absorbed some of the radical energy that might otherwise have gone somewhere else.

I had intended to study English and history, but the Keele foundation year persuaded me to abandon English and study history and philosophy, mainly so that I could go into the wonderful, freethinking Keele philosophy department and hear the great Anthony Flew, a key figure in the linguistic philosophy of the period, teach more or less the pure gospel of A. J. Ayer and logical positivism. From Flew I learned that there isn't a God, that this messy, haphazard life is all there is. From his colleague John Grundy I learned that it's possible to work out, and live by, a moral system that does not depend on a vengeful God who will make you fry for ever unless you obey him. We atheists can be just as good as Christians. Better, maybe, because when we are kind, or truthful, or unselfish, it is not simply because we are terrified of the horrible things God will do to us if we are not. There must be some intrinsic good in us.

Theirs was the wonderfully liberating doctrine that nothing – nothing at all – may be taken for granted: nothing we are told, and not even the evidence of our own senses. 'It does not normally occur to us that there is any need for us to justify our belief in the existence of material things,' says A. J. Ayer. But there is such a need. What we perceive is not the objects themselves, but what Ayer calls 'sense data'.[16] It was a wonderful preparation for what was good about the sixties, which was its freethinking; and a wonderful antidote to what was bad about the sixties, the magic and superstition, the idea that mind-altering drugs brought you in some way closer to spirituality.

In other, less thoughtful of the decade's many chambers, religious ideas were developing that seemed even nuttier than the God of our fathers. 'Like a lot of people at the time, myself included,' wrote Marianne Faithfull, 'he [Brian Jones of the Rolling Stones] was convinced there was a mystic link between druidic monuments and flying saucers.'[17] It would be easy – a great many people did it in the sixties – to replace divine revelation with mysticism. For students brought up to accept without question the assertions of ministers of religion, or inclined to be taken in by the mystics of the sixties, or tempted by Marxist historicism, a session with Tony Flew was always a little like having a bucket of ice-cold water thrown over you. He had a grand contempt for vague, metaphysical statements, and loved stripping arguments down to their skeletons. 'Can you hit it with a hammer?' he would ask when confronted with a particularly nebulous concept.

Forty years later I learned that, in his eighties, Anthony Flew, before dying in 2010, decided there is, after all, a God. And I thought: is nothing sacred?

7. The end of the adventure: 1968

The sixties began in 1956 with Soviet tanks rolling into Hungary, and ended in 1968 with Soviet tanks rolling into Czechoslovakia. They started in 1956 with the British government impotently furious with Washington for refusing to let us fight in Suez, and ended in 1968 with Britons furious that the Americans insisted on fighting in Vietnam.

The sixties opened with the instinctive radicalism of youth searching for an outlet, shouting in despair, 'There are no good, brave causes left,' and ended with so many different and conflicting outlets for radicalism that youth did not know where to put itself.

When they started in 1956, hope and inspiration seemed to come from America. The year they ended, 1968, was the year American hope and inspiration seemed to die. Martin Luther King was assassinated in April and Robert Kennedy in June. Eugene McCarthy, the hope of the young and the sixties generation, after a storming start on the presidential campaign train in New Hampshire in March, found his campaign snuffed out by the time of the Democratic Party convention in August. President Lyndon Johnson was succeeded by a very right-wing and rather corrupt Republican, Richard Nixon.

The sixties came to Britain from America in 1956, and emigrated to France in 1968. Left-wing student politics in France in 1968 have been accurately described as 'such a dense and dangerous jungle that only those raised in it really ever know their way about'.[1] This sectarian spirit was tightening its grip on British student politics too.

The spirit of the age was for revolutionary slogans under which could shelter a host of theories, political grouplets, and one-off causes. Of the causes, the first was opposition to the American war in Vietnam. But even this was not a simple matter. There were those who demanded simply that the Americans should stop tormenting the Vietnamese people with bombs and napalm, and get out of their country. And there were those whose slogan was 'unconditional support for the struggle of the Vietnamese people' – that is, for the forces that fought under Ho Chi Minh. Among these were numbered what the French called the *enragés*, who were, in essence, left-wing provocateurs and saw their task as to provoke the establishment into exposing its true, brutal colours. The name was taken from a radical group active in the French Revolution of 1789.

The position of the more radical faction was strengthened at the start of the year when the North Vietnamese launched their stunningly effective Tet Offensive, and a South Vietnamese general was photo-graphed executing (or rather murdering) a Viet Cong prisoner. In just one week in February, 543 Americans were killed in action and 2,547 wounded. And in March came the dreadful My Lai massacre, though it was a year before the world heard about it: three hours of frenzied killing by American troops, in which 500 Vietnamese civilians, from the very old to the very young, lost their lives.

In London, March 1968 saw a great demonstration against the Vietnam war in Trafalgar Square, organised by the Vietnam Solidarity Campaign, whose chief spokesman was Tariq Ali, the founder of the International Marxist Group, one of the tiny warring Trotskyist sects. Tariq Ali, in his mid-twenties, came from a prosperous Pakistani family and had been president of the Oxford Union. The VSC campaign, said Ali, was 'committed to the victory of the Vietnamese people against the war of aggression and atrocity waged by the United States,' which sharply distinguished it from the traditional pacifist group, the British Council for Peace in Vietnam.

Between 10,000 and 25,000 demonstrators assembled in Trafalgar Square to march to the American embassy in Grosvenor Square. There, Vanessa Redgrave, the actor and leading light of another Trotskyist sect, the Socialist Labour League (SLL), later to become the Workers Revolutionary Party, delivered a letter of protest; and the police tried to make the crowd disperse. Protesters hurled mud, stones, firecrackers and smoke bombs. Mounted police charged into the tightly packed crowd. More than 200 people were arrested.

John Lennon was against the demonstration. 'Don't expect me to be on the barricades unless it's with flowers,' he said. Mick Jagger was for it, or so it seemed: he was there on 17 March, and went home and wrote 'Street Fighting Man'. The revolution helped turn him into a multi-millionaire.[2] The song rather suggested he thought the demonstrators ought to have been much more violent: '. . . in sleepy London Town there's just no place for a street fighting man.'

How those demonstrators remember the events of the day varies, according to what, in retrospect, they think of the sixties. João Monjardino, who was barred from a medical career in his native Portugal because of his opposition to the Salazar regime and settled in London in 1961 to do cancer research, told *The Guardian* in 2008:

> I remember the strength of feeling of the demonstrators, and the strength of action – brutality would be a better word – of the police. I am as strong an opponent of the war in Iraq today as I was of the Vietnam war then. At least at the time Britain was shamed only by its association with the US, but had the wisdom not to send troops to assist them.

Donald Fraser, then a postgraduate student from New Zealand and now a retired lecturer in English at Strathclyde University, recalls

> somehow being fairly near the front, where I was surprised to find a number of people in the crowd urging us to rush forward and storm the embassy steps. The rumour was that US Marines armed with machine guns were behind the doors and would fire live ammunition, so I was pretty reluctant! I also remember feeling sorry for the police horses, as there was talk of throwing ball-bearings under their hooves.

But he adds that the demonstrations

> helped force the US out of Vietnam. They really did mean something, I'm convinced of that. I'm not one of those who jeers at the sixties. I'm not a heavy-duty activist and I wasn't one then; I couldn't bring myself to chant, 'Ho, Ho, Ho Chi Minh' or 'Victory to the Vietcong'. But 1968 was a hugely significant moment. Even in this class-ridden country, life – socially, culturally, politically – just opened out.

March 1968 'had a big impact on the outlook of many of my generation, and on the political culture we inhabited,' said Gordon Coxon. But then, he wonders, 'What do I know? . . . Pretty soon after I was living in a commune in south London, consuming large quantities of pot and playing drums in a rock band. Then came the hallucinogens – and the world really changed.'[3]

Here's how Tariq Ali himself sees it, forty years on.

A storm swept the world in 1968. It started in Vietnam, then blew across Asia, crossing the sea and the mountains to Europe and beyond. A brutal war waged by the US against a poor south-east Asian country was seen every night on television. The cumulative impact of watching the bombs drop, villages on fire and a country being doused with napalm and Agent Orange triggered a wave of global revolts not seen on such a scale before or since.

If the Vietnamese were defeating the world's most powerful state, surely we, too, could defeat our own rulers: that was the dominant mood among the more radical of the 60s generation . . .[4]

Well, perhaps it was the mood, but it's impossible to avoid the feeling that polite, well-educated, prosperous young people like Tariq Ali and Mick Jagger were playing at revolution.

Ali has over the years found himself a comfortable niche as a sort of licensed radical in a society that today is far further away from the ideals he embraces than it was in 1968. And Jagger? He was not at all a street fighting man. He was a middle-class grammar-school boy from Kent with rather reactionary social opinions, known today as Sir Michael and by all accounts delighted to be so. But in 1968, such was the confused ferment of the time, he did briefly consider entering politics – though not the sort of politics of which Tariq Ali would have approved, had he known about it. The legendary Tom Driberg, a flamboyant left-wing Labour MP whose homosexuality had been public knowledge long before it became legal, and who probably spied for both the Russians and the British, made an approach. Marianne Faithfull writes that Driberg is the one person who might have tempted Jagger into politics: 'Tom was utterly charming and beautifully dressed. Such a perfect model for Mick, too, because he had a lot of money . . . A real socialist of the old school, with ideals and all that.' Well, maybe. Anyway, Driberg assured Jagger that 'we wouldn't expect you to attend to the day-to-day ephemera of the House. Not at all. We see you more as, uh, a figurehead, like, you know . . .'

'The Queen?' said Mick.

'Precisely!'

Faithfull got carried away. 'Mick Jagger, leader of the Labour Party! And me, the little anarchist in the background, pushing the great man further into folly!' It's doubtful whether Driberg was serious, though Faithfull thinks he was. Driberg's real interest was probably revealed more in another of his remarks to Jagger, when Jagger was wearing tight trousers: 'What an enormous basket you have.'[5]

Only a man of the thirties like Driberg could have said this in 1968. Someone from the fifties would have been far too buttoned down. Marianne Faithfull's book shows that she and Jagger felt more comfortable with old thirties figures than with the generation immediately above theirs. Driberg once brought the poet W. H. Auden to dinner. Aiming to shock, Auden said: 'Tell me, when you travel with drugs, Marianne, do you pack them up your arse?' 'Oh, no, Wystan,' said Faithfull. 'I stash them in my pussy.' Sixties one, thirties nil.[6]

Ali and others produced a great many revolutionary slogans, but – and this may be the key to the failure of the sixties – they don't seem to have meant them. They played at outflanking each other on the left, so that the Vietnam Solidarity Campaign turned its most furious verbal fire on the British Council for Peace in Vietnam for its failure to demand a Vietnamese victory. They were playing games of lefter-than-thou. Newspapers and television whipped up a great ferment of fear among Britain's suburban middle classes, but not a lot was going on, really.

A few of those in Grosvenor Square that day have subsequently devoted much of their lives to rubbishing what they appeared to stand for in 1968. They stare across the four decades that separate them from their youth, and wonder what on earth they were thinking. Peter Hitchens, now a right-wing columnist on the *Mail on Sunday*, was in Grosvenor Square that day. Hitchens was the seventeen-year-old son of a retired naval commander and, as described in Chapter Three, had been to a strict public school.

Of such things was the anger of 1968 made, which is why the smash hit film with the educated young in 1968 was not some politically improving fable about oppression, but Lindsay Anderson's If . . . , about a group of public-school boys finally turning on their oppressors.

Going on the anti-Vietnam war demonstration in Grosvenor Square was at least as much an act of rebellion as of political conviction, and today Hitchens is thoroughly ashamed of it. What he had to say about that day in Grosvenor Square forty years later tells us something about the spirit of the sixties that no reflective liberal recollection can offer. With his permission, I quote it at some length.

> Very soon it will be the 40th anniversary of the day I threw lumps of mud at the police in Central London. I had precious little idea why I was doing it, though I can confirm that riots are fun for those who take part in them, and that rioters usually riot because they enjoy it.
>
> I wasn't oppressed, deprived, abused, underprivileged, poor or any of the other things people give as justifications for this sort of oafishness. I had no excuse then, and offer none now. I was a self-righteous, arrogant, spoiled teenage prig . . .
>
> This is not a piece of nostalgia about the wonderful Sixties. It is a shameful confession, and an attempt to explain why my generation has, in general, been so destructive and wrong . . .
>
> I can vividly remember the intense, rapid, thrilling moments as the demonstration against the Vietnam War turned nasty; the sudden, urgent shoving, the unsettling feeling of being surrounded by strangers, supposedly my allies, the clatter of hooves, the struggle to save myself from being pushed to the ground, the wordless yelling all round me, the feeling that I could cast off every rule I had been brought up to believe in, and get away with it. It was exhilarating, and wholly stupid . . .
>
> We weren't pacifists. We were clueless rebels, indulging in childish shock-tactics to annoy our elders. We thought we wanted the communists to win, and I am pretty certain I carried a North Vietnamese flag and that I joined in with the moronic chant 'Ho! Ho! Ho Chi Minh! We shall fight and we shall win!' among others . . .

His explanation is mass insanity – he calls it the 1968 disease:

> In that year, several strands of folly came together in the happy, free, wealthy West. We had our little festival of manufactured wrath in London. French students had a far greater one in Paris. Though most of us had little idea of what we wanted, we succeeded almost completely in overthrowing the society we had grown up in, with the miserable results we now see.
>
> Was there something in the air of that year that made us all susceptible, like the mysterious shiver that goes through the landscape in early spring?

Or was it the result of the great baby bulge that had come after the Second World War ended in 1945? Were there just too many adolescents, hormones churning, concentrated on the European landmass all at once? . . .

This organised selfishness was the main reason behind the May 1968 riots in Paris. Selfishness needs to attack things that demand self-sacrifice – family, marriage, duty, patriotism and faith. And above all, it needs weakness and confusion among those in charge, if it is to succeed as it did then, and still does.

Leafing through the newspapers of four decades ago, I was reminded sharply of how authority seemed to have lost its nerve, and people to have lost any sense of belonging. Perhaps it was the accumulated shame and defeat of Suez, seeping into every institution. Perhaps it was the Profumo affair, after which our politicians and judges all seemed funny and deflated . . .

I remember beginning to notice, around about the time I was twelve, in 1963 and 1964, that authority had begun to lose the will to live. It was easier to get away with things – bad manners, sloppy schoolwork, lateness, laziness, breaking and above all bending the rules. I learned quickly to exploit every weakness.

That great destroyer, Lenin, advised his fellow apostles of chaos: 'Probe with the bayonet: if you meet steel, stop. If you meet mush, then push.' And more and more, it was mush we met. The year before my first riot, in 1967, I remember still being at school when Mick Jagger and Keith Richards were arrested in the famous West Wittering drug bust . . . The very idea of Jagger, Richards and Marianne Faithfull, clad only in a rug, roosting subversively in this cosy place was revolutionary in itself. Was nothing sacred? Jagger was not just a rock star, but a herald of cultural revolt.

He had recently declared, moronically: 'Teenagers are not screaming over pop music any more, they're screaming for much deeper reasons. We are only serving as a means of giving them an outlet. Teenagers the world over are weary of being pushed around . . . they want to be free and have the right of expression, of thinking and living without any petty restrictions.' Richards, even more of a Blairite before his time, had said: 'We are not old men. We are not concerned with petty morals.' Now both were in the dock, and Judge Leslie Block (a naval veteran who had genuinely fought for human freedom) sent them to prison – Jagger for three months, Richards for a year . . .

> Lord Rees-Mogg . . . then editor of *The Times*, said the sentence was
> unfair and denounced as 'primitive' those who thought that the future Sir
> Michael Jagger had got what was coming to him. This, plus an expensive
> legal team, led to Jagger's rapid release . . .
>
> I watched greedily, and concluded with absolute certainty that night
> that nobody was in charge, and that I could do anything I liked from now
> on. And I duly did.[7]

Of course, even if Hitchens himself was only in Grosvenor Square
for kicks, it is not true of many, perhaps most, of the others; and a
year in prison for possessing cannabis was over the top, even if Judge
Block was, like Commander Eric Hitchens, a naval veteran. But there
is enough left here to disturb those of us who do not share the naval
commander's son's robust reactionary prejudices. Much of what happened that day was about Vietnam, but there was a big part of it that
was merely about the battle between youth and age – a battle that is as
old as the hills, but in the sixties tilted decisively towards youth. To the
sixties generation, that battle was never far from sight, and often took
precedence over such matters as war in Vietnam.

Hitchens is an extreme case. There are not many people who have
turned with this sort of self-hatred on their younger selves. But they are
as authentic a part of the baby boomer generation as Marianne Faithfull,
or Greg Dyke, or me.

Or Paul Mackney. While Hitchens was throwing lumps of mud at
the police, eighteen-year-old Mackney was preparing to start at Exeter
University – and to join the International Socialists. Bob Dylan influenced him – 'Only a Pawn in Their Game' spoke to Mackney of working-class people being wound up and cynically used by racist Southern
politicians. So did a holiday in Greece in 1967, while the country was
run by an American-backed military dictatorship; gun-toting soldiers
split him from his friends because there were six of them, and more
than four was an illegal gathering. After attending a school run by ritual
bullying, Mackney was not disposed to think much of capitalist society.

Mackney's views haven't fundamentally changed in the forty years
that have elapsed, even though, six years later, he was expelled from
the IS. Groups like the IS hoovered up a lot of baby boomer anger,
and never knew what to do with it. Arriving at Exeter in September,

Mackney found that the IS expected him to go to Exeter Station every morning, collect newspapers and deliver them all round the town. On Saturday he had to go to all the people to whom he had delivered and try to get money from them. The mantra for young student activists was to build bridges between students and workers, and Mackney found himself helping to organise strikes throughout the West Country, starting with a hotel strike in Torquay in 1968.

He did have time for more common student pursuits. 'I remember trying to buy a condom in Swanage in 1968,' he says. 'One chemist was a Roman Catholic and wouldn't sell them. The other two asked if I was married and they knew I wasn't. Eventually I bought them from a small ad in the *New Statesman*.' It was not all free love in 1968.

*

Tony Blair's 1968 was a lot less interesting than Peter Hitchens's. He was fifteen and busy trying to preserve his long locks from the attentions of schoolmasters intent on marching him to the barber. Even if it had been permitted, it would never have occurred to him to go to Grosvenor Square. Neither, for very different reasons, would it have occurred to seventeen-year-old Gordon Brown.

Tony Blair and Gordon Brown, though neither had heard of the other, were physically very close to each other that year. Just a couple of miles separated the portentous old pile that is Fettes College from the centre of Edinburgh, where Brown lodged in his first year at Edinburgh University. Blair, just starting on his A-Levels, frequented the student pubs, dodging Fettes masters. It's perfectly possible that they might have been in the same pub at the same time, and a startling contrast they would have made: Blair and a couple of like-minded friends, raucous, wealthy, anglicised, apolitical, public-school ersatz rebels, full of the spirit of the sixties; Brown, with drinking companions a year or two older than himself, tweed-jacketed, serious-minded, left-wing, clever, a Scottish 'lad o' pairts' – a young man of talent and promise.

Fettes, with the reputation of an English public school that just happened to be in Scotland, provided exactly the sort of education that Blair's hero Mick Jagger thought was ideal. Jagger the supposed rebel had said two years earlier, 'It takes a conventional upbringing in the English style to produce a normal human being. It gives you an equilibrium, a balanced view.'[8] Blair admired the Rolling Stones musically and modelled himself on Mick Jagger. It would be comforting to think the association was just musical, but in the sixties music was never just music.

Blair was not alone in modelling his revolution on the Rolling Stones. 'We all thought the Rolling Stones were revolutionary, but actually the Beatles were much more revolutionary,' I am told by Tim Gopsill, a veteran of the London School of Economics occupation in 1967. Jonathon Green dismisses the Stones perhaps too harshly, but it's a symptom of disappointment. The Stones were, he writes, 'pasty white boys . . . only recycling the music of black American men, and making it palatable for the masses'.[9]

The Beatles, on the other hand, had in 1967 transformed their image, from nice young men in identical smart suits and haircuts who sang about love, to hippieish young men with individual styles and left-wing (or at least anti-war) political views, for whom drugs were at the core of their music. For a while they outflanked the Rolling Stones. That self-appointed spokesman for youth, Kenneth Tynan, called the album *Sergeant Pepper's Lonely Hearts Club Band* 'a decisive moment in the history of western civilisation'. But it contained as little striving for a better world as anything the Stones had done. The spirit was still the primacy of gilded youth, most clearly in a rather cruel song about how the Beatles' parents' generation grew old in poverty, called 'When I'm Sixty-Four'. The Beatles sang about scrimping and saving – derisively, for that was not something any of the Fab Four would ever have to do again. The rather sad old fellow in the song contemplates a cottage on the Isle of Wight, if he can afford it, and being happy doing chores in house and garden – who could ask for more? Their young listeners knew the answer to that one: we could ask for more, all of us. We want freedom. For Jagger it might be the freedom to smoke dope, for Hitchens it might be freedom from having to write out 'Few things are more distressing to the well-regulated mind than to see a boy who ought to know better disporting himself at improper moments' over and over again.

British students took some of their revolutionary politics from their French counterparts. *Les événements* in Paris in May 1968 offered a magnified vision of the divisions and manoeuvring among the British left. A student protest beginning in the Sorbonne spread within twenty-four hours to the provincial universities, and became suffused with wild, unfocused hope and optimism. Scrawled on a faculty wall were the words 'Here, imagination rules'. As the police with tear gas and fire hoses moved to break up the huge demonstrations, demonstrators counter-attacked with barricades, sticks and cobblestones torn up from the streets.

At first the students had public opinion on their side. Despite, or perhaps because of, the absence of clearly set out objectives, the French middle class rallied to their children's cause, and were horrified to see the police attacking them. Leading left-wing intellectuals like Jean-Paul Sartre and Simone de Beauvoir supported them. The government seemed frozen – unable to clear the students from the streets, unable to offer concessions – and running street battles in the Latin Quarter were the result. The leader of the Trotskyist Fourth International, the Belgian Ernest Mandel, watched his own car burning and exclaimed joyfully, '*Ah! Comme c'est beau! C'est la révolution!*'[10]

Students, many of them only teenagers, threw themselves and any missiles they could lay their hands on, bravely and joyfully, into the battle for – well, for whatever it was they were fighting for. The police, clad all in black with masks, goggles and helmets, charged, again and again, and drove the students from their defences.

Here is a contemporary description of what the occupation of the Sorbonne looked like, by people who saw it for themselves:

> Within hours of its occupation, the walls of the Sorbonne were covered with wild, joyful graffiti, and the formal classical courtyard, festooned with red and black flags and decorated with portraits of Mao, Lenin and Marx, Trotsky, Castro and Guevara, became a bazaar for trafficking in revolutionary ideas. A youngster thumped out jazz tunes at a grand piano . . . Scores of young people just lay about in this august place hugging each other, pluck-ing guitars . . . cocking a snook at the grownup world which would have had them stand up straight and comb their hair.[11]

Decisions were made in the General Assembly, which each night elected a fifteen-man occupation committee, with a mandate limited to just one day, lest power should corrupt it. The rooms in the building were given over to debating issues of the day – African affairs, women's liberation, the place of art in capitalist society. Everyone debated the struggle between reformists and revolutionaries, endlessly. And what was going on in the Sorbonne was replicated, more or less, in universities throughout France.

France was paralysed, for the workers had followed the students – it was the dream of every European Trotskyist. It was this that gave les événements their real significance, that made them far more important than the wave of university occupations that was soon to wash over Britain. And it was the refusal of the French Communist Party to back the strikes that pitted the old left against the new left.

The left thrives on allegations of treachery, and the Communists are said to have betrayed the 1968 revolution. The truth is rather more complicated, and is summed up in a slogan from a wall in the Sorbonne: 'We will claim nothing. We will ask for nothing. We will take. We will occupy.' The harsh lesson of France, May 1968, was that if you claim nothing and ask for nothing, you get nothing.

By 30 June, De Gaulle's government had been returned in the elections with a bigger majority than ever, a renewed sense of purpose, and a new confidence. The left were pretty well wiped out. Still making the best of a bad job forty years later, Tariq Ali wrote:

> The police failed to take back the Latin Quarter, now renamed the Heroic Vietnam Quarter. Three days later a million people occupied the streets of Paris, demanding an end to the rottenness of the state and plastering the walls with slogans: 'Defend The Collective Imagination', 'Beneath The Cobblestones The Beach', 'Commodities Are The Opium Of The People, Revolution Is The Ecstasy Of History'. The revolution did not happen, but France was shaken by the events. De Gaulle, with a sense of history, considered a coup d'état.[12]

So long as we stick to easy generalities – 'the rottenness of the state' is unlikely to find many defenders, and 'defending the collective imagination' sounds like a cool idea, whatever it means – Paris 1968 can be called a success. It provided the model for dozens of British student occupations in 1968 and afterwards, all of them accompanied by razzmatazz from their leaders, hysterical denunciations from journalists and politicians, and, in the long run, not a lot else.

*

Amid all this colour and excitement, real domestic politics rather took a back seat. How could Harold Wilson hold a candle to Tariq Ali, or his Employment Secretary Barbara Castle to Vanessa Redgrave? And how could the grey, proletarian men at the TUC stand comparison with the new wave of exciting young middle- and upper-class student leaders emerging on British campuses all over the country?

Yet in the real world, real things were happening. Trade unions really were moving to the left, and that really did matter. Today, no one under forty knows what it is like to live in a society where trade unions are a force in the land, but in 1968, and for many years after that, they were.

For years the unions had been the right-wing praetorian guard of Labour Prime Ministers. Clement Attlee had relied on them, not only to keep their own hotheads under wraps, but also to use their voting power to keep the Labour left wing off his back. Hugh Gaitskell had used union leaders as a battering ram against the Bevanites.

All that was changing. In 1968, left-wingers were elected as the heads of Britain's two biggest and most powerful unions: Jack Jones at the Transport and General Workers Union and Hugh Scanlon at the Amalgamated Engineering Union. Jones spearheaded the shop stewards movement, which aimed to give shop stewards in every workplace vastly more power. Strikes were becoming more common, and more working days were being lost to industrial action than ever before.

The effect of all this was nothing like as great as has been claimed. Both the unions and their enemies inflated its importance. More working time was lost to illness than to strikes, and the impact on productivity was negligible.[13] But politically Harold Wilson believed he could not afford to be thought to be in the pockets of powerful union leaders. In April Barbara Castle was appointed to head the new Department of Employment and Productivity, and set to work to produce a white paper called 'In Place of Strife'. This brought Wilson's government into open confrontation with the unions.

On the opposition benches, 1968 was the year that Enoch Powell made his famous speech on immigration:

> It almost passes belief that at this moment twenty or thirty additional immigrant children are arriving from overseas in Wolverhampton alone every

week – and that means fifteen or twenty additional families a decade or two hence. Those whom the gods wish to destroy, they first make mad. We must be mad, literally mad, as a nation to be permitting the annual inflow of some 50,000 dependants, who are for the most part the material of the future growth of the immigrant-descended population. It is like watching a nation busily engaged in heaping up its own funeral pyre . . . As I look ahead, I am filled with foreboding; like the Roman, I seem to see 'the River Tiber foaming with much blood'.

Opposition leader Edward Heath fired Powell from the Conservative front bench at once. Four months later, black cricketer Basil D'Oliveira was surprisingly omitted from the touring party for South Africa, although his record justified inclusion, for what were almost certainly thoroughly discreditable reasons to do with not offending South Africa's apartheid regime.

The departure of Powell was also a defeat for the wing of the Conservative Party that Powell represented. Powell had resigned from Macmillan's government over economic policy, and was an early monetarist. His dismissal looked like an affirmation that things could only get better, or at least lefter. Of course, a decade later Powell's wing of the Conservative Party triumphed under the leadership of Margaret Thatcher.

However much Tariq Ali, Vanessa Redgrave and the student leaders seemed to matter in 1968, the people who were going to matter when 1969 dawned were the middle-aged politicians and union leaders: Harold Wilson, Ted Heath, Enoch Powell, Barbara Castle, Jack Jones. In 1968, few of the young apart from the small cadre of committed revolutionaries thought trade unions had a part to play in their vague vision of utopia. Trade unions produced middle-aged men in suits and white shirts who went on television and said, in plonking proletarian voices, 'I 'ave to consult my executive committee.'

Within a couple of years, trade unions would suddenly become of great significance to the generation of 1968. The students decided that the unions were, after all, the instruments of the revolution, if only they could be radicalised and made to see their historic mission. This, of course, was going to require turning out all the old, boring, reactionary leaders. We stormed into the trade unions, bringing our frantic, fetid student politics with us, and we destroyed them. But in 1968, we did not even know we cared about them.

*

That year produced a long, hot summer – a languid summer full of dope and drowsiness, if you were that way inclined; a frantic summer driven by wild political optimism, if that was what turned you on. Seventeen-year-old Rosie Boycott, the daughter of an army officer and a product of Cheltenham Ladies College, who thirty years later was to edit three national newspapers, sat on the grass in Hyde Park in a loose flowered dress and smoked her first joint. It made her happy, and seemed a much better way to get high than her parents' nightly sherry or dry martini. But more experienced druggies like Marianne Faithfull already knew that the languid anything-goes torpor of dope-smoking groups was a fraud. 'Hipness itself was part of the problem,' she writes. 'One of the biggest barriers was hip protocol . . . A lot of that had to do with smoking too much dope . . . Subjects of any seriousness or personal concern were totally *verboten*.'[14]

While Rosie Boycott was enjoying the first of many leisurely joints in the warm summer sunshine, James Greenfield and John Barker were tearing up their Cambridge finals papers as a protest against the Vietnam war and leaving Cambridge to strike up an alliance with a veteran of the Paris *événements*, Chris Bott, a postgraduate student at Essex University, and two young women undergraduates at Essex, Anna Mendleson and Hilary Creek. All five were moving towards the London revolutionary scene, the scene of communes and squats. All of them, like Peter Hitchens, were from comfortable, suburban middle-class families, and they were to become the strangest young revolutionaries the sixties produced – the Angry Brigade.

While the Angry Brigade were establishing themselves in a house in London and preparing to fill it with bomb-making equipment, 22-year-old Tony Elliott, a product of the public school Stowe, was walking out of Keele University a year before he was due to sit his degree, armed with a £70 legacy with which he proposed to go to London and found a listings magazine called *Time Out*. He and I talked, just before he left. We had done our A-Levels together at a further education college in

London, and had worked together on a Keele literary magazine. He thought I should leave too, that Keele was dreadfully inward-looking and juvenile, that there were real opportunities in London. I told him I thought his idea quixotic and pointless, and he might as well hang on for another year with the rest of us and enjoy the Keele experience.

In 2008 the *Time Out* Group had an annual turnover of over £45 million.

Tony Elliott left behind a campus in fashionable turmoil. That hot summer, Keele University students occupied the university registry, a little late: Warwick, the London School of Economics, Hornsey College of Art and other radical campuses had got there up to a year earlier. I look back on my part in Keele's occupation, not with any of the shame and disgust with which Peter Hitchens recalls his part in the Grosvenor Square events, but not with any particular pride either: more with puzzlement. I cannot work out quite what I was thinking, and I suspect that in this I am not alone.

Vietnam was there in our thinking somewhere – it always was in 1968. I am sure that dissatisfaction with the doings of the university was a part of it – one of our science professors was said to be involved in experimentation to produce chemical weapons.

But the paternalism of Keele in those days had more to do with it than any of these. The Keele authorities had not adjusted well to students who were no longer willing to be told whether they might be permitted to buy contraceptives in the student union shop, or where and with whom they might use them. Keele still seemed to think it was in *loco parentis*. And it had not moved quickly enough to dilute the regime of examinations, then the only form of testing for undergraduates. Students resented not being represented in its highest councils.

I see from documents that a friend and contemporary has kept that we called the university 'paternalistic in outlook, privileged in atmosphere and non-participatory in structure'; and that we tried to adapt Marxist class politics to the university, with students playing the part of the proletariat, which was a rather strained intellectual exercise.

The occupation started after I was asked to a terribly secret meeting of four or five folk convened by a young man called Martin Yarnit, who was short, tanned, saturnine, thoughtful and a little mysterious, with a soft voice, a sardonic smile, a jet-black beard and a reputation as an aesthete, though his real interest was politics. We called ourselves Action for a Free University, and Martin is still proud of it today, writing to me in 2008:

> The grounding concept was the notion of a community of scholars without distinctions of rank which made its rules together rather than imposing them on the majority (the students). Ground down by arbitrary regulations, such as the (unwittingly gay-friendly) one forbidding members of the opposite sex from spending the night in halls of residence, the students rose up with a mighty cry of 'Freedom!' and occupied the Administration Block.

This small group – and principally Martin – planned the occupations of the next few days in some detail. We all tried to maintain the fashionable sixties myth that there were no leaders, that revolution happened spontaneously, man, but none of these events would have happened without someone to make them happen, and at Keele that was Martin, buzzing from meeting to meeting on a neat but noisy motor scooter. 'I always saw him whizzing around campus on his scooter with a very revolutionary air,' recalls the novelist Marina Lewycka. Martin and I were delegated to go to the Keele branch of the Association of University Teachers, explain ourselves, and ask for support.

The students' union president, Malcolm Clarke, tried to head off the threatened occupation, but the senate did not give him anything like enough concessions, and against his opposition we carried a vote for direct action at a Union General Meeting. Clarke resigned. Leadership passed to his successor, Godfrey (or God) Smart: tall, rangy, charismatic, with a huge motor bike and leathers – a rocker to Martin Yarnit's mod.

We occupied seats at high table at lunchtime, we broke the hours rules en masse and challenged the authorities to do something about it, we stood round the Vice Chancellor's house and sang 'We Shall Overcome' and 'The Internationale', we called off our sit-in in the library when it was time for the staff to go home, and, most importantly, we occupied the registry.[15] I advocated the occupation eagerly at first, but swiftly found myself being outflanked on the left, in conflict with younger, sharper-toothed students who felt I did not show the proper revolutionary spirit. Being outflanked on the left was a new and uncomfortable feeling, but one that I was to have more and more often as the colourful sixties turned into the grinding seventies and eighties.

Outflanking on the left was the game the 1968 generation learned from France, and it played the game throughout the seventies and early eighties, in the trade unions, in the Labour Party, in the many campaigns that sprang up, until everyone forgot that there was anything in the world to fight apart from our rivals on the left.

But perhaps I deserved to be outflanked. Instead of sleeping on the registry floor so as to keep watch for a night raid by the authorities, as the most committed did, I would spend the evening drinking in the student union bar, or rehearsing (for I was due to direct a show at the Edinburgh Festival fringe that summer for the Keele Theatre Company); and at closing time I would amble 50 yards to the occupied registry and perhaps share a joint, then walk a couple of hundred yards to my comfortable little room in one of the halls of residence. I was much more exercised about the show I was directing, though I could hardly have admitted that at the time.

Our trawl through the secret files the university kept on us did reveal, as we suspected, that the authorities were frequently foolish, frequently wrong, and their judgements sometimes distorted by snobbery. 'Comes from a poor family,' noted her tutor on one of my contemporaries. Oxbridge, of course, was far worse, and the playwright Steve Gooch's tutors at Trinity College, Cambridge, observing his theatrical activities and the girlfriend whom he sneaked into his rooms at night, noted in their file, which Gooch managed to see some time later, 'Gooch has led a bohemian existence, for the son of an artisan.' What we failed to do, of course, was follow this up and challenge it. Baby boomer tutors are now doing the same with our children, only more so.

Of all these Keele characters, Malcolm Clarke tells us most about the sixties, because in the same way that he was not a part of the occupation, he was not really a part of the sixties; he was attached to them only by the accident of being born at about the right time. He was very tall, and somewhat ungainly – I used to get a laugh by describing him as 'a man of many parts, clumsily assembled'. Slightly eccentric and entirely unfashionable, he kept his hair quite short and wore flannel jackets and shirts, and a deerstalker hat to keep his ears warm, and to this day he does not really know what cannabis smells like. Anyone less like a sixties product it would be hard to imagine, but he was greatly liked and trusted, and only the strange enthusiasms of the sixties could have persuaded us to ignore his advice. His failure to prevent direct action distressed him greatly, but today he says, 'Tension had been building up anyway over the year, as part of a wider sea change not only in this country but abroad – and the Senate wasn't intelligent enough to give me, as President, anything to work with back at the ranch.'

The next term, a strange young Dutchman called Ralph appeared on the campus from nowhere. He was a voracious consumer of forbidden substances, and a supplier of the same, and although not a student he found campus life rather comfortable, and seemed to settle in, becoming the centre of a hippieish sort of circle.

One day the idyll was shattered. A police car screamed on to the campus, sirens blaring, and skidded to a halt beside Ralph, who had the presence of mind to scream 'Fascists' just before they bundled him into the back seat. A crowd of thirty or so students assembled quite fast, shouting 'Pigs' and other opprobrious epithets, as the police car revved up. And at that moment, a very tall, gangly figure in flannel trousers charged through the crowd, opened the door of the police car, and swung himself into the back seat beside Ralph just as the car drove off with a squeal of tyres.

Anyone can shout 'Pigs'. Malcolm was doing the one thing that might be useful to Ralph, and that no one else had the presence of mind to do: going with him to make sure he wasn't mistreated. At the police station he got the union's lawyer out of bed to defend Ralph, a difficult task since Ralph would only talk of the beauty of the universe. A few weeks later Malcolm launched an appeal to pay the lawyer, and some of Ralph's campus friends declined to contribute because they were against giving money to bourgeois lawyers. That's very, very 1968.

*

The occupation ended when the term ended. Everyone had other things to do – I had a few weeks in which to earn enough money to spend the rest of the summer in Edinburgh – and the campus was empty when, one day in August, with shocking suddenness, Soviet tanks rolled into Prague. The new Czechoslovak regime, which had tried to bring in a free and democratic sort of socialism – 'socialism with a human face' – was brutally suppressed, and its Prime Minister Alexander Dubček arrested.

It was really the end of the road for the British Communist Party, though it struggled on until 1991. It had been in long, slow decline since 1956, kept alive by a revival of Soviet subsidies. Even without the Soviet Union to give it a bad name, it was out of tune with the mood of 1968. For all practical purposes, it had long since abandoned its revolutionary pretensions, and offered only slightly more radical an agenda than the Labour Party. The revolutionary banner had been picked up by the Trotskyist groups that led the events of 1968. Could they make a better job of the revolution? As it turned out, the answer was no.

The next month, the victory that most typified 1968 was won. The abolition of stage censorship, which Parliament had agreed in February, came into force on 26 September. It was a long overdue reform, and let in many good things that we might otherwise not have been allowed to see. Unfortunately, the first show to benefit, opening the very next day at London's Shaftesbury Theatre, was not one of them. *Hair* was everything that was trashy and pretentious about the sixties.

I went to see it with my girlfriend, and we sat in silence on the tube home, because neither of wanted to be the first to say, 'That was rubbish.' To dislike *Hair* seemed like a denial of our youth, a denial of the great demonstrations, a denial that the end of censorship was important. W. A. Darlington in the *Daily Telegraph* called it 'a complete bore. It was noisy, it was ugly and quite desperately unfunny.' Milton Shulman told *Evening Standard* readers: 'The effect was like being a voyeur at an orgy of Boy Scouts and Girl Guides.'[16] We had been sure that was simply the establishment doing it down. But the critics were right.

Yet *Hair* was a commercial success. It said just one thing: 'Nothing is sacred.' And in that, I suppose, it is a decent representative of the spirit of 1968, except that this message was already being conveyed far more eloquently and with more subtlety in the mass medium of television. For 1968 saw the first episode of *Dad's Army*. The Second World War was not yet twenty-five years away, and even a couple of years previously the idea of mocking the Home Guard would have seemed deeply offensive. In 1968 it was precisely in tune with the spirit of the times, for the point about the Home Guard was that it consisted, mostly, of elderly men.

Hair disappeared into well-deserved obscurity, and the 1968 play that everyone remembers was *Forty Years On* by Alan Bennett, which premiered almost exactly a month after *Hair*. It is set in a decaying public school, Albion House. The old headmaster, played by that magnificent relic of an earlier era Sir John Gielgud, is to retire and be replaced by a younger and more 'progressive' one. 'When a society has to resort to the lavatory for its humour,' says Gielgud, 'the writing is on the wall.' References to naked breasts in the school play draw from him the reflection that 'if everyone who caught an unlooked-for glimpse of the female bosom chose to publish it in book form, civilization would very shortly grind to a halt.'

For all its witty historical allusions to the twenties and thirties, *Forty Years On* had something quite profound to say about the sixties. In 2008, exactly forty years on from *Forty Years On*, Peter Hitchens, long after he had completed his long march across the political arena, wrote:

> If you had wanted a summary of the ideas which lay behind the new humour of the 1960s, you could not have found a better one. Not only do we have the left wing myth of Munich, which is used to strip the old governing classes of their right to carry on ruling; we also have a conviction that Britain is finished, has lost its reason for existence and is an untenanted, decaying estate in need of new masters and plenty of modernisation and improvement. And why? Because of the absence of 'social justice', which led to the cancelling out of the great words – honour, patriotism, chivalry and duty . . . The fact that it is done with some affection and style does not make it any less of a manifesto, or any less harsh or misleading.[17]

It takes a baby boomer who was once a Trot to enter the new millennium sounding like a reactionary fifties colonel in his favourite corner of the Athenaeum. But, as he sometimes does, Hitchens has stumbled on something important here, though he does not know what it is. Albion House was just the sort of school that he and many of the student radicals of the sixties attended, and it shows Britain's governing class stumbling obliviously through the decades from one crass error to another. That is what the baby boomers liked about it. Also, it offered no solutions at all. The baby boomers liked that too, for the moment you offer a solution, someone else will offer a more radical-sounding one, and then where are you?

8. How the baby boomers destroyed the trade unions and made Thatcherism: 1969–79

Tariq Ali tells a story about appealing for funds from readers of the IMG magazine *The Black Dwarf* in 1968–9. A stallholder on Portobello Road gave the magazine £125 every fortnight, explaining, 'Capitalism is so non-groovy, man.'[1]

If that was all that was wrong with capitalism, the sixties and seventies put it right: by 1979, capitalism was definitely groovy. For while the sixties sometimes sounded fiercely anti-capitalist, and sometimes, as their libertarian rhetoric ran away with them, fiercely pro-capitalist, it was the pro-capitalist strand that won in the long run. The long-term legacy of the sixties was Thatcherism.

The right won because, though much less in fashion than the left in the sixties and seventies, they were clearer about what they wanted to achieve. A revolution that exclaims defiantly that it will ask for nothing lacks a few basic nuts and bolts for the building of a new society. In a muddle, anyone with a clear objective starts out with an advantage. And the sixties were a real muddle. 'Certainty had vanished, conviction was vanishing, will itself was crumbling,' wrote Bernard Levin, 'as those behind cried, "Forward!" and those before cried, "Back!" and both sides were constantly drowned by a mysterious muttering of "Sideways! Sideways!" which came none knew whence.'[2]

Tariq Ali calls the sixties 'the glorious decade'. But they were glorious as a storm over the sea is glorious. The best things in them disappeared as fast as you could glimpse them.

The satire boom, the irreverence of the sixties, was quickly snuffed out. *TW3* never returned from its banishment before the 1964 election, and in 1969 the BBC launched the comedy programme that was to set the tone for the seventies, *Monty Python's Flying Circus*, which was glorious fun, owing its inspiration to the likes of N. F. Simpson, but was never going to get up the noses of the powerful. The BBC's moment of bravery was over. It was not until 1984 that mainstream television returned to the sort of programming that makes famous people cringe, with *Spitting Image*.

The alternative press of the sixties turned into nothing more than a short cut to Fleet Street. Rosie Boycott of *Spare Rib* and John Lloyd of *Ink* and *Time Out* were two of many who eventually became the newspaper establishment of their day, Boycott at the *Daily Express* and Lloyd at the *Financial Times*, and both ended up close to Tony Blair. *Time Out* survived because its founder Tony Elliott, who never really thought of it as an alternative magazine, shrewdly repositioned it as he and his readers got older.

Oz tried to preserve the sixties faith into the seventies. In 1971 it produced a schoolkids' issue with a lot of sex in it, and got school students (one of them was Hilary Benn, later a cabinet minister) to work on it. The three editors were given prison sentences. Felix Dennis got a shorter sentence than his two co-accused because Mr Justice Argyll, aiming to hurt, said he was the least intelligent of the three. Mr Justice Argyll was an ass. Dennis, after being acquitted by the Court of Appeal, founded his own magazine publishing company in 1973, pioneering personal computer magazines; he made millions, and today is one of the wealthiest people in Britain.

One of his two co-defendants, Australian Richard Neville, later summed up what the problem was with the 'alternative' press of the sixties, and it could apply to the decade as a whole. 'We knew what we were against but what were we for? . . . [We] liked to think of ourselves as lovers of the new, but we defined the new only by tearing into the old.'[3]

Oz was one of many things that looked lovably revolutionary in the sixties and started looking ugly in the seventies. Student protest, too, acquired a harsher, more sectarian feel. At Keele they surrounded the Vice Chancellor's house, chanting and apparently trying to levitate it, and there were running battles between demonstrators and vigilantes. At Exeter University, says Paul Mackney, 'you had the RSSF [Revolutionary Socialist Students Federation] people saying we should provoke the police to come on campus to show what they were really like.'

For the Rolling Stones, the sixties dream turned very sour. In the summer of 1969 Brian Jones, full of far too many drugs and far too much alcohol, drowned in his far-too-warm swimming pool. And in December, the remaining Stones played at Altamont in northern California and hired Hells Angels to provide the security, not realising that California's Hells Angels were a lot more violent than their British counterparts who had policed earlier Stones concerts. The Hells Angels started indiscriminately laying into everyone with sawn-off pool cues. Mick Jagger stood on stage, impotently appealing for calm, while they stabbed and kicked a young man to death and injured many more. As the frightened musicians were carried away from the scene in a helicopter, they must have known that the sixties had fled before them.

The sixties turned nastiest of all for the half-dozen mostly well-educated middle-class young people who had come together in 1968 to campaign for better treatment for the poor and against the Vietnam war, and called themselves the Angry Brigade. Their London home was raided in 1971, bomb-making equipment was found, and they served long prison sentences. The bombs were not great, lethal IRA weapons but smallish lumps of gelignite and, if they had actually managed to kill anyone, they would have been horrified. 'For one thing we were libertarian Communists believing in the mass movement and for another we weren't that serious,' one of them, John Barker, has said, while the only working-class member, Jake Prescott, has called them 'the slightly cross brigade'. Some of them emerged physically and psychologically permanently damaged from the long (and very harsh) prison sentences that were handed down.[4] The baby boomers talked a lot of nonsense in the sixties, and those in the greatest danger were the ones who took every word seriously.

*

The baby boomers retained into the seventies their precious ability to focus on what mattered least. As 1969 began, the children of the sixties were interested in Home Secretary James Callaghan's refusal to modify the penalties for smoking cannabis, and they were triumphant about the takeover of the National Union of Students by the left. Throughout the ferment of 1968, the NUS remained in the hands of the old guard who had refused to flay Harold Wilson for not condemning the US war in Vietnam. The new left saw the NUS leaders as reactionary fifties hangovers, with their suits and their short hair and their polite lobbying and their demure presence at government receptions, when they should have been taking to the streets. 'Tio Pepe diplomacy,' they called it, and it was meant to hurt.

In 1969 the old guard was swept from office by a new, young, thrusting radical, a magical sixties figure with long, dark hair, piercing eyes, left-wing fervour, an attractive slight hesitancy of speech, a gift for a soundbite, and an impossibly romantic and evocative name: Jack Straw. Straw, then twenty-three, the product of a London grammar school and Leeds University, came to office at the head of the Broad Left, then a coalition of Communists, Trotskyites and young left-wingers from the Labour and Liberal parties, in which the Communists dominated. A new dawn had broken.

Or rather, it hadn't. It was just a stage on Jack Straw's journey to becoming the grey, pompous, reactionary senior politician we know today. This shiny product of the new left didn't actually believe anything different from the old right he displaced. Like much else in the sixties, Jack Straw's radicalism was all done by smoke and mirrors.

In the long term, none of the things that seemed important to the children of the sixties was going to be of the slightest importance in the future: not Callaghan and cannabis, where the debate has hardly moved on from 1969, and certainly not the brave new world offered by the student leaders of 1969, whether they were Tariq Ali or Jack Straw.

The 1969 events that were to matter, they hardly noticed at the time. In January Barbara Castle produced her proposals on trade union reform, in a white paper called 'In Place of Strife'. The trade unions forced the government to withdraw the proposals, and Harold Wilson had to settle for a 'solemn and binding' assurance to deal with unofficial strikes. Solomon Binding became a name for promises you do not intend to keep. In June came the announcement that high-grade crude oil had been found under the North Sea, and the print unions approved Rupert Murdoch's proposed takeover of *The Sun*. And on 21 October, Conservative leader Ted Heath appointed a new shadow education spokesperson called Margaret Thatcher.

All of these things were to change Britain fundamentally, and mostly in ways that would horrify the children of the sixties. It was as though Thatcherism had erected its fortifications, carefully planted its gun emplacements, and then sat quietly with a glass of vintage wine in its hand, wondering how long it would be before the baby boomers looked away from the pretty coloured lights long enough to notice.

*

If I realised a little faster than some others that the sixties were over, it was because I spent the last three months of 1969 trawling all over the place where they began. I was chosen to be one of the two-man student debating team sent that year to tour the USA. I addressed a huge peace rally on Moratorium Day, with all the arrogance of youth – how could I talk about keeping the anti-war faith when in my audience were young men from whom it might require the courage to go to prison?

In a town called Gunnison, Colorado, I saw signs saying 'Keep America beautiful – take a hippie to a barber shop.' The students of Gunnison had very short hair, because the sign was not just rhetoric. If the cowboys caught you with long hair, they often did not bother going all the way to the barber shop – they held you down and did the job with sheep shears. And you stayed still, for sheep shears are big, clumsy instruments, even in the hands of someone who cares about whether he hurts you or not, which the cowboys didn't.

In the Midwest I came across a college where men were forbidden to wear beards – except during one week, Founder's Week, when they were obliged to grow beards. Whatever is not compulsory is forbidden, and whatever is not forbidden is compulsory, I muttered, and my hosts smiled uncertainly. Had they realised I was comparing their university with the Soviet Union, they might have been less kind and welcoming.

In Texas I found a university which decreed that all students must believe in God. Failing to do so was punishable by expulsion. I said from the platform during the debate that it was the opposite of everything a university ought to stand for. One corner of the audience started to clap – and stopped at once as the lecturer who chaired the debate glared in that direction.

It would all be different, I thought, when I got to California. And so, at first, it seemed to be. There I met a young man with a permanent joint hanging from his mouth, who assured me that, if his number came up, he would go to prison rather than fight in Vietnam. He told me America was in thrall to what he called 'the military industrial complex'. But when I suggested a small dose of nationalisation and a welfare state, he recoiled as though I had advocated going to every family in California and murdering their firstborn. 'That's big government, man. Like, big government, like, that's death, man.'

I was seeing the campuses of the land of the free in 1969, the campuses from which the mood of the British sixties had come, and suddenly I understood. The sixties were an American import. How could we have imagined that they would possess some sort of political direction? Much of sixties radicalism consisted of a vague feeling that things could be done better, and that the way to have them done better was to have them done by the young. Like most ideas that depend on who governs, rather than the principles upon which they govern, it turned out to be a disappointment.

*

In the seventies came a concerted effort on the left to turn that vague feeling into a philosophy. So the broad spirit of vague sixties optimism became a game of 'lefter than thou', with each sect trying to outdo its rivals in radicalism. If you didn't sound quite revolutionary or pure enough, your opponents on the left would spit deadly words like 'reformist' at you. So the left descended into a dark pit, where we all fell on each other with a ferocity that astounded those who stood at the top of the pit, unnoticed by the combatants, and peered down, fascinated and horrified at the same time. The left was clearly in no state to take on the outside world: so intent was it on its battle with itself that it often seemed not even to realise that the outside world was there. As Henry Kissinger once said of academic politics, the battle was all the more vicious because there was so little at stake.

The game of 'lefter than thou' was popular in trade unions, in radical magazines, even in the arts, where political commissars made the world of left-wing artists almost uninhabitable. In the theatre, Vanessa Redgrave's Workers Revolutionary Party stood ready at the drop of a hat to brand socialists who did not get the line right as agents of capitalism and reaction. 'You had to be lefter than everyone else,' recalls Steve Gooch, then starting his career as a playwright in London and helping to found the Theatre Writers Union (now amalgamated with the Writers Guild). 'Whatever issue came up, you had to take the further left position, preferably with a new angle that made it hotter for lefties. That was what was used to guilt-trip people with, the fear that someone else might be more extreme in their views than you were.'

Gooch says the public-school people in the theatre were in the International Socialists (IS), and that was the next stopping-off point for Peter Hitchens, whom we last met throwing mud at the police in Grosvenor Square. Hitchens was eighteen in 1969 and had been having some serious rows with his parents. His father, Commander Hitchens, now the bursar of a small preparatory school in Oxford, was not at all pleased to hear that his son had led a charge against a police line outside Oxford Town Hall. Peter, however, was astonished that the police let them through: 'We had no idea what to do next, a moment of sharp revelation that nagged at me for years afterwards, and may have helped me recover.' What he calls the 'collective lunacy' would 'eventually carry me into a revolutionary organisation just a few inches from the borders of terrorism, and at one of whose meetings I had a nasty confrontation with a man I am now certain was an IRA killer.'[5]

He means the IS. Hitchens joined it, he told me, at least partly because he needed a sense of order, and felt that the authority figures he had grown up with could no longer provide it. He had been thrown out of the home of a friend's parents, where he was staying, and his friend took him to a squat at 144 Piccadilly which had had some publicity at the time. He did not feel comfortable there, and left, but as he walked out he was picked up by the police and spent two nights in Cannon Row police station. Later that same week he had a serious motor bike crash and might have lost his leg.

All this suddenly concentrated his mind. He realised he needed order and discipline. He joined IS and applied to university, arriving at York University in October 1970. He found that the biggest sect on the York campus was Tariq Ali's IMG, and they managed a respectable turnout for Ali when he came to speak. Hitchens, in the true spirit of sectarian rivalry, decided he would devote himself to making the IS the biggest sect on campus instead. Despite all the years that have passed, and all the loathing he now feels for the politics he adopted then, I think he is still just a little proud of how his aggressive propaganda succeeded. IS did displace IMG as the biggest sect on the York campus. Two years later, when Paul Foot of the IS came to speak, 'we easily filled the hall,' Hitchens told me, trying to keep the pleasure out of his voice.

I suspect he cut quite a figure at York – serious, intense, with a dark-brown voice, and a revolutionary fervour somehow heightened by a strong public-school accent. That's what he sounds like now, as a very right-wing columnist for the *Mail on Sunday*, and it is probably not that different from what he sounded like then. For Greg Dyke, a fellow York student, noticed the same phenomenon that Steve Gooch picked up in the theatre: 'People like Peter Hitchens and all his mates from public school were all Trots.' Hitchens, he says, was the leader of the hard left, and Dyke recalls him arriving at a meeting and explaining his lateness by saying he had 'been out working for the revolution.'[6] Hitchens denies it, but Dyke stands by his story and says it was 'exactly what Peter was like'. Hitchens adds that he remembers Dyke as 'looking like a walking mountain-range, and favouring yellow T-shirts, the last Labour Party supporter in the university'. That's true too, Dyke told me.

A mature student, Dyke had arrived at York at twenty-four after working at Marks and Spencer and then as a local newspaper journalist. 'I'd busted up with a girlfriend and I decided to go to university. I'd been the organiser of the trade union on the paper, and I thought I was a lefty, and you turn up at university and discover you're a revisionist.'

Peter Hitchens's contempt for someone who supports the Labour Party, as Greg Dyke did, has not changed over the years. He feels it now, as a right-winger, in much the same way as he felt it then as a Trotskyite, for the same sort of reasons. It seemed wishy-washy, lacking ideological navigation, like the sixties.

Today Hitchens offers me an interesting reason for becoming a Trotskyite. The baby boomer generation was the first not to have to do national service, and Hitchens is one of those who think a spell in the army would have done him good. Those years in IS, he told me, were 'the nearest my generation could get to national service. As a Trot I got enormous contact with people not of my social background. Without national service, there was no other way of getting it. I ran a small Bolshevik cell in a coal works in Scarborough, I met people who dig coal out of the ground.'

The IS, he is saying, provided the structure that his prep-school masters, his public-school masters, his father, had all tried to provide, that national service might have provided – and that Hitchens needed, as some people do. He was not alone. Ultra-left politics in the early seventies often fulfilled a psychological need at least as much as a political conviction. Baby boomers in power have been keen to make the young do the national service they escaped, and may be about to get their way. I suspect the likes of Jack Straw and David Blunkett are spiritually closer to Peter Hitchens than they would care to admit.

So is that it, then? Revolutionary politics as a substitute for the order and discipline and certainty once offered by schoolmasters, priests, parents and military service? Children ignoring Hilaire Belloc's advice, running away from nurse and finding something worse? Not entirely. The world was and is awry; there was, and is, anger at injustice and inequality. But just as there was once, in the thirties and forties, a surprising level of interchange between the Communist Party and the Roman Catholic Church because both organisations offered a complete answer to every question, so now the Trots offered the same refuge for those fleeing from the old certainties but unwilling to abandon certainty itself.

And because the sixties were so muddled and many of the children of the sixties needed – or thought they needed – order and discipline, in the seventies they joined tiny, intolerant sects. The Communist Party, IS, the IMG and the rest believed subtly different things, but they believed them with absolute certainty. They would accuse opponents of having an 'incorrect analysis'. And that was deadly. A vague preference for capitalism might be forgiven, but an incorrect analysis reserved you a place in front of the firing squad, come the revolution. In earlier decades, communists had accused opponents on the left of having 'incorrect politics'. In the seventies the now splintered far left talked of things being 'politically correct'. It started as a way of denouncing rivals on the left, and ended up being adopted by the far right as a rallying cry. 'Political correctness gone mad' will make a page lead in the *Daily Mail* any day.

And so they splintered and splintered, as the theological differences grew sharper and more exact, and interpretations of Marxist texts grew more sophisticated, each sect encouraged in its ideological rigidity by young men and women like Peter Hitchens, who were using them as substitute schoolmasters.

One of the Keele Trots, a young man with a double-barrelled name, sought out my friend Malcolm Clarke at the start of the seventies.

He had always, he said, respected Malcolm without agreeing with his Labour Party views, and would be glad of Malcolm's view on the manifesto for the new political group he and some others were starting in Birmingham. Malcolm asked how many people were in the new party, and was told that, while there was great potential for growth, the current headcount was, er, five. Malcolm took the proffered eight-page manifesto and glanced through it. The first four pages were the statement of the minority.

Also in Birmingham, Paul Mackney was working his way up the ranks of the local trades council – the regional TUC organisation. He divided his time between agitation in Birmingham, where he worked, and in the West Country, where he had been at university. He was also writing some rather good Dylanesque protest songs for use on picket lines in West Country industrial disputes – this one to the tune of the Weavers' hit 'Goodnight Irene':

Come gather round me comrades
A story I want you to hear
About some brave strikers from Devon
Who've been out for over two years . . .

But Greg Dyke, now on the verge of his television career, was sure the young Trots were wasting their time: 'People at university went on for years about Paris in '68 where workers and students came together and all the rest of it. But workers and students had nothing to do with each other, workers were working and students were a bunch of middle-class kids.'

*

Just before the 1970 general election, Opposition Leader Ted Heath took his shadow cabinet and top advisers for an awayday to a hotel, Selsdon Park, near Croydon. He had to meet the press before much work had been done, and, rather off the cuff, he announced that the Conservative priorities in office would be tax cuts; union reform; immigration control; law and order, including a new law on trespass that would stop the anti-apartheid demonstration that had disrupted the

South African rugby and cricket tours; and more money for pensioners aged over eighty. Harold Wilson denounced 'Selsdon Man' as 'a lurch to the right . . . an atavistic desire to reverse the course of twenty-five years of social revolution. What they are planning is a wanton, calculated and deliberate return to greater inequality.'[7]

In fact, Heath wasn't like that. He had been influenced in the thirties by the depression and the poverty he saw around him; by Clement Attlee's favourite economist John Maynard Keynes; and by a book called *The Middle Way*, an attempt to create a sort of left-wing Conservatism, by a young Tory MP who was then considered not much better than a Communist by many of his colleagues, and whose name was Harold Macmillan. However, Selsdon Man helped convince the baby boomers that the worst they had to fear was a Heathite Tory. It was another decade before they discovered their error.

Right up to the election, Labour was expected to win, but the voters gave Heath a thirty-seat majority. The story of the Heath government is the story of the zenith of trade union power. The 1971 National Union of Mineworkers conference demanded a substantial pay rise, and called for strike action if it was not conceded. It was not, and, for the first time since 1926, a national coal strike was called, starting in the depth of winter, on 9 January 1972, so that the lack of coal had a swift effect. The coal that there was could not be used, because members of other trade unions refused to cross the NUM picket lines.

Heath was forced to declare a state of emergency a month after the start of the strike, and a few days later he agreed to set up a court of inquiry into miners' wages. He tried to persuade the miners to go back to work while it was sitting, but failed, so Lord Wilberforce, the enquiry chairman, was told to work at breakneck speed. He did – his report was done in just two days. He was also under pressure to recommend paying the miners enough to get them back to work, and he did that too.

The strike had another effect, of even longer-term significance than the NUM victory. Before it, no one outside Yorkshire and delegates to NUM conferences had heard of Arthur Scargill. By the end he was on the way to being a household name. Journalists loved him: he was dashing, and fluent, and quotable, and happy to talk up his own role.

'We took the view that we were in a class war,' he told *New Left Review*. 'We were not playing cricket on the village green, like they did in '26.'

He told the *Observer Colour Supplement* that he ran a 'strike operations room' like a military headquarters, with a map showing ports, power stations, steelworks and mines, and from there he despatched pickets 'like shock troops'.[8] But what really made his name was what became known as the Battle of Saltley Gate. On 7 February Scargill led 400 Yorkshire miners to the gates of Saltley depot in Birmingham, to stop coke leaving the depot bound for power stations. A battle between police and miners raged for three days, while television cameras recorded every twist and turn and Scargill directed his men through a megaphone. After three days, he persuaded unions in the city to call a one-day strike, and thousands more miners came, from all over the country. The chief constable closed the gates, as Scargill wanted.

That day the government appointed Lord Wilberforce's Court of Enquiry, which is the basis of the myth that Scargill and Saltley won the strike for the NUM. In fact, though its symbolic importance was enormous, its practical importance was not that great. The coke heap in Saltley, which was a fraction of the size Scargill claimed, would have been used up in a fortnight.[9] But that myth was key to the unions' thinking and the thinking of the baby boomers. Like Peter Hitchens in Grosvenor Square, they took from it the message that they could do anything, and that if only they were militant enough, they would always win. Jack Jones of the Transport and General Workers Union, perhaps the most powerful union leader Britain has ever known, and far too old and wise to fall for the shibboleths of the sixties and seventies, tried to get the Heath government off the hook. Jones promised that a settlement with the miners would not be used to hike up wages generally. 'If the miners are allowed to negotiate directly with the coal board, whatever they get will not be quoted by us or used as a lever to get a similar increase.'[10] Left-wing baby boomers who had once admired Jones started to have doubts about their man's ideological purity.

In 1973, with the value of what they had won being eroded by inflation, the miners called another strike. This time there was an added pressure on the government: the Yom Kippur War in the Middle East, which drove up oil prices. The strike was called for 9 February and, before it began, Heath called a general election for 28 February 1974. A victory in the election would be interpreted by the government as a mandate to stand firm against the miners. Heath declared a state of emergency, and limited industry to a three-day week. Shops and offices could not use electricity in the evenings, and television channels had to close down not later than 10.30 p.m.

During the election, Aims of Industry called for a guerrilla campaign against left-wing unions, with sit-ins at their headquarters and phone-ins to block their switchboards. Graffiti appeared saying, 'Vote Jack Jones, cut out the middle man.' The perception that the unions were immensely powerful was already creating a backlash, so effectively that, although Labour won the election, it polled slightly fewer votes than the Conservatives. Another straw in the wind for the unions was that the proportion of trade unionists voting Labour had gone down from three quarters in the sixties to little more than half.[11]

There was not much money around, and voters, encouraged by a bitterly anti-union press, thought this was all the fault of over-mighty trade unions. In 1976 the city editor of the *Sunday Telegraph*, Patrick Hutber, published a polemical paperback called *The Decline of the Middle Class – And How It Can Fight Back*.[12] The writing was on the wall. Wise old union leaders like Jack Jones could see that union power was a bubble that was threatening to burst. But there were plenty of less wise folk insisting on the idea Arthur Scargill had helped sell to the baby boomer generation, that the purer your socialist militancy, the more assured you were of success.

After the election, Harold Wilson waited in the Labour Party general secretary's office with Jack Jones for the summons from the queen. Their conversation well illustrates the power the unions had, and the power they did not have. Jones limited his advice to the one matter in which the unions had a legitimate interest, and in that one matter he prevailed. He told Wilson that the unions would not stand for Reg Prentice being made Employment Secretary. 'We agreed that Michael Foot would be the ideal choice,' wrote Jones in his autobiography, and Foot got the job.[13] The unions had power. If operators like Jones, who knew its limitations, had remained in control, they might have kept it.

*

In the summer of 1971, eighteen-year-old Tony Blair walked in to Biba in Kensington High Street and purchased a pair of white flared trousers, so tight that he had to hold his breath to get them on, with lace-up flies. They went well with his purple and blue striped jacket, which was an old school blazer from someone else's former public school.[14]

Barbara Hulanicki had opened the first Biba store in Kensington, an expensive and fashionable part of west London, in 1964, and a second in 1965. At first, in the manner of the sixties, Biba looked like a statement, but we soon realised that it was just another clothes shop. But it was a clothes shop that sold you things of which your schoolmasters would have disapproved. If, like Blair, you came from a reactionary boarding school that had strained to hold back the tide of the sixties and was obsessed by the length of your hair, then you might well see tight white flared trousers as more than just something to cover the nakedness of your lower limbs.

Instead of going straight to St John's College, Oxford, Blair took a gap year and came to London, with nothing but a guitar, a change of clothes, the names of friends of friends who might give him a floor to sleep on for a few days, shoulder-length hair, an ambition to be a rock promoter and a passable imitation of Mick Jagger.

Kensington in 1971 was a haven for people like Blair – ersatz rebels, mostly from public schools, filling in time before turning their minds to respectable careers, trying to out-sixties the sixties by having longer hair, stranger clothes and more cannabis than old fogies from 1968 ever dreamed of, and saying outrageous things in public-school accents.

After a while Blair realised he was not going to make a fortune as a rock promoter, and he found a job in the food department of Barker's in Kensington High Street. The department manager liked him, and told him that if he worked hard, there might be a career there for him. How Blair laughed. Sad little careers in department stores were not for gilded seventies youth.

In 1972 he went to Oxford and did his celebrated Mick Jagger impressions with a band in the Junior Common Room at St John's. One of his contemporaries was Peter Mandelson, at St Catherine's, but they never met. Later, Mandelson put this down to the fact that 'I was interested in politics.'[15]

The year Blair arrived at Oxford, Gordon Brown was elected as the Rector of Edinburgh University. He had just graduated with a first in History, and his election was a direct result of the student power movement of the sixties. Past Rectors, elected by all members of the university, had been chosen from the great and the good, but it was in the spirit of 1968, the year Brown had started at the university, that the students should demand, and get, one of their own as Rector.

The university put up the usual grey industrialist. Brown ran a lively campaign in which mini-skirted girls called Brown's Sugars wore T-shirts saying 'Gordon for me', and he won a spectacular victory. He involved himself at once in the NUS grants campaign. At that time, students paid no tuition fees, and were entitled to a means-tested grant for living expenses. The grant was £455 a year, and the NUS claim was for £510.

Brown wanted greater powers for the Rector, and a new principal elected directly by the staff and students. He also wanted to democratise the composition of the Court. The university became very sick of him, and in April 1973 the Court proposed a rule change to end the Rector's right to chair Court meetings. Brown took the Court to the courts, and won.

Brown ended his term of office in summer 1975, and the university has never again elected a student Rector, because Brown did a deal. He agreed that in future students could not stand, trading this concession for a student seat on the Court as of right. So Brown was succeeded by the establishment candidate. The idea of a student Rector at Edinburgh went the way of most of the advances for student power won by the baby boomers: it was not passed on to their children.

Blair and Brown were to be the only baby boomer Prime Ministers Britain would ever have, for there will never be another one – the baby boomers' time has come and gone. They were men of their generation. Blair was a fashionable style rebel. Brown, superficially more grounded, a serious-minded son of the Manse, later regretted making waves at Edinburgh and thought the Rectorship was a mistaken adventure. Neither was the stuff of which revolutions are made, but both, as young men, looked rather revolutionary, in their very different ways. They were already the opposite of Labour's great revolutionary Clem Attlee. When he was their age, he looked and sounded like the mildest and least revolutionary of men.

*

In 1975, the year Gordon Brown finished his term as Rector and Tony Blair left Oxford, the Sex Pistols formed in a rundown part of Chelsea called World's End. Their success was a sign that music had parted company with radical politics, and in October the same year another singing star of the seventies confirmed it, with the sort of reflection no sixties band would have contemplated – or could safely have contemplated. David Bowie said, 'You've got to have an extreme right front come up and sweep everything off its feet and tidy everything up . . . It'll do something positive, at least, to cause a commotion in people and they'll either accept dictatorship or get rid of it.'[16]

The sixties alliance between music and politics could not survive the new sectarianism. Years later, during the 1997 election, Tony Blair told a meeting in Stevenage, 'I am a modern man. I am part of the rock 'n' roll generation – the Beatles, colour TV, that's the generation I come from.' The divorce between music and politics, which had seemed inseparable in the sixties, was now absolute.

Also in 1975, there was another new president of the National Union of Students, a big man with a big bushy beard called Charles Clarke, who led demonstrations for student grants to be raised, and for an end to the means test, which meant that all but the poorest were humiliatingly forced to top up their grants from the parental wallet. If we had been told in 1975 that one day a cabinet of which Jack Straw, Charles Clarke and Gordon Brown were all members would take the decision to remove grants from most students and force them to pay tuition fees, we would have considered the joke to be in very poor taste.

In 1975 Clarke had a reasonably receptive audience in government circles – certainly a much more receptive one than he would have provided to a young man bringing him the same sort of message when he was Education Secretary a quarter of a century later. They may not always have got everything they asked for, but he and his predecessors were listened to with respect and attention by Education Secretaries of both parties. The cult of youth was not yet over, and our elders still tended to bow their heads with attention and respect when we spoke.

In Clarke's first year as president I was the NUS press officer. When I was interviewed for the job, the sensible middle-aged accountant who ran the organisation asked me where I expected to be when I was thirty. In true baby boomer spirit I replied, 'Oh, I'll be dead by the time I'm thirty.' He laughed indulgently and agreed to appoint me.

*

By the mid-seventies, all the factions on the left had chosen the powerful trade union movement to be their battleground.

Back in 1951, the British Communist Party leader Harry Pollitt had announced a strategy of working for the revolution through the unions. Since 1951 the communists had been remarkably successful in getting into key union positions, but Communists like Ken Gill at the draughtsmen's union TASS and Mick McGahey at the miners seemed, to disappointed young revolutionary baby boomers, to have gone native. They were often satisfied with mere industrial victories giving their members a better standard of living. Had they forgotten they were there to work for the revolution? Now the young idealists of the baby boomer generation, after three years of intense student politics, were streaming into the unions, and their first task, as they saw it, was to get rid of the 'Stalinists' who had betrayed the revolution, and show the unions their duty to the working class. Where else could they go, if they thought Parliament was a dead end?

They made the late seventies and early eighties the golden age of syndicalism – the idea that trade unions can be used to make a better world. Their inspiration was the young, fluent, passionate president of the Yorkshire mineworkers, soon to be president of the National Union of Mineworkers, Arthur Scargill. John Mortimer interviewed him for the *Sunday Times*, and asked him if he wanted to be a Labour MP. Scargill, he reported, was quite offended. 'I was asking King Arthur if he'd care for a post as a corporal. He has been offered four Labour seats, but why should he forsake the reality of union rule for the pallid pretensions of Westminster?' Scargill had briefly been a Young Communist, but had found the party restrictive and reactionary.

The British Labour Party was the creation of the unions, so the unions could offer not only an industrial weapon, but access to the levers of power in the Labour Party too. When, years earlier, Communist Party industrial organiser Bert Ramelson had boasted that he had only to 'float an idea early in the year and it would be official Labour Party policy by the autumn' he exaggerated, but not much.

So whether the baby boomers wanted a socialist society or workers' control or gay liberation or abortion on demand, the unions were the instrument through which they thought they were going to get it. Minor trade union posts suddenly became fiercely contested as the baby

boomers sought to make a clean sweep of the old guard, the right wing
and the Stalinists. Union leaders whose faces did not fit in with the new
wave found themselves under unremitting daily siege. The left seemed
to believe that unions were all-powerful, and you had only to get your
hands on the levers of trade union power to change the world. And
the right believed it, too. Doom-laden books of the period included
Anthony Burgess's novella 1985, published in 1978, which predicted
a dictatorship by the unions.

The IS, or Socialist Workers Party as it became in 1977, was well
to the fore in all this. In each union it set up a 'rank and file' organisation, effectively a rival to the official union leadership, with its own
meetings, its own caucuses, even its own newspaper. In one of the
civil service unions, which had an official magazine called *Red Tape*, the
rank and file magazine was called *Redder Tape*. Other unions saw journals
springing up with names like *Hospital Worker*, *Journalists' Charter* and *Rank and
File Teacher*.

Rank and file was a misleading term because the IS was not remotely
interested in the rank and file, only in those few members of it who
supported the IS. The aim was to convince union members that their
interests were opposed to those of trade union leaders and officials
(except Arthur Scargill). They appeared to believe that the workers were
straining at the leash to unseat capitalism by force, held back only by
their bureaucratic union leaders (except Arthur Scargill); and that exist-
ing trade union leaders, unenlightened by having been at university
in the late sixties, were greedy bureaucrats and traitors to the working
class (except Arthur Scargill). Therefore, anything that could be done to
weaken their powerbase should be done.

By then, the IS was having to do without the services of most of
those who had sustained it at the start of the seventies. Peter Hitchens
was one of many who, soon after graduating, began a sharp sprint
rightwards. But probably more were expelled than left of their own
accord. Paul Mackney was expelled in 1975. In Birmingham, where he
worked, he had done a deal with local Communists, with the approval
of the IS high command, that they would support an IS candidate for
a trade union position, if the IS would support their candidate for
another such position. When the time came for Mackney to deliver on
his side of the bargain, the policy had changed and he was told not to

do it. He aligned himself to something called IS Opposition, and the letter expelling him hangs in a frame on the wall of his home to this day: 'Dear Paul, The Central Committee has today expelled you from the organisation for refusing to accept the discipline of the organisation by refusing to dissociate yourself from the IS Opposition Faction. Yours fraternally, Jim Nichol, National Secretary.'

Roger Protz was fired from his job as editor of the IS newspaper *Socialist Worker* for some ideological deviation or other, so he applied for a job as a trade union official at the National Union of Journalists, and was expelled from the IS for making this application, because its members were not allowed to apply for appointed positions as 'trade union bureaucrats'.

It was extraordinary to watch this tiny grouplet behaving as though its decisions mattered, and I had a grandstand view, as a member of the NUJ executive and eventually, as the seventies turned into the eighties, its president.

I also found myself in as wretched a place as any baby boomer has known – in the firing line of the late seventies battles over feminism. There were the socialist feminists, who talked to me guardedly, and the revolutionary feminists, who did not talk to me at all but frequently shouted at me; and the two factions hardly spoke to each other. The former faction thought the unions should be harnessed to the feminist cause, while the latter faction took the view that the unions were just another exploiter of women. Both made the seventies mistake of supposing the trade unions to be immensely powerful.

Marsha Rowe, one of the founders of *Spare Rib* and a sixties icon, started to go to trade union conferences because 'it seemed to be important what women could gain through the trade union movement.' But when she got there, she thought dismissively, 'Oh, middle-aged men'.[17] It's not clear whether their primary sin was to be male or middle-aged. It was silly enough, and harmless enough, until we woke up a few years later and realised that the myth that the unions were the principal obstacle in the way of equality for women helped Margaret Thatcher to destroy them in the next decade. 'We just thought that we were making our own world,' Marsha Rowe told Andy Beckett three decades later, with a great, wide smile. A lot of baby boomers thought that. She was, reports Beckett, sitting in her immaculate flat, beautifully and expensively dressed, with just a splash of lipstick, and Beckett speculates: 'Perhaps there was something about people who had lived through revolutions that made them want orderly lives in the decades after.' Perhaps. Or perhaps people like Marsha Rowe were, essentially, comfortable middle-class people with tasteful, orderly homes, rather than radicals.

Marsha Rowe's feminist comrades ran a vigorous campaign to get the NUJ to support abortion on demand. Any man who wanted to be elected to anything was careful how he voted on this, as also was any young man wanting a sexual adventure at the union's annual conference. It was a massive set-piece battle. On one side were the fiercest of the female baby boomers, taking a break from sitting grimly at the back of union meetings and waiting for some man to say 'he' instead of 'he or she' so they could pounce on him and tear him to pieces. On the other side were a few raddled religious monomaniacs taking a break from standing at street corners with placards saying 'Be sure your sins will find you out' and picketing theatres showing plays they didn't like. Neither side was at all interested in anything else the NUJ did; they just wanted a battleground, and our union would do fine. 'Oppressors of women,' shrieked one side, and 'Murderers of children,' shrieked the other, and one of the religious monomaniacs held aloft at the annual conference an aborted foetus he happened to have about his person.

I let myself be bullied into supporting the proposal to adopt abortion on demand, fearful of being branded a male chauvinist or a reactionary, despite the harmful effect I knew it would have on the union. It wasn't my finest moment. It mattered not a jot in the debate about abortion. Not a single mind was changed by our decision. The pros and the antis used us as a battleground for their private war, and left the battleground devastated, as battlegrounds always are, while they took their war to the next battleground. It was a typical baby boomer political operation: ugly and pointless.

Neither am I especially proud of my role in helping expel NUJ members. The 1977–8 provincial newspaper strike, the biggest journalists' strike in living memory, ended in partial victory, but then came the demand to expel from the union anyone who had gone back to work before they were given permission to do so. Quite why I agreed to serve on the travelling assize that went round the country expelling journalists from their union, I am not sure. I do remember expressing some doubt about its wisdom as I returned from one such round of bloodletting with one of the most enthusiastic witchfinders, who replied with a misquote from Lenin: there would be 'fewer but better Russians'.

The baby boomer illusion that, during the seventies, the trade unions were immensely powerful resulted in fierce, bitter, divisive political campaigns being waged for even minor union positions. When Bernard Levin led a right-wing rebellion against the takeover of the NUJ's London Freelance Branch by the far left in 1976, the monthly branch meetings, which had always struggled to get a quorum, were suddenly crowded out with hundreds of people, whipped in by both sides. Levin used his *Times* column to call his supporters in and give his side their voting instructions. The campaign, writes one of his left-wing opponents, Hilary McCaskill, 'brought in celebrities hitherto (alas) indifferent to trade union affairs, such as Woodrow Wyatt and Marghanita Laski. At one meeting Arianna Stassinopoulos [a well-known American author, who lived with Levin] sat on the arm of my chair, reading a book, but putting up her arm to vote when Levin did.'[18]

They were fighting for control of one branch of one small trade union, and a branch whose members, being freelance journalists, had virtually no industrial muscle. Yet such was the perceived power and importance of the unions that no one thought this at all disproportionate.

It suited both the unions and their enemies to pretend they were far more powerful than they were. It suited the unions because it was good for recruitment, and may have alarmed some employers into giving concessions they might not otherwise have given. It suited their enemies because it helped make voters frightened of the unions, and therefore of the unions' allies, the Labour Party.

The reality was illustrated by a dispute at a photo processing company called Grunwick in Willesden, London in the hot summer of 1976. It was the sort of workplace where the women's toilet breaks were timed. Pay was appalling. A group of Asian women workers went on strike for trade union recognition. The pickets were augmented by a coachload of Yorkshire miners led by Arthur Scargill, who was arrested at Grunwick. Yet in the end the strike was lost: coachloads of strike-breakers were escorted through the pickets by the police, and the work continued. Faced with a company which really was exploiting vulnerable workers, and under a Labour government, the massed weight of the trade union movement could do nothing.

*

The idea that the unions might co-operate in the Wilson government's attempts to get pay restraint, and thus ease the government's economic woes, seemed to those who were young in the sixties to be a betrayal of the revolution. But some older union leaders, and crucially Jack Jones, were becoming alarmed at spiralling wage rises. Hyper-inflation, said Jones, was no good for working people. In July 1975 the unions and the government agreed a so-called social contract aimed at preventing this, with a ceiling for wage rises of £6 a week for all workers earning less than £8,000 a year. This resulted in a dramatic decrease in the level of wage increases and in wage inflation being reduced to single figures by early 1978. But sterling remained under pressure and in November Chancellor Denis Healey had to negotiate additional special drawing rights with the IMF. The next year Healey negotiated a voluntary agreement for 1977/8 of a minimum wage increase of £2.50 per week or 5 per cent, whichever was the higher, and a maximum increase of £4 per week.

Healey was rapidly earning the wholehearted loathing of Labour's younger and more vocal supporters. As a student at Oxford in the thirties, Healey had been in the Communist Party, and now he reflected that student Communists used to debate the question of who would do the dirty work under socialism. After 1974 'I learned that the answer was: Denis Healey.'[19]

After Wilson announced his surprise resignation as Prime Minister in 1976, his successor James Callaghan's first speech to Labour's conference as leader seemed to attack all the old certainties on which Labour policy had been built ever since Attlee walked into Downing Street. 'We have been living on borrowed time,' he said. 'We used to think you could spend your way out of a recession . . . by cutting taxes and boosting government spending. I tell you in all candour that that option

no longer exists.' He wanted 'our labour costs [to be] at least compa-
rable with those of our major competitors', better productivity, and an
end to the printing of 'what Denis Healey calls confetti money to pay
ourselves more than we produce'. To put it another way, Callaghan was
an early and unlikely convert to monetarism. No wonder he did not get
the leader's usual standing ovation, and some of his colleagues on the
platform did not even clap.[20]

But when the IMF demanded cuts before it would give Britain a
loan, Callaghan and Healey negotiated hard over the level of the cuts,
and what they agreed was as far as possible in line with Labour's
instincts. Education, the health service and welfare benefits escaped
relatively unscathed. The big cuts were in defence, in money to stimu-
late employment, in nationalised industries and road building, in
housing and food subsidies. As Andy Beckett notes, 'Clement Attlee died
in December 1976, but the Callaghan government was not ready to
dismantle his welfare state just yet.'[21]

In 1978, the third year of pay restraint, Jack Jones wanted to continue collaboration with the government. Jones told his union's 1977
conference, 'The benefits of North sea oil and an improved balance of
payments are on the horizon. If this government fails you will hand
these to the party of privilege. You will put back the mighty in their
seats and kick the people of low degree in the teeth.'[22] But he knew – he
had warned ministers – that he could not hold the dam much longer.
Now, just months from Jones's retirement, the old left and the new left
combined to defeat him for the first time. Ministers pleaded with his
successor, Moss Evans, to try again next year. Evans replied, 'If they did
that to Jack Jones, what do you think they'd do to me?'

That year, at the Trades Union Congress in Brighton, the engineering
union leader Hugh Scanlon, the second most powerful trade unionist
in Britain, tried to hold the line on pay restraint, and failed. Dozens of
young men and women who had grown up in the sixties surrounded
Scanlon as he left the conference, and followed him back to his hotel,
jeering and shouting. It suddenly looked very ugly. These were fit young
people surrounding and bullying a man of sixty-four who was accompanied only by one colleague almost as elderly as himself.

Scanlon had been outflanked on the left by the baby boomers. It
happened to the lefties of his generation a lot in the seventies.

It was also the last time for some years that a major union leader walked round during TUC week unprotected. A couple of years later I saw TUC general secretary Len Murray walking just 20 yards from his hotel to the new conference centre with a heavy police guard. That sort of sight became common, and lasted for years, until the unions were too insignificant for anyone to care much what they did.

It rather suited the Trots in 1978 to have union leaders protected by the police. They felt it showed the working class that their union leaders were not really their people. And of course it did, but the beneficiary was not the left.

Almost everyone expected Callaghan to call a General Election in the autumn of 1978. When he announced that he would not do so, TUC leaders thought they had been bamboozled: they were sure he had given them as clear a private hint as he could that there was about to be an election. The decision looked like electoral suicide – and, as it turned out, it was. Both the TUC and the Labour Party conference (controlled largely, as it was, by the block votes of the trade unions) rejected his proposed pay restraint overwhelmingly. The 5 per cent limit was going to mean a real cut in living standards, because inflation was running at 8 per cent, and the unions were not going to go along with it.

Callaghan tried to impose a pay ceiling without the support of the unions. The result was the 1978–9 'winter of discontent' – the public sector strikes that seemed at the time like the fulfilment of all the dreams the baby boomers had dreamt since 1968.

The Transport and General Workers Union had put in huge pay claims at Ford and British Leyland and in the road haulage industry. Ford workers went on strike and won 17 per cent, so other workforces took 17 per cent as the benchmark. Another strike by oil tanker drivers won a 20 per cent pay rise. By the time the Prime Minister flew to Guadeloupe on 4 January 1979 for a summit with the US, France and West Germany, Callaghan's pay policy lay in ruins.

While he was away, Liverpool gravediggers refused to bury the dead, there were food shortages brought about by a road haulage strike and panic buying, and many families found it difficult to heat their homes because heating oil was not being delivered. On Callaghan's return on 10 January, he managed to sound complacent, saying, 'I don't think other people in the world share the view that there is mounting chaos.'

The Sun the next day splashed a headline: 'Crisis? What Crisis?' Of course Callaghan had not said that, but the headline was to haunt him. Strikes spread from industry to industry – rail, water, sewage. Secondary picketing at ports and depots prevented goods from being distributed. Public sector workers brought chaos to schools, ambulance services and hospitals. On 22 January a million and a half public sector workers came out for a day in support of a £60 a week minimum pay deal for public service workers. At the end of January Health Secretary David Ennals announced that 1,100 of the 2,300 National Health Service hospitals were carrying out emergency operations only.

The Government relaxed the 5 per cent pay limit on 16 January for those earning less than £44.50 a week, and a mechanism was found to enable some public employees to have more than 5 per cent. The powers of the Price Commission were strengthened to prevent companies automatically passing on the cost of wage increases to consumers. Callaghan met the entire TUC General Council on 29 January and found them in a contemplative mood. They had been shocked at the ferocity of some of the picket lines and also the backlash in public opinion against trade unions. The baby boomers thought that by defeating Jones and Scanlon they had won a victory. But they had shot themselves in the foot.

Jones and Scanlon had both just retired. They were the last two trade union leaders to be powers in the land, and the last two to carry great weight and influence both with their own members and outside. When Jones stepped down, the Prime Minister and several members of his cabinet attended the day-long leaving ceremony at the Royal Festival Hall, where tributes were read by actor Prunella Scales, and Mike Yarwood did a joke about Callaghan needing Jones's permission to form a government.

Jones was the last union leader to have this sort of treatment. Today, even people who have studied the seventies think it strange: Andy Beckett, who was a child at the time, feels the need when he reports it to sneer at 'Emperor Jones' in the 'stately Attlee-style auditorium' of the Royal Festival Hall.[23] It's a measure of how low the baby boomers have brought the reputation of the unions, as well as of how high it had once been.

*

In 1945, when the new Parliament met for the first time, the new, young Labour MPs, among them Harold Wilson, Jim Callaghan and Michael Foot, shocked their elders by singing 'The Red Flag'. It never happened again until 28 March 1979, when Callaghan's wafer-thin majority finally collapsed and the government fell. That day, Labour MPs struck up 'The Red Flag' once again, this time led by a member of the war baby generation, Neil Kinnock. Labour then proceeded to lose the 1979 general election by a landslide to the new, radical Conservative Party under Margaret Thatcher. Over the next few years, the Attlee settlement of Britain's affairs ended, and the Thatcher settlement began. The Attlee era began with the first-ever rendering of 'The Red Flag' in the chamber of the House of Commons. It ended with the second, and probably the last.

9. The radical conservatives: 1979–97

Thatcherism, nurtured privately throughout the sixties while the baby boomers' attention was distracted, had been crouching beneath the bridge of the seventies like a malignant troll.

It was born just before the dawn of the sixties, in 1959, the year there was a run on the pound, caused largely by rumours of devaluation, the weakening of the pound after Suez, and the devaluation of the French franc. Harold Macmillan's Chancellor, Peter Thorneycroft, was persuaded by his young financial secretary, Enoch Powell, to control the money supply and keep wage settlements down (see Chapter Five). Thorneycroft's measures, which included sharp bank-rate rises and cuts in public spending, did not have the impact he expected, and he urged more of the same, including deep cuts in welfare spending, abolishing children's allowances and family allowances, and higher prescription charges. It went against all Macmillan's instincts, and Thorneycroft was forced to toe the line or resign. He resigned, along with Powell and economic secretary Nigel Birch. Powell never got over his loathing for Macmillan. He later complained that Macmillan's habit was to offer 'a quid pro quo to the workers for co-operation in an inflation-free planned economy'[1] and that Macmillan and Heath inhabited 'a never-never land where it would be possible – given "moderation" on all sides – to enjoy the sweetness of inflating the currency without suffering the punishment which follows'.[2]

The 'one nation' Conservatives had won the first round, but not the last. Macmillan suffered the fate of many politicians with his precious skill for balancing irreconcilables: in the end he satisfied no one. For many in his own party, he moved to the left far too far, far too fast, but for the early sixties baby boomers, he was too old, too cautious, too cunning. They wanted a revolution, they said. And they got one, two decades later. It was not the left-wing one they dreamed of: it was Margaret Thatcher's. But hey, it was a revolution. Who's quibbling about details?

For Margaret Thatcher did the things that Peter Thorneycroft, Nigel Birch, Enoch Powell and her intellectual mentor Keith Joseph had dreamed of doing. The result was not the libertarian society that the children of the sixties might have dreamed of, but the opposite: a more centralised bureaucracy than Britain had ever known. As Will Hutton put it in 1995, 'intermediate institutions that even faintly expressed an alternative political agenda have been summarily subordinated to the will of the centre.' Norman Tebbit was remarkably frank about the reason for abolishing the Greater London Council: it was 'Labour dominated, high-spending, and at odds with the government's view of the world'[3]

Such parts of local government as remained were stripped of their powers to decide anything important, or to spend money except as decided by central government. They could not even decide how to administer such services as they were instructed to administer. Mostly these services had to be contracted out to private companies under a set of regulations so detailed and complex that ever since then, any company wanting a local government contract must fill in a form amounting often to several hundred pages. Local government contracts – and central government contracts too – have become playgrounds for big business, because small businesses cannot afford to speculate several weeks' work on form-filling.

Debased local government produced a debased political culture, because top national politicians from both political parties once cut their teeth in local government. They seldom do so any more, because local government has so little power, and they arrive in Parliament with no experience of being democratically accountable.

A debased political culture produced the totemic local government figure of the Thatcher era: Dame Shirley Porter, elected Leader of Westminster City Council in central London when money was God and Mrs Thatcher his prophet. Porter threw poor people out of council homes and into dreadful bed and breakfast accommodation, at enormous cost, because they lived in marginal wards, and she wanted to sell their flats to people more likely to vote Conservative. She knowingly housed families with young children in tower blocks stuffed with asbestos, because these blocks were in safe Labour wards, and she wanted to move the families – presumed to be mostly Labour voters – out of the marginal wards.

Porter was dependant on the sharp-toothed right-wingers of the baby boomer generation: she recruited youthful right-wing Conservatives – there were a lot of them about in the eighties – to pack the public gallery during council meetings. They got a kick out of jostling the relatives of those buried in the three cemeteries Porter sold for less than £1 – the relatives who had come to complain that the graves were no longer being looked after and were being desecrated by vandals. When a Labour councillor read letters from relatives, these unpleasant young men began to simper and snigger.

Porter was admired in the eighties because she had limitless inherited wealth (her father founded Tesco). Limitless wealth sometimes brings limitless arrogance. As her biographer Andrew Hosken puts it, people 'listened as she referred to residents as "customers" and argued the need for the council to be run on "business lines", and concluded that the magic of Tesco had rubbed off on her. But Porter had no real business experience.'

In 1995, she was to fly on holiday to the US. Her last instruction was that successful managers should be given leather Filofaxes, and underachievers should get plastic ones. Her assistant chief executive knew Porter would forget, and intended to do nothing about it. Then came a call from the airport. 'Now, I don't want you slacking while I'm away . . . I want you to develop an adopt-a-granny scheme . . . And I also want you to reward the top ten time managers with leather personal organisers.' 'Yes, Leader.' 'Oh, I've got to go now, the pilot wants to take off.' The pilot was asking Lady Porter for the return of his radio before taking Concorde to the runway.[4]

The trade unions were another potential source of dissent from 'the government's view of the world'. If capitalism was a perfect system, but a capitalist enterprise was not working perfectly – and many of them were not – there must be some external reason. The unions seemed the obvious one. 'Attacking the institutions of collective bargaining . . . was seen as the absolute priority of Conservative policy,' wrote Will Hutton. Unions were 'over-mighty subjects' and as dangerous to Conservative policy as strong local councils.[5]

The unions had rendered themselves vulnerable in the seventies, and never quite knew what hit them in the eighties. But it was like an armoured train. In 1979, five million people were in closed shops, where, by agreement between unions and management, everyone had to be in the union; by 1993 the closed shop had been outlawed. In 1979, 13.3 million people were in unions (perhaps slightly fewer, for some unions inflated their membership figures in order to increase their block vote at the Labour Party conference); by 1993 it was under nine million, and only a third of employed workers belonged to a union – the lowest percentage since 1946. In 1979, nearly three quarters of the workforce were covered by collective bargaining agreements; by 1993 it was less than half.

A series of Acts of Parliament reduced the unions' bargaining strength dramatically. Secondary picketing – picketing an organisation other than the one that employs you – was banned, which was serious because a strike could often be made entirely ineffective if a supplier or a customer carried on working normally. Ballots before strike action became a legal requirement, and the ballot regulations were made very complex and difficult to fulfil. It became illegal to discipline a union member, for example by expelling him from the union, for breaking a strike. Companies could not be forced to recognise unions, and could issue individual contracts that undermined collective agreements. Thus encouraged, companies rushed to derecognise unions and scrap industry-wide collective bargaining agreements.

Key to destroying the power of the unions was ending Britain's dependence on strongly unionised heavy industries, especially coal, iron and railways; and the moment when Thatcher finally defeated and humbled the unions was the great miners' strike of 1984–5. The strike was called to defend the mining industry against the huge pit closure programme planned by the government, and ended with total victory for the government.

Unemployment, which had been seen as a scourge by governments of all parties between 1945 and 1979, was considered by the Thatcherites to be at worst an acceptable consequence of the free market, at best a positive good because it depressed wages and undermined the power of the unions. Unemployment rose steadily, from 4 per cent of the labour force in 1979 to more than 11 per cent in 1986. It reached three million in 1983. The government's response was to reduce the levels of unemployment benefit and income support, and make them harder to obtain.[6] In Chancellor Geoffrey Howe's first budget, the link between pensions and earnings was broken. Those on state pensions were in future to be allowed to get relatively much poorer than those still working. The nostrums of the Attlee settlement, even the welfare state, were no longer sacrosanct.

The pensions decision meant little to the baby boomers at the time – they were aged between twenty-four and thirty-four in 1979, and not inclined to worry about the standard of living of old folk who had failed to follow Bob Dylan's advice and get out of the way of the new world. It would not have stopped them voting for Mrs Thatcher in 1979, which many of them did. But they are noticing it now, as I write, in 2010.

The National Health Service was (and is still, despite everything that has happened to it) easily the most popular institution in Britain. Every government, even a Thatcher government, promises to defend it, and cannot break that promise too openly; that would court electoral disaster. When Marianne Faithfull at last freed herself of her sixties drug addictions – expensive therapies having failed, and her money having evaporated – she did so in the NHS, and started to understand what her generation had taken for granted: 'Only on the NHS could you do something like this.'[7]

But even so, the baby boomer generation did not value it enough, and the edges of the principle of 'free at the point of use' were chipped away in the Thatcher years, with, among other things, much higher charges levied for prescriptions and dentistry, and charges being introduced for eye tests. The NHS was forced to put such services as cleaning out to tender among private companies, which produced complicated tendering procedures that favoured big companies, and lower-paid staff. General practitioners were brought as far as possible into the commercial world by being made fund-holders, holding budgets from which they bought services for their patients. Big hospitals were encouraged to opt out of regional health authority control – Nye Bevan had sweated blood to bring them in – and to become self-governing trusts. Private health care flourished as it had not done since 1947, though most people could not afford it, and it could not deal with complex illnesses. By 1990 the BMA was saying that shortage of money represented a crisis for the NHS.

The government's vast privatisation programme became a crusade in the name of freedom, and sharp-suited young men and women of the baby boomer generation made fortunes by buying public assets for less than they were worth. The eighties were golden years for the City of London, the years of legendary excess. A young person who went into the city in the early eighties and stayed there would have to be pretty thick to fail to be a millionaire several times over by the time he or she was fifty, the age at which many of them retired and started wondering vaguely what to do with their time and money.

British Telecom, British Gas, British Airways, Rolls Royce, the British Airports Authority, British Steel, the water companies, the electricity companies, the railways and many more are huge enterprises in which the taxpayer – every citizen – once had a stake, but does not have a stake any longer. Harold Macmillan likened the privatisation programme to 'selling off the family silver'.

While some of the baby boomers were lining their pockets in the City of London, the young in the inner cities erupted in 1981. London, Liverpool and other cities saw riots of the dispossessed young against a society that gave them no hope. A Conservative publication admitted two years later, 'Only half of Britain's school leavers are trained compared with nine tenths in Germany and four fifths in France.' Yet the government saved money by abolishing sixteen of the Industrial Training Boards, which organised training for specific industries, keeping only seven.[8] The next generation was not high on the agenda. It was the baby boomers who mattered still, when electoral calculations were made. They could make and break governments.

The age of individualism came to mean individual ownership. The Thatcher years were dominated by the certainty that owning things was the road to freedom; that the more that was privately owned and the less that was publicly owned, the freer the society. So in 1979 only about 15 per cent of the population owned stocks and shares; by 1992 it was 22 per cent. In 1979 just over half the population owned their homes; it was nearly three quarters in 1992. The baby boomers joined the property owners. Ownership seemed like a wonderful thing in the boom years, and a very bad thing on Black Monday, 19 October 1987, when £50 billion was wiped off the value of shares on the London stock exchange.

One of the few winners on Black Monday was Greg Dyke, who had just been given stock options in the company that employed him as its director of programmes, London Weekend Television. Their value was based on the average price of the shares over a short period in October 1987, and the lower the price, the better it was for him. He became very rich, very quickly.

Two years later Dyke was promoted to managing director and sent on a management programme at Harvard Business School to learn how to do his new job. 'This was 1989, the height of Thatcherism, he writes,

> when everyone in Britain still believed that successful management was all about being tough with your staff, the unions, your competitors, and virtually everyone else. I had never believed that, and [a Harvard professor] reinforced my view of the world . . . the most successful organisations in the world were those that treated their staff properly.[9]

It was not a lesson that the Thatcher era wished to learn.

*

Thatcherism was as much a legacy of the sixties as free love. In the sixties, the baby boomers talked of freedom, meaning the sort of freedom John Stuart Mill wrote about in 1859 in On Liberty: 'If all mankind minus one were of one opinion, and only one person were of the contrary opinion, mankind would be no more justified in silencing that one person than he, if he had the power, would be justified in silencing mankind.' As they crept towards middle age in the eighties, the baby boomers started to put the word 'economic' in front of the word 'freedom'; they started to identify with their bosses, to champion the right of the rich to do whatever they wished with their money, to identify taxation with threats to freedom, to imagine that ours would be a freer society if everything was privately owned.

And so the greedy eighties became the beneficiaries of the indulgent sixties. Sixties man twenty years older became eighties man: sleek, sharp-suited, and ready to harness the language of liberation to the cause of capital. He was identified by John Betjeman:

> You ask me what it is I do. Well, actually, you know,
> I'm partly a liaison man and partly PRO.

Essentially I integrate the current export drive
And basically I'm viable from ten o'clock til five.[10]

It was back to the fifties with a vengeance. No one learned that the
times they were a-changing back again more painfully than Marianne
Faithfull. She had held fast to the sixties mantras as she understood
them, but she had watched Mick Jagger start to take seriously all the
things they had laughed at together, such as debutantes' parties. Jagger
was embracing the establishment, and Faithfull recalls his shame and
mortification when she, full of drugs, passed out at the dinner table of
an earl.[11] One by one, her old sixties friends deserted her as she clung
to the things that had worked for all of them in the sixties, like drugs
and a grand disregard for money, and she found herself ostracised and
eventually sleeping on the streets.[12] Reflecting years later on the death of
Jimi Hendrix in 1970, she thought, 'We must really have fucked up.'[13]
By 'we' she meant the golden boys and girls of the sixties.

In the eighties the right-wing baby boomers, those who had never
been part of the ersatz revolution, came into their own. Andrew Neil,
born in 1949, who had languished in the seventies in the widely despised
Federation of Conservative Students (which was wound up in the eighties, having become too right-wing even for Thatcher's Conservative Party)
became editor of the *Sunday Times*. Kelvin Mackenzie, born in 1946, took
over *The Sun*, and Michael Portillo, born in 1953, began what looked like
an unstoppable political rise as a government adviser in 1979.

The idea that all the baby boomers were, at one time or another,
lefties or faux lefties was mistaken. The right were always there, and
their unfashionableness in the sixties and seventies made them the more
determined to put their stamp on Britain when the chance came. Unlike
the baby boomer left, when their moment came, it turned out that the
baby boomer right meant every word of their rhetoric, and it was in
the eighties that we heard a phrase that seemed like a contradiction in
terms: radical conservative.

Neil and Mackenzie helped create the mood in which Thatcherism
could flourish. They redefined 'freedom' to mean freedom from taxes
and regulations, and developed, as Mark Garnett puts it, 'a context in
which Conservative supporters could have their cake and eat it; they
could enjoy the benefits of the permissive society while blaming their

political opponents for its perceived excesses.'[14] In their world, the freedom of the rich to spend their money however they wished was sacrosanct, and so was the freedom of *The Sun* to print soft porn and sell it over the counter; but the freedom to attack sacred pillars of the state was licentiousness, and the 1979 film *Life of Brian*, which made wonderful fun of Christianity, was banned in several parts of the country. 'Blasphemous as well as tasteless,' stormed the *Daily Telegraph*.[15] Twenty years later Peter Hitchens wrote furiously that the film 'did more damage to faith among young Britons than every pamphlet and lecture which ever issued forth from the earnest spokesmen of rationalism and humanism,'[16] which may well be true.

*

The new managerial hippie often came armed with another sixties innovation – an MBA, or Master of Business Administration. The MBA arrived quietly on these shores from the USA in 1964, and it rose to become a symbol of eighties managerialism. In 1964, no British university had a business school, and the first British MBA students studied for the degree at the London Business School (which was, and is, independent of the universities). By the end of the eighties, every university felt it had to have its own business school and run its own MBA course. They could attract commercial sponsorship as no other department could. And they alone could teach the approved ideological gospel that a society was only free if the rich were free to do whatever they liked with their money, and that only people with capital were 'wealth-creators'.

Germaine Greer, who among her many accomplishments is Professor Emeritus of English Literature and Comparative Studies at Warwick University, has written of how she glowers resentfully from her office window at the building from which Warwick Business School operates – so much more expensively equipped than her department, and with access to riches of which literature students can only dream. On the other hand, John Kay resigned as director of Oxford University's Said Business School because the Oxford academic establishment would not allow him to offer his faculty salaries that were massively higher than those of other Oxford academics. Greer resents business schools having more money than other departments; Kay thinks the difference between what business schools get and what other departments get is not big enough. And it is Professor Kay, not Professor Greer, who represented the spirit of the age. The Regius Professor of Semiotics was swept aside by the Enron Professor of Profits.

It was the MBA and its associated 'business gurus' who performed the intellectual confidence trick of turning sixties freedom into an instrument of big business. The business schools persuaded many people that the only freedom worth defending was the freedom of the ultra-rich to do whatever they liked with their money, and make as much more of it as they could. Never mind your freedom or mine to go where we like, think what we like, wear what we like, do what we like, say what we like – if, as often happens, these freedoms conflict with economic freedom, they must take second place to it. The logical consequence was that you could not have freedom *and* a mixed economy, for anything owned by the state inhibits the freedom of investors to do what they wish with their money. You could not have freedom *and* strong trade unions, for an organisation that places limits on what management may do must necessarily be against freedom. It was even hard to defend the welfare state, because that requires the state to take away private money and use it in ways that those to whom it originally belonged might not have chosen.

This led to the view, which was conventional wisdom in 1920 and unthinkable between 1948 and the election of Margaret Thatcher as Tory leader in 1976, that the only sort of education, healthcare and outdoor relief that should be provided to the poor is whatever the rich choose to provide out of the goodness of their hearts.

And there was no shortage of young and early-middle-aged people to argue that very thing. The distinguished right-wing educationalist Professor James Tooley believes there is 'no justification for state intervention in education, not in terms of provision, funding or regulation'. Things were much better, he says, before 1870, when almost the only education available was what you paid for yourself. He sums up his prescription for putting it all right in one of those handy three-word soundbites of the sort that normally encapsulate something pious and reactionary: the three Fs, 'freedom, family, philanthropy'.

'Freedom' in the mouths of Thatcherite ideologues usually means the freedom of the rich to bully the poor. 'Family' in those circles is used as a way of attacking state welfare provision: when Margaret Thatcher used those famous words 'There is no such thing as society,' she added, 'There are individual men and women, and there are families.' But the key word here is 'philanthropy'. Take away the state, says Professor Tooley, and leave it to the rich and to business to decide what provision, if any, should be made for the poor. Charitable money would be raised and 'administered with discretion and discernment'.[17] As this idea caught on in the last two decades of the twentieth century, charities became very big, and very powerful. 'The voluntary sector,' as they self-importantly call themselves, has been handed huge powers and huge sums of our money.

The Attlee philosophy appeared dead in the eighties, murdered by the baby boomers. Clement Attlee had listened to Lord Beveridge, whose 1944 report advocated government action to slay 'the five giants', and to Maynard Keynes, who advocated public spending. Margaret Thatcher listened to Friedrich von Hayek, who argued that the state should not involve itself in the welfare of its citizens, and Sir Keith Joseph, who told her that money supply should be limited and public expenditure cut. For some of the baby boomers, Thatcherism seemed to be everything they had fought for: a small state, a liberalised economy, power in the hands of individuals and companies rather than the state. They were turning in their early middle age into the hard-faced men and women who did well out of the eighties.

*

For the more recognisable baby boomers, the sixties rebels turned seventies ideologues, Thatcherism was of course the enemy, but the Labour Party was even more of an enemy, for it pretended to be on the side of the working class. And the worst element of the Labour Party was those on its so-called left like Michael Foot and Neil Kinnock, for they taught the working class that advance could be achieved without accepting every nostrum of whatever grouping the speaker attached himself to.

So the dull settlement that had given the baby boomers all their chances in life, created by the Attlee government and maintained by Macmillan, Wilson, Heath and Callaghan, had few defenders among the children of the sixties, being too radical for some and not radical enough for others. It was not until Thatcher had been in power for some years that many of them started to see how privileged they were, and stirred themselves to defend the welfare state; and the National Union of Public Employees produced a T-shirt for them, proudly bearing the slogan 'Born in the NHS'.

For the first few years of Thatcher government, the left among the baby boomers still thought their brand of student politics mattered. So in 1979 the Bennites manoeuvred through the Labour Party conference a system by which the leader and deputy leader would be elected, not by Labour MPs, but by an electoral college which would give 40 per cent of the votes to the trade unions and 30 per cent each to MPs and to grassroots party members. This was clearly going to direct an unwelcome spotlight on the way the trade union block vote was cast. It would make the unions the key, almost the only, power-broker, and ensure that no one could become leader without owing a huge political debt to the leaders of the biggest unions. This was bound to damage both Labour and the unions in public esteem. But the baby boomers had grown to believe that unions were impregnable, and union leaders were not wise enough to spurn this massive, but temporary, addition to their powers. It was to be a very costly mistake.

Michael Foot was by now Labour leader, and he wanted his right-wing rival for the leadership, Dennis Healey, to be elected unopposed as deputy leader, to unite his party. But Tony Benn stood against Healey, and his ambassador to the baby boomer generation, a sharp-toothed young man called Jon Lansman, had a ready answer for those who thought Benn's campaign might not be a good idea: 'You don't believe in democracy then?' Arthur Scargill, never guilty of knowingly understating a case, told the Scottish Miners Gala that anyone who criticised Benn was 'sabotaging not only the candidature of Tony Benn but the principles of socialism which are basic to our movement.'

That set the tone. No self-respecting child of the sixties could be seen to sabotage the principles, etc., etc., never mind where it might lead.

The six-month campaign centred on how the big unions were going to vote. It looked like what it was: a fight for trade union patronage. When the executive of the building trade union UCATT took its voting decision, the headline in the next day's *Sunday Times* read: 'How three top Communists swung 200,000 votes to Benn'. Labour's popularity plummeted, and by the time Healey's desperately narrow victory was announced, Labour had as good as lost the 1983 general election.

The Labour Party was in a state of civil war. At its 1980 conference, Terry Fields, the MP who was also a member of the Militant Tendency, said:

> We need co-ordinated action by the whole of our class to get the Tories out and the democracy that is being pumped out in the capitalist press is their democracy, not ours. We will found a new democracy when we have created a socialist state in this country . . . To the weak-hearted, the traitors and cowards I say: 'Get out of our movement. There is no place for you. Cross the House of Commons . . .'

The next speaker, former Chancellor Denis Healey, to shouts of 'Out, out', said, 'We certainly will not win the next election if . . . instead of meeting the real needs of people, we go on ideological ego-trips or accept the clapped-out dogmas which are now being trailed by the toytown Trotskyists of the Militant group . . .'

While the Labour Party collapsed in ideological warfare, so did all the far left groups, tiny splinters splitting into even tinier splinters. The Communist Party was involved in a bitter civil war. One faction was the older folk grouped around the daily newspaper, the *Morning Star*, and the other, broadly the baby boomers, was grouped around the theoretical journal *Marxism Today*, edited by a very sixties figure called Martin Jacques. Tariq Ali's International Marxist Group was splitting between 'right-wingers' who supported Tony Benn and Arthur Scargill, and purists who considered Benn and Scargill to be tainted with reformism. The Workers Revolutionary Party, which, as everyone on the left knew, really was secretive and rather sinister, was about to feast on its own flesh over an accusation that its leader, Gerry Healy, then in his seventies, was guilty of 'sexual debauchery' – using young female members of his party as sexual playthings. Over at the Labour left-wing weekly magazine *Tribune* there was another furious, bitter and hard-fought battle as editor Chris Mullin, Bennite and baby boomer, heaved the magazine's policy away from its support for Michael Foot and swung it behind

Benn, thus provoking a bitter and widely publicised war with some of his trustees. The whole of the British left appeared to be engaged in a hideous battle to strangle itself.

The baby boomers had adopted a chillingly intolerant view of the workers' movement, in which everyone was playing at being prolier than thou. If you wished to be, or purported to be, on the left, a whole range of litmus tests were devised to test your true devotion. It might be uncritical support for Tony Benn, or for Arthur Scargill. It might be getting exactly the right line on which method of electing Labour's leaders was the most democratic. Whatever it was, you either supported the line, the whole line and nothing but the line, or you were a traitor to the working class. Failure to have exactly the correct line on any one of a dozen or so issues was a fatal character defect.

Unemployment reached three million in 1981 for the first time since the thirties, but the left was so busy tearing itself to pieces that it hardly noticed.

Out of this atmosphere came Margaret Thatcher's second crushing election victory in 1983 and the great miners' strike of 1984–5. The miners' strike could not have happened at any time apart from one at which the left had become frightened of its own shadow, where the fear of being denounced for moderation or reformism, or just being a stooge of the capitalist press, was so great that decisions that were obviously foolish and self-defeating went more or less unquestioned. Decisions were made by the miners' leaders, effectively by their president Arthur Scargill, that make almost no sense until you see them as part of this determination not to be outflanked on the left: the decision not to allow the members to ballot; the decision to pass up several negotiated compromises in pursuit of a total victory that, it was clear fairly early on, was not obtainable. Arthur Scargill 'always seemed to want to appear further left than anyone else,' according to a member of the miners' executive committee.[18]

Paul Mackney, still in Birmingham and now a key figure on the city's trades council, spent the strike organising support for the miners, hampered by internecine struggle on the left. He found Communists demanding full support for the miners' leaders in public, but in private one of the Communist party's two wings, he writes, was trying to isolate Scargill from early on, and opposing mass picketing. Mackney's and Peter Hitchens's old comrades in what was now called the Socialist Workers Party, who had expelled Mackney for ideological deviancy ten years previously, got themselves into a terrible ideological tangle over putting together food parcels for miners who needed them. SWP leaders described food collections derisively as charity work that kept people away from the important work of joining the picket lines.[19]

The baby boomers seemed to split between those who created this atmosphere; those who recoiled from it, like Peter Hitchens; those, like me, who tried hard, for much too long, to appease the ideological monster at our heels; and those – Tony Blair, Gordon Brown – who took the spirit of the sixties into government in 1997.

The generation of 1968 had emerged from its universities and made the left not only unelectable but uninhabitable.

*

Thatcher was forced out in 1990 after eleven years in Downing Street, when she overreached herself with the widely unpopular poll tax. The idea that everyone should pay exactly the same for local services, whether they were multi-millionaires or on the breadline, was a Thatcherite step too far. She was replaced with the less abrasive John Major, who led the Conservative Party into the 1992 election. That election was the baby boomers' last chance to stop the Thatcherite bandwagon, to save the gentler, more caring society inaugurated by Attlee. Its failure was terminal, because by the time Labour did return to office, in 1997, it had lost the will and the courage and confidence to champion the underdog.

Labour entered the 1992 election campaign marginally ahead in the polls, and then, somehow, lost. John Major returned to Downing Street with an overall majority of twenty-one seats. And that defeat, even today, is the wound the Labour Party still touches, and finds that it still hurts. Even today, Labour people (and former Labour people like me) will fall out about why it happened and whose fault it was.

There are those who say it was Shadow Chancellor John Smith's fault for producing a shadow budget that could be unfairly characterised by the Conservatives as 'tax and spend'. (This, by the way, is the most meaningless of all political slogans, for taxing and spending are what governments – all governments – do, and if they had to stop doing it, they could not govern.)

There are those who say it was all the fault of the Sheffield Rally – a great, vulgar, triumphalist television spectacular a couple of days before the election, which spectacularly misfired and made Labour and Kinnock sound threatening.

And there are those who blame Labour's spin machine. Labour's communications in the years leading up to the election were destroyed by personal and political infighting. When it came to the election, Labour had the worst of both worlds: a reputation for an invincible spin machine, and the reality of an ineffective one.

Actually, though all of these things played a part, the real villains were the generations of the sixties and seventies. To take advantage of their last chance to salvage a fair society, the baby boomers who believed in that sort of society had to get behind the Labour leader, and he was the wrong generation for them. Neil Kinnock, born in 1942, was a war baby. A little younger, and he would have been one of their own, like Tony Blair. A little older and he would have been so far removed from them that he would have been just another elderly politician who could not be expected to understand, like Michael Foot. And he had made a series of grubby com- promises, for example ditching his own long-standing belief in unilateral nuclear disarmament because it was an electoral albatross. Too few of the left among the baby boomers could bring themselves to get behind him. It was that very sixties problem of losing face if someone else was seen to be more left-wing than you were, or even just a bit less ideologically correct.

I first met Kinnock in 1982, when I was Labour's press officer for the Peckham by-election at which Harriet Harman first entered parlia- ment. The grim, sectarian, ultra politically correct chairperson of the Peckham Labour Party Women's Committee watched Kinnock exchang- ing rugby reminiscences with a senior policeman sent to look after our walkabout, and muttered furiously, 'How macho!' Her name was Sue Goss, and she is now a revered figure in New Labour. But she and her like helped to ensure Kinnock's 1992 defeat.

There was then – and still is, even now, though they are getting rather long in the tooth – a collection of keepers of the pure faith who were young men and women in the sixties and seventies, and were growing increasingly intolerant and embittered as they grew older.

I watched these grim folk, holding their ideological correctness to themselves like a comfort blanket, make what may have been their last appearance en masse one night in 2009, when Arthur Scargill addressed a London rally to celebrate the 1984–5 miners' strike. He told them, 'If Neil Kinnock had have called on the whole working class to support us, Thatcher would have been out in a year.' And they cheered him to the rafters, even though most of them must have known it was nonsense in a silly hat. They still could not bear someone else to be seen to be more radical than they were.

They are there to this day, confined to their ideological dugouts, spitting hate and venom at their enemies on the left, and to this day the litmus test of ideological purity is the long irrelevant belief that Arthur Scargill was a great working-class leader who could have led us to the promised land had he not been betrayed by reactionary class traitors like Neil Kinnock. There is no word too harsh and bitter for anyone who criticises their hero.

Kinnock had to face the baby boomers from the far left, who would comfort themselves with muttering 'class traitor' in the sure knowledge that, while they would change nothing, at least they could not be out-lefted; and the baby boomers from the far right, to whom Thatcher represented the promise of 1968. But worst of all, perhaps, he was surrounded by a third sort of baby boomer: the ones who wanted to turn him into a svelte, branded product that the now upwardly mobile children of the sixties and seventies would find attractive. He listened to them – to his chief of staff, Charles Clarke; to Labour's head of communications, Peter Mandelson – and they told him that all the things that made him attractive had to go: the noise, the passion, the bons mots, the houndstooth suits. He was to wrap himself in grey flannel suits and grey woollen phrases, to give up the direct, passionate language that won hearts, and deliver his thoughts in vast, shapeless bundles of words.

So he did his best. It became hard to recall what an exciting politician he had been before leadership descended on him like a frozen shroud. He started to deliver his thoughts in vast, shapeless bundles of words. They told him that, when asked a difficult question, he was to flannel until the time ran out, and he did, though he felt foolish doing it.

Despite relentless rebranding and repackaging, something of what he really was still showed, and his advisers insisted that there were still vestiges of the old Kinnock to be suppressed. Peter Mandelson wrote privately to deputy leader Roy Hattersley that Kinnock's 'values and rhetoric are still tied strongly to the "have-nots." He cares too much. He's too much of a socialist.' It didn't work, and if the communicators had understood their trade better, they would have known why. You can build on the product you have, but you can't pretend that it is a completely different product. It took the children of the muddled sixties and seventies to make that simple error.

*

In 1995, just two years before New Labour came to power, in an influential book called *The State We're In*, Will Hutton counted the cost of Thatcherism. Britain, he wrote, had become a country divided against itself as it had not been since before the Attlee settlement, 'with an arrogant officer class apparently indifferent to the other ranks it commands', a class which 'is favoured with education, jobs, housing and pensions.' He wrote this thirteen years before the world knew of Sir Fred Goodwin, the Royal Bank of Scotland Chief Executive who steered his bank into the rocks, and now, having reached the age of fifty, is permitted to draw a pension of £693,000 a year for the rest of his life (which under pressure he agreed to reduce to £493,000).

Sir Fred's pension is largely paid for by taxes on what Hutton called 'the new working poor, who were created when the Thatcher government removed employment regulations, and by cutting the benefits of those who live off the state in near poverty, Hutton wrote that the poor were in a trap, and all paths out of it were closing down. 'The world in which they are trapped becomes meaner, harder and more corrupting.' Those in work are much less secure than they used to be, 'fearful for their jobs in an age of permanent downsizing, cost-cutting and casualisation, and ever more worried about their ability to maintain a decent standard of living'.[20]

Hutton summed up what was in 1995 a commonly held view: 'The great ideological contest of the twentieth century has been settled. Free market capitalism has won; state planning and communism, of which social-market capitalism is alleged to be a sub-set, has lost.'[21] The conventional view was that 'a minimal welfare state, low taxation and little business regulation would allow the economy to take off into a virtuous circle of capitalist dynamism.'[22] Sixties freedom had been redefined.

Twelve years before Hutton was writing, in the week of the 1983 general election, Neil Kinnock, who later that year would be elected leader of the Labour Party, told an election rally:

> If Mrs Thatcher is re-elected as Prime Minister on Thursday, I warn you. I warn you that you will have pain – when healing and relief depend upon payment. I warn you that you will have ignorance – when talents are untended and wits are wasted, when learning is a privilege and not a right. I warn you that you will have poverty – when pensions slip and benefits are whittled away . . . If Mrs Thatcher wins on Thursday, I warn you not to be ordinary. I warn you not to be young. I warn you not to fall ill. I warn you not to get old.[23]

10. The baby boomer Prime Ministers: 1994–2010

Tony Blair and Gordon Brown were the first Prime Ministers of the baby boomer generation, and they will be the last. The baby boomers' obsession with youth, and newness, and modernisation, has rebounded on them.

For Tony Blair, it served its purpose. It made him, at forty-four, the youngest Prime Minister since 1812.

The baby boomers had triumphed, impatiently jostling to the front, pushing aside the old men and women. But it had not occurred to the baby boomers that they too would get old. No longer did it seem desirable, or even tolerable, for someone to become Prime Minister in his sixties, as Churchill, Attlee and Macmillan all did. The baby boomers' obsession with newness created an age when a leader of the Liberal Democrats, Menzies Campbell, could be hounded out of office for the crime of being in his sixties.

But baby boomers in 2010 are between fifty-five and sixty-five, and they have had their day. They did not die before they got old, as Roger Daltrey had urged; but they might as well have done.

The victorious 1997 Labour Party – New Labour – was the party of the baby boomers and of the sixties: Tony Blair, the self-proclaimed modern man and member of the rock 'n' roll generation, who had fought bitter battles with his schoolmasters over the length of his hair and came to London for a Bohemian year in 1971; Gordon Brown, rebel student politician at the end of the sixties who beat the establishment to become Rector at Edinburgh University; Peter Mandelson, who had been leader of the British Youth Council in the seventies.

There too were the NUS presidents who once made sixties radicalism the dominant feature of student politics and led huge demonstrations in the late sixties and the seventies for higher student grants, Jack

Straw and Charles Clarke. There too was Alan Milburn, proprietor in the seventies of a radical bookshop in Newcastle upon Tyne called Days of Hope, known locally as Haze of Dope from the delicious smells that emanated therefrom; John Reid, former Communist and researcher for the Scottish Union of Students; and David Blunkett, who led Sheffield City Council in the days when Sheffield was called the 'Socialist Republic of South Yorkshire' and fronted a group of left-wing Labour councils determined to launch the assault on Thatcherism that they claimed Labour's then leaders were too timid to mount.

So there it was, the first baby boomer government – and a baby boomer parliament too, for the old guard were swept out of safe seats to make room for them.

John Gilbert, Labour MP for Dudley East, was one of many: he was asked to quit to make room for Blair's former roommate and fellow lawyer Charles Falconer, and offered a peerage and a job in his favourite department, the Ministry of Defence. Unfortunately Dudley East refused to have Falconer – they were not impressed to learn that he sent his children to fee-charging schools – and Blair had to give him a peerage too. Stuart Randall became Lord Randall to clear his Hull West seat for a favoured Blairite trade unionist, Alan Johnson. Peter Mandelson told the Daily Telegraph, 'Isn't it good to get all these bright young Blairites into the House?'[1]

No government had ever looked so young, and fresh, and radical, and prepared to change the world. No government ever proved so conservative, and timid, and reactionary, and sure that the established order and conventional wisdom must be right. The chance to change the world had gone with the departure of the war babies – the resignation of Neil Kinnock in 1992 and the death of John Smith in 1994.

If Smith had lived to lead Labour into the 1997 general election, much would have been different. Labour would still have been elected with a comfortable majority, for the Conservatives were in meltdown at the time and Smith was the most popular and respected Labour leader since Attlee, whom he resembled in many ways. Bob Worcester of MORI, the greatest living expert on political polling, tells me the majority would not have been the 197 that Blair had, but something between 90 and 100.

Smith would have led a very different sort of Labour government. We would never have heard of New Labour. When the government had to decide if it should side with the rich and powerful, rather than with the poor, we would not have the sinking, miserable certainty that it would choose the rich and powerful.

He would not have pledged, as Blair did in *The Sun* during the 1997 election, to 'fight any bid to foist on Britain the high costs which are hampering business on the Continent.' 'High costs which are hampering business' is well-understood code for laws that give rights to employees, and this was a message aimed more at *Sun* proprietor Rupert Murdoch than *Sun* readers. Blair was as good as his word: he ran Labour's first ever anti-union government.

Jon Cruddas, now MP for Dagenham & Rainham, was in Congress House, the TUC headquarters, on the night of the 1997 election, and recalls union leaders' growing apprehension as they saw the scale of the election victory. They knew that the stronger Blair was in Parliament, the less chance they had of getting a pro-union government. 'Many of them thought, we ought to jump before we're pushed,' he says. 'They thought, this means the full Blairite agenda, including ditching the unions.'

They didn't jump. Instead, TUC general secretary John Monks and Jon Cruddas formed a partnership to lobby the government on behalf of the trade unions. Cruddas says, 'Tony Blair is unlike any previous Labour leader in that he does not think a Labour government ought to enhance collective bargaining. Every previous Labour leader has believed that trade unionism is basically a good thing and union membership ought to be encouraged.'[2]

To the war baby generation of Labour politicians, the unions, for all their faults, were the only way the interests of workers could compete with those of business. To the baby boomers of both left and right, from Thatcherite to Trotskyite, unions were old-fashioned, reactionary, a drag on progress. The left among the baby boomers had agitated within the unions in the seventies to turn them into the vanguard of the revolution; the right in the eighties had made out they were exactly that, and eviscerated them for their revolutionary pretensions. Now the first Blairite Prime Minister was to show them that they had no friends left, even at the head of the political party they had created. To Blair as much as to Margaret Thatcher, the trade unions were the enemy within.

Jon Cruddas did not know it, but just before Blair became Prime Minister, in 1996, the leaders of the Confederation of British Industry, the employers' body, asked for a meeting with Blair, to be kept secret from everyone, including the TUC. They told him they were concerned about the rights given to workers and their unions by the European social chapter that Labour was committed to sign. Blair told them he had to sign the social chapter because it was a Labour Party commitment, but he would block any other pro-worker and pro-union proposals. Any help to employees the EU felt like giving on such matters as maternity benefits, or health and safety, would be fiercely fought by the British government if the CBI required it.

So when TUC leaders continued to besiege the Blair government with requests, and Cruddas continued to argue for them inside the 'den', the Prime Minister was already secretly pledged to turn them down.

Never was a pledge so amply fulfilled. The European Commission wanted a directive on information and consultation, designed to stop employees hearing on the television (or in some notorious cases by text message) that their factory had been shut and they were out of a job. But the moment Blair became Prime Minister, the European Trades Union Congress, which represented European trade unions in Brussels, was startled to find that the directive had a determined enemy in the new British government. 'Britain went to war to block the directive,' is how John Monks, now general secretary of the ETUC, put it to me. 'The British government led the opposition in the corridors of Brussels throughout.'

It also led opposition to the proposed directive on agency workers, which would give these workers the same rights as permanent workers. 'The British government blocked that ferociously,' says John Monks. 'We would have it without the British government.'

Later there was the working time directive, which Blair also blocked. The directive said that normally no one should work more than forty-eight hours a week. European social democrats, and even Christian Democrats, were amazed at how determined Britain was to block this. A Dutch ETUC official was shocked to be told by a brisk young Blair aide, 'We don't do collective bargaining.'[3]

Blair was particularly scathing about the trade unions' use of their block vote, right up to the time when it came to selecting a Labour candidate to be the first Mayor of London. But then he realised that the only way to stop Ken Livingstone getting Labour's nomination was to have a system by which the unions could use their block vote, and to invite them to do so. Union leaders, by now thoroughly tamed, cast their block vote as instructed and delivered the nomination for Blair's candidate, Frank Dobson. Much good it did them. Dobson as Labour's official candidate lost the election to Livingstone, and if Blair was grateful to the unions, it never showed.

John Monks tried to paper over the cracks between Labour and the unions, telling BBC Radio 4's *World at One* that he did not expect more privatisation from New Labour. 'I wouldn't expect a Labour government to go down the direction that the Conservatives have been down – which is to clear out every potentially lucrative bit of the public sector,' he told the programme. If he really believed that, he learned different quite fast. Privatisation continued as though Thatcher had never left office. Fifty Labour MPs opposed the privatisation of air traffic control on safety grounds after hearing British Airways' concern that a private company should not 'have profit as a primary objective.' The pledge to undo the privatisation of the railways was never fulfilled.

Big companies were permitted to fleece the taxpayer. Chancellor Gordon Brown forced London Underground to sign contracts with private companies for maintaining the tube system on the companies' terms. Professor Tony Travers, director of the Greater London Research Unit at the LSE, commented at the time, 'The preferred bidders can add any number of noughts to the deal and wait until they get it. The government demands a quick deal at any price – any price is what they will get.'

In education, there was to be no more of that egalitarian nonsense about ending the Eleven plus, to which Labour was pledged, and which had been part of Labour's programme since Harold Wilson's day. Selection, school uniforms, tight discipline, those hallmarks of fifties and early sixties secondary schools before the lax late sixties came along, made a comeback under Blair. So did university tuition fees, which had been abolished for the baby boomer generation. In their middle age, the baby boomers wanted their children to have all the restrictions and limited horizons that they themselves had rejected. New Labour, whose leaders had almost all benefited from free university places and student grants, pulled up the educational ladder they had climbed.

When Labour had last been in office, under Wilson and Callaghan, it had begun to get rid of selection at the age of eleven and the widely hated Eleven plus examination. When it left office there were just 166 grammar schools left, with the right to choose which pupils they taught and force neighbouring schools to teach the children they did not want. When New Labour took office in 1997, the 166 grammar schools were still there. They still are. New Labour has also found several new ways of enabling certain schools to select a proportion of their pupils.

New Labour completed the Thatcherite policy of taking control of schools away from local authorities and handing it to business and religion. Teachers and parents were removed from governing bodies to make way for business people. The city academy programme is the crudest example. City academies are schools paid for by public money (except for a small contribution from the sponsor) but entirely controlled by the sponsor – normally a business or charity or religion. The sponsor has a majority of seats on the governing body, and controls the key appointments, the curriculum, the management of the school, in perpetuity.

Even Blair's old boss Neil Kinnock publicly attacked New Labour education policy – the only time he has ever criticised any of his successors, for he makes a fetish of loyalty. Only on education could Blair have brought out the old Neil Kinnock. Kinnock is old enough to know that free and equal access to education is new and precious and to be nurtured and protected. He has known all his life that he is a product of the 1944 Education Act.

New Labour's first contribution to the National Health Service was pure Thatcherism. Foundation hospitals are hospitals that opt out of government control and become independent not-for-profit organisations, able to borrow money on the private markets and set their own financial and clinical priorities. Their enemies said they would create a two-tier NHS, where some patients would get the best treatment from the best funded hospitals, which were able to offer higher salaries to get the best staff, and other patients would get second-rate treatment.

In Labour's first term, 1997–2001, public spending grew more slowly than it had done under John Major. Each year that Labour refused to put more money into them, the state of the public services grew worse, and the time it would take to put them right grew longer. For those four years, pretty well nothing was done to repair the under-investment of the Thatcher years.

Compare that with the only other Labour government to have had a big majority. In three years the Attlee government of 1945–51 created the National Health Service, implemented the 1944 Education Act, including raising the school leaving age and building hundreds of new schools, and created Britain's first comprehensive welfare system. And Attlee inherited a war-ravaged economy.

Attlee also narrowed the gap between rich and poor. Blair and Brown widened it.

*

The children of the sixties talked a lot about peace and love, and they went on great demonstrations against the American war in Vietnam. But twenty-nine years after 1968, the children of the sixties led the twentieth century's most bellicose British government. Two of the countries in which it went to war are still in turmoil, Afghanistan and Iraq. To get them both off the ground, Tony Blair persuaded President George Bush to offer a sweetener to Russia's President Putin: Blair and Bush would classify Russia's war in Chechnya as part of the 'war on terror'.

In January 2002 the first of hundreds of chained and hooded people were herded on to a US cargo jet and flown to Guantanamo Bay. Today, eight years later, we still do not know everything about what crimes they are suspected of committing, what evidence there is that they committed them, or exactly what methods have been used to extract confessions from them. We do know that they have been tortured, that some of them are British citizens, and that their government does not seem very concerned about whether they will ever receive justice.

There was a time when the idea that the British government might be complicit in torture would have been deeply shocking, not least to the baby boomer generation.

We also know Blair told Parliament that Iraq had weapons of mass destruction and could launch them at forty-five minutes' notice, and that he knew it was probably untrue. The generation that had preached peace and love and truth in the sixties produced the first war that Britain has ever entered because its government lied to the people.

It was the Iraq war that finally ended Greg Dyke's long love affair with New Labour. Dyke had made serious money in independent television, and some of it went into Blair's leadership election campaign and then Labour's 1997 general election campaign. He had quelled the doubts that rose up in him when he first met Tony Blair and Blair said to him, 'I want to serve my country by being a Labour MP.'

In 2000 Blair made him BBC Director General. One of the first complaints to the new DG came from Dyke's old York University Trotskyist contemporary Peter Hitchens, now harrumphing from the far right about 'political correctness gone mad'. Dyke says, 'Peter Hitchens complained to me that the BBC guidelines said the BBC shouldn't use the word housewife. I said, "For God's sake, Peter."'

On 29 May 2003, at 6.07am, reporter Andrew Gilligan said on the BBC's *Today* programme: 'We've been told by one of the senior officials in charge of drawing up that dossier [alleging that Saddam Hussein had weapons of mass destruction and could launch them at forty-five minutes' notice] that actually the government probably knew that that 45-minute claim was wrong, even before it decided to put it in.' The claim was not repeated: it was dropped from Gilligan's subsequent reports that morning. We now know that Gilligan was right.

The government had already spent a lot of time and effort trying to discredit Gilligan's reporting, and Dyke had been drawn into a war of words with his old friend Blair. Two months before the famous broadcast he had written to Blair:

> Frankly, and I do not mean to be rude, but having faced the biggest ever public demonstration in this country and the biggest ever backbench rebellion against a sitting government by its own supporters, would you not agree that your communications advisers are not best placed to advise whether or not the BBC has got the balance right between support and dissent?[4]

It was no good. Dyke and his chairman Gavyn Davies were eventually forced to resign after the government put pressure on the BBC governors. Here is what Dyke wrote in 2004 of the first government of the baby boomer generation:

> Gavyn Davies and I left the BBC because we were criticised . . . we think wrongly and unfairly, for failing to ensure the BBC's editorial controls were sound on a particular story broadcast on one BBC radio station at seven

minutes past six one May morning. Tony Blair took Britain into a war in which thousands were killed, including many British troops, on the basis of shoddy intelligence. Some of that intelligence he knew was unproven; and some of it he should have questioned and didn't. He is still the Prime Minister.[5]

*

The Labour Party had waited eighteen years to get their people into government. The baby boomers had waited much longer – twenty-nine years, ever since 1968. When both succeeded, they placed in No. 10 Downing Street a man who read not Marx or Keynes but (so he once claimed, and there is no reason to doubt it) everything written by management writer turned religious philosopher Charles Handy.

Handy is one of the small company of 'business gurus'. 'Guru' is a wonderful sixties word, and British business schools are a sixties invention. When a guru speaks, you are not supposed to subject his words to any of the normal tests of logic or consistency. It is equivalent to divine revelation. And business people of the baby boomer generation, as they climbed corporate ladders in the eighties and nineties, treated the lightest word from a business guru much as John Lennon in 1968 treated the lightest word from Maharishi Mahesh Yogi. Tom Peters, C. K. Prahalad, Gary Hamel, Charles Handy – you sit at their feet and learn, you don't question them.

Paul Mackney, who became the leader of the college lecturers' trade union in the same year that Blair became Prime Minister, told me at the time that if he had the power, he would ban all college principals from going into airport bookshops, because that was where they picked up the work of Tom Peters, and what Peters told them was that management was God.

Charles Handy was the most fashionable British business guru. (Most business gurus are American.) He poured scorn on the idea of having a safe job, and urged us all to become business entrepreneurs, holding up John Birt as a shining example. For the first six months of Birt's time as Director General of the BBC, Handy pointed out, Birt was not employed directly by the BBC; instead, the BBC had a contract with Birt's private company, which enabled Birt to earn much more money. Handy thinks this was visionary.[6] Most people thought it was just greedy.

Professor Handy also offered a sort of simplistic piety which at one stage earned him a regular gig on the *Today* programme's godspot. He is in the wealthiness-is-next-to-godliness school of management thinking. So Handy pressed all the buttons for Blair, and for what the children of the sixties had turned into: God; the infallibility of revealed truth; the moral worth of material success; and the striving for an ideal society in which everyone understands that the purpose of life is to watch for a chance to make a quick buck.

Management brought with it its own dead language, in which nothing is ever changed and improved, things are always 'transformed'; in which nothing is ever started, it is always 'kick-started'; in which you have to pretend to be 'passionate' about whatever dull consumer product you are paid to promote ('I am passionate about sub-prime mortgages'); in which you push the envelope and think outside the box. (Only exceptionally dull management types use this last phrase. Anyone who is really capable of creative thought doesn't know where the box is.) In its first three years New Labour set up no less than forty 'taskforces' as well as a variety of 'tsars'; a senior police officer became 'drugs tsar' and a 'fast track' for heart patients was overseen by a 'heart tsar'. The 'fast track' was, of course, part of a 'national crusade'.

Managementspeak is a matter of cramming the maximum number of feelgood words into the smallest amount of meaning. It was what middle-aged former hippies used as a replacement for the studied vagueness of their sixties language. The slogan on the wall of the Sorbonne in 1968 read, 'Here, imagination rules.' It sounded fine, but it didn't mean anything. In the nineties, the consultants Capita wrote to Railtrack: 'In a facilitated workshop with senior management, Capita first identified communications objectives to underpin Sentinel [the safety system]'s newly defined vision and values, identified and analysed key stakeholder audiences, and outlined and secured agreement for desired messages.' After that frenetic activity, the exhausted consultants were going to 'establish and agree a programme of research to capture the "big picture", ensuring all relevant stakeholder views were sought.' Suddenly, 'Here, imagination rules' sounds pregnant with meaning.

Cap Gemini won an MCA award in 2005 for work with Inland Revenue to create 'a global ecosystem of technology partners as a means of accessing greater access to innovation.' Only Blair-era management types can access greater access. And only management types think you can have access to innovation.

Blair gobbled up the theories of management gurus like Handy. And the one bit of solid meaning he was able to glean from them was that he should tear down all the bureaucratic civil service structures, all the paraphernalia of meetings and minutes and consulting; he should do it like the business leaders he admired, on the hoof, in his shirtsleeves, latte in one hand and mobile phone in the other. Run Great Britain PLC as though it were a city investment company.

So New Labour's ways of operating had a very sixties feel about them. None of that stately old-fashioned stuff about minuted meetings; none of the formal Attlee style where you might call your Foreign Secretary Ernie in private, but round the cabinet table you called him 'Foreign Secretary'. The Blair court was a loose, fluid group of baby boomers that took momentous decisions over coffee in what they called the 'den'.

Blair's religion is a very sixties thing too. He is a Roman Catholic, but an eclectic one, open to all sorts of ways of finding God, like a new age hippie at a séance. He is interested in spiritualism. Cherie Blair wears a 'magic' pendant. On holiday in Mexico in 2001, the Blairs visited a temascal, a steam bath enclosed in a brick pyramid. Journalist Nick Cohen described what happened:

> It was dark and they had stripped down to their swimming costumes.
> Inside, they met Nancy Aguilar, a new age therapist. She told them that
> the pyramid was a Mayan womb in which they would be reborn . . . They
> smeared each other with melon, papaya and mud from the jungle and then
> let out a primal scream of purifying agony . . .'[7]

You can't get a lot more sixties than that.

If he is so very sixties, how come Blair preached against sixties libertarianism? What he was really attacking was the Attlee settlement that had given the children of the sixties the freedom to be what they were. In the sixties, a generation was growing up in Britain that, for the first time, was educated and never had to fear unemployment, near-starvation, being unable to pay for their medical treatment, or being unable to provide schooling for their children. That sort of security gives people freedom, and no generation ever had it before.

Whatever we expected of New Labour, I suspect most of us thought that it would seek to increase that freedom. Perhaps not a lot, not as much as we hoped, but that would be the direction of travel. After all, most Prime Ministers tug the centre of political gravity a little in their direction. They cannot pull too far, or they lose the middle ground entirely. But they tug it as far as they can, and how far they go depends on how good they are at it. Clement Attlee tugged the centre of gravity towards the things that Labour stood for, so successfully that what his government did became the new political consensus for nearly thirty years. Margaret Thatcher tugged the centre of gravity in her direction, and equally successfully.

Blair did the opposite. He did not pull the centre of gravity; he pushed it. He adopted Thatcherite economic policies wholesale, and built on them. His core beliefs are the vague ones of the sixties, homogenised into management jargon for the new millennium. In 1996 he published a book called *New Britain – My Vision of a Young Country*. That gets three key feelgood words into a short book title: new, vision and young. I opened the book at random and all these headlines hit me at once: 'A young country that wants to be a strong country', 'Modern public services for the people', 'Strong Britain', 'Democratic Britain'.[8] I recalled that Dennis Potter wrote three years earlier:

> Each age, even each decade, has its little cant word coiled up inside real discourse like a tiny grub in the middle of an apple. Each age, even each decade, is overly impressed for a little while by half-way bright youngish men on the make who adeptly manipulate the current terminology . . .

The little cant word of the nineties, he wrote, was modernisation.[9]

*

In a dreadfully sixties way, Tony Blair knew next door to nothing about the history and philosophy of the Party he led, often appearing to believe that it came into existence fully formed in 1994, when he became its leader. History, to the children of the sixties, was never much more than a burden.

If Blair had known his party's history, he probably could not have changed it so fundamentally. Roy Hattersley calls him the soldier who crossed a minefield in confident safety because he did not know that the mines were there. Because he neither knew nor cared about what Labour had once stood for, he was able to lead the most remarkable revolution in modern political history . . . The ideas which had inspired a century of democratic socialism were ruthlessly discredited. They had survived since Attlee's day and were therefore, by definition, too ancient to be of any value in New Labour's brave new world.[10]

Labour before Blair was the party of the underdog. This, to the baby boomer generation, was a dreadfully old-fashioned thing to be.

Some of his fiercest supporters had started by supporting Tony Benn, for in the Benn camp they found the intolerant certainty they craved. The more ideologically inclined, like Dr John Reid, were once intolerant and sectarian left-wingers. They had played the game of lefter-than-thou with ferocious abandon. It was an easy transition for them to become equally intolerant Blairites, for the Blairites, like the Bennites, police ideological purity strictly. New Labour is what Labour politicians of the baby boomer generation have bequeathed to the next generation.

So old Trots have unexpectedly prospered under New Labour. The group of council leaders who made Neil Kinnock's position difficult in the early eighties was led by the fiercely left-wing leader of Sheffield City Council, David Blunkett. He worked his passage back under Blair by moving so fast to the right that the journey was over before most people knew it had begun.

Paul Boateng was one of Ken Livingstone's chief lieutenants in the eighties, even embarrassing Livingstone with the fury of his convictions. He once called on the Labour Party to 'have the guts to support workers who have the guts to fight Thatcher.' In working his passage back – as old Trots must do, for Blairism is as rigid and unforgiving a religion as the one they have deserted – Boateng's penance when he became Chief Secretary to the Treasury was to be wheeled out to attack Livingstone's bid to become London's Mayor. He did it with all the fire and fury and personal unpleasantness that he used to direct at Livingstone's enemies.

Chris Mullin's fate was particularly hard. The one-time fiery Bennite editor of *Tribune*, who helped smash the Labour Party apart in the early eighties because he did not consider Michael Foot or Neil Kinnock sufficiently left-wing, was forced to work his passage back by oversee-ing the privatisation of air traffic control, perhaps the most brutal affirmation that the Labour Party Mullin had fought for in the eighties was not the Labour Party of whose government he was now a part.

Old Trots and old Stalinists glower at each other across the Cabinet table, where they feel at home because New Labour demands the religious loyalty they were used to.

They do not talk a lot about their shared sixties experiences, but one day in 2007, at a gathering organised by the National Union of Students, Lord David Triesman, then a minister at the Department for Innovation, Universities and Skills, found himself talking to Jack Straw, Minister of Justice. Before they put on grey suits, grey hair, and gravitas, Triesman and Straw were student radicals – in 1970 Triesman led a famous occupation at Essex University. Triesman said, 'What shall we occupy?' And they both laughed, indulgently.

*

Greg Dyke now says that the baby boomers produced the weakest Labour politicians ever, and the most conformist. 'It's only with this government that I've rejected the belief in the Labour Party that I've always had,' he says. 'The Labour politicians of our generation thought they were there to get jobs, not to hold the PM to account. How easily that generation rejected Thatcher but bought into the values! Thatcher created New Labour.'

He puts their desire to conform partly down to the fact that, unlike previous Labour cabinets, most of the Labour Party baby boomer politi-cians did little before becoming MPs outside student politics and being political advisers. Jack Straw was NUS President, then adviser to Barbara Castle MP, then an MP. Gordon Brown was student Rector at Edinburgh University, briefly a television researcher (Dyke does not rate Brown's television experience highly), then an MP.

'What is his experience of life?' asks Dyke.

Did he ever think about anything else, did anything else ever dominate his life? His life has been Westminster. The baby boomer generation of politi-cians became professional politicians, they had never done anything else.

Jack Straw, what the fuck has Jack Straw ever done? Apart from not standing up over Iraq.

Westminster, Dyke says, is

a very conditioning environment where if you don't buy in you don't do anything. Ken Livingstone did not buy in, and when he went to Westminster he found he was hated by most of the Labour Party and he never achieved anything at Westminster. He only achieved anything by being a populist when he came back out again.

This, says Dyke, is why New Labour politicians put business chiefs and management gurus on a pedestal: because they know nothing of the world.

I remember going to dinner at the Financial Services Authority, full of bankers, they just gave Gordon Brown a terrible time, said you've got to keep regulation away from us, no red tape. The great tragedy of New Labour was that Brown and Blair believed these people. But these people, their job when they meet ministers is to get in there and get them to do things that maximise their profits, that's their job, and Brown and Blair began to believe these people, they thought they were saying these things to do something worthwhile.

And that is why the baby boomer generation of Labour politicians have let us all down, he says. 'There have been three massive opportunities in the last century when the government could make massive social change. The first was the liberal reforms [of 1910], the second was under Attlee, the third was 1997. The first two times, it was done. The third, they did nothing.'

As I finish this book, in May 2010, the political era of the baby boomers has just ended, after thirteen years in which to create a better world. The second of Britain's two baby boomer Prime Ministers, Gordon Brown, has departed, and there will be no more. Almost every member of the new government is too young to be a baby boomer, with the obvious exceptions of Kenneth Clarke and Vince Cable, who are too old.

The society we have now is the baby boomers' political legacy, and so is the new government, which represents the triumphant return of the old ruling elite. Most members of the cabinet are seriously wealthy, and as for the new Parliament, the TUC's deputy general secretary Frances O'Grady summed it up at a union conference just after the election: 'More Oxbridge graduates than women, twice as many old Etonians as ethnic minorities, and around a quarter categorised as coming from one occupational group – bankers – though lots of them had second jobs, as consultants to hedge funds.'

Does New Labour have any core beliefs at all? Yes, it seems to; but they have nothing at all to do with what the Labour Party used to stand for. To judge by what New Labour does, it appears to believe the following things: that there is nothing the public sector can do that the private sector can't do better; that trade unions are at best a burden on business; that the best hope for the world is the pax Americana, and Britain should hug America close and not be seduced by either our European neighbours or dangerously idealistic talk of international action through the United Nations; and that Britain, America and Christianity between them can create a new and better world order.

*

So how did this conventional and rather reactionary set of opinions come out of what once looked like the most radical generation since 1945? How did intolerant student rebellion turn into intolerant middle-aged conformism?

It happened because the rebellion never meant anything in the first place.

Back in 1968, Mick Jagger went home from the demonstration in Grosvenor Square and wrote 'Street Fighting Man'. He did not know then that, in an old granite building just outside Edinburgh, a public-school boy called Tony Blair was honing his imitation of him. But forty-five years later Prime Minister Blair gave Jagger a knighthood, though Sir Michael had to work his way back to respectability, putting his hand in his deep pockets to sponsor Britain's gymnastic team for the Los Angeles Olympic Games, and by finding God, in Jagger's case by adhering to the fashionable kabbalah creed. The singer also helpfully clarified that there was nothing to rebel against any more, so the young might as well conform. After his investiture he told the press, 'I don't think the Establishment we knew exists any more.'[11] To this day he apparently does not realise that the establishment is just where it always was – but he's now a part of it.

Others took their revolutionary inspiration from Bob Dylan. Many now ageing baby boomers still do. Had he not told mothers and fathers throughout the land not to criticise what they didn't understand? Well, yes, but quite what it was they shouldn't criticise he never spelled out. And when, in 1985, he played in the famous concert organised by Bob Geldof to raise money for the starving of Africa, he 'gave the worst performance of his life and then said, hey, shouldn't we, like, y'know, give some of this money to American farmers.'[12]

In the sixties the baby boomers used to sneer at people they called middle-aged, middle-class and middle-brow. The baby boomers are the masters now, and they call them Middle England and defer to them. We have come full circle. Hilaire Belloc might have been writing of the 1997 election, rather than the 1906 one:

The accursèd power which stands on Privilege

(And goes with Women, and Champagne and Bridge)

Broke – and Democracy resumed her reign:

(Which goes with Bridge, and Women and Champagne).

11. The children of the baby boomers

We have forgotten how much political courage and will the creation
of the welfare state required. The press was unremittingly hostile, and
many of the wealthiest and most powerful in the country were incan-
descent with rage. The mild-mannered Prime Minister, Clement Attlee,
was compared to the Gestapo. Britain was bankrupt, and even many of
those who did not condemn the idea outright wanted to wait for better
economic times.

But the government did it, and for two decades after that it was
pretty well impregnable, protected by people who remembered how
dreadful things were before we had it.

But most of those people are dead now. The welfare state is in the
hands of the baby boomers, who do not know how bad things were
for their parents without it, or how bad they will be for their children
without it.

Ten years into the new millennium, six decades after its birth,
Britain's welfare state is in the worst danger it has ever known.
Commentators and politicians sneer at it and undermine it while legis-
lators chip away at it. The political will in the Labour Party that created
it has gone.

The baby boomers inherited it and were the first generation to
benefit fully from it. They could easily be the last.

A trip to the hospital is still free, but you pay through the nose to
park your car there. More and more bits of the health service – prescriptions, dentists – cost more and more. The principle that no one
should die of a treatable disease was breached long ago; if the treatment
is very expensive, it may not be provided on the NHS. The solution now
being proposed is not that the NHS should be properly funded so that
it can provide the treatment people need. Instead, sleek commentators of the baby boomer generation are slyly proposing that wealthy
patients should be enabled to 'top up' their NHS treatment. This is being

presented as a way of giving more freedom, and if we are seduced into going along with it, then before we can say Nye Bevan, topping up will become the rule not the exception, and the NHS will be no more.

The proposal for wealthy patents to top up NHS treatment comes from a group called Doctors for Reform, which calls for 'liberalizing the public sector, breaking monopoly and extending choice'. This is code for handing control to private companies and instituting payment for those who want top quality treatment. 'Single provider, single payer, tax-based health systems are doomed,' says one of the founders of Doctors for Reform, Professor Karol Sikora, who runs the medical school at Britain's only private university, the University of Buckingham. Cynically, Professor Sikora tries to turn the young against the NHS, writing, 'Most healthcare costs are spent on retired people, who pay little tax.'[1]

Top Conservatives, including Cameron confidant Michael Gove, say in a recent book that the National Health Service isn't 'relevant in the twenty-first century'. One of the authors, Daniel Hannan MEP, calls the NHS a 'sixty-year-old mistake'.[2]

When the NHS was created in 1948, the vested interests that made money from health fought it tooth and nail. It was 'suggestive of the Hitlerite regime now being destroyed in Germany', said one delegate to the British Medical Association conference, who was cheered to the rafters for saying it.[3] A former BMA Secretary, Dr Alfred Cox, wrote that the NHS was a big first step towards 'National Socialism as practised in Germany'.[4] Today, opponents of President Barack Obama's healthcare plan said that these plans, too, were 'Nazi'. Anton Chaitkin, right-wing ideologue and history editor of the *Executive Intelligence Review*, called them 'a revival of Hitler's euthanasia killing program'.[5] That is how much national healthcare systems are hated, and if the NHS's defenders do not realise its value, they will lose it.

The careful balancing act between church and state control of education contained in the 1944 Education Act has been destroyed by the explosion of faith schools under New Labour. Control of much of the education system has been handed to priests (and a few rabbis and imams) as well as to some charities and some private companies. As state schools struggle with budget cuts and different systems of control, fee-charging schools (which some people, mistakenly, call independent schools) have had a new lease of life. They remain, absurdly, classed as charities, with all the tax breaks that brings.

In the thirties, bright children from poor families who won scholarships to the grammar school were unable to take them up because they could not afford the expensive uniform required. Today, we are racing back to that time. The most popular state schools are asking parents for 'voluntary' donations, and forcing them to buy their uniforms from stores that sponsor the school.

Oaklands Catholic school in Waterlooville, near Portsmouth, was in the news in 2009 for forcing parents to buy a uniform from one outfitter, or direct from the school, for between £78 and £97 (scarves, coats, PE kits and the rest are extra), when perfectly serviceable school uniforms are obtainable for a fraction of that amount.[6]

The move against selection at the age of eleven has been halted and reversed, and New Labour is more addicted to it than the Conservatives: there is more selection now than there was in 1997, because New Labour has allowed its favoured schools – the Trust schools and the academies – to select up to 10 per cent of their intake.

The principle of equal access to university education for rich and poor alike has been effectively axed by New Labour. At the end of the sixties, my student grant gave me enough to live on (my widowed mother being demonstrably penniless) and I did not have to work in termtime, or beg from older relatives, or build up a mountain of debt, as my own children have to do. I and my friends studied what we enjoyed, instead of doing what we now tell our children to do, which is to take whatever Gradgrind course will commend itself to employers. I had small seminar groups, and tutors who saw their task as to encourage my intellectual curiosity. Our children and grandchildren have none of these things.

I last revisited Keele University in 2008, for a reunion dinner. The student union building that I knew has now to accommodate many times the number of students, so they have divided it meanly into lots of grubby little shut-off spaces. The great open staircase is closed off and shuttered so as to make a little room out of every nook and cranny. It was a grand sixties building. It now looks and feels mean and miserable, for a mean and miserable decade.

Dr Chris Harrison went to Keele as a student in 1964, and has just retired as a lecturer there, having spent most of his life on the campus. His generation and mine, he writes, wanted a society in which 'Authority whether political or academic should be challenged.' The students he sees today have no such demands, perhaps because 'our leaders, both political and academic, are more authoritarian and dirigiste than they have ever been. The irony is that these leaders come from the same generation that forty years ago challenged authority.'[7]

In the sixties and seventies, Oxford and Cambridge universities were slowly beginning to lose their reputation as finishing schools for the rich. That process ground to a halt in the early eighties, and the social compositions of Britain's two most prestigious universities have hardly changed since then. They still take about half their students from the 7 per cent of children who go to fee-charging schools. They claim they do so because most state school pupils are not up to their standards. Insofar as that's true, it's because state schools have been relatively starved of money, and fee-charging schools can teach in smaller classes. But state school pupils are still turned away from Oxbridge for pupils from fee-charging schools with poorer A-level grades.

We looked briefly as though we were becoming a classless society, but class is back with a vengeance.

The landmark 1944 Education Act was about creating a level playing field. The playing field has since then been decisively tilted against the poor, but many people did not notice until the summer of 2009, when university places contracted because of the economic crisis, and it quickly became clear that pupils from fee-charging schools were destined to elbow aside those from state schools for the diminishing number of places. Between 2002 and 2008, fee-charging schools have increased their A-grades at A-Level by 9.1 per cent, compared with 3.9 per cent at comprehensives and 8.3 per cent at grammar schools.[8]

Those who claim unemployment benefit have to telephone a premium rate line and pay 40 pence a minute to speak to the job centre. The value of state pensions is decreasing every year.

Kat Fletcher, who was President of the National Union of Students between 2004 and 2005 and was born in the year Margaret Thatcher became Prime Minister, pointed out to me that there will be no occupational pensions for people of her age: the baby boomers have taken them all. 'There will be a big crisis when my generation reaches their sixties,' she says.

The welfare state's enemies smell blood.

Today it is stuck together with Sellotape, starved of money, and struggling under the weight of great, bullying, bureaucratic initiatives designed to give it the appearance of a market, because nothing that does not at least look like a market is apparently acceptable in the Britain the baby boomers built.

Most capital expenditure for education and health no longer comes from the present-day taxpayer, but from the next generation, because the baby boomers have been too stingy to pay for the welfare state. This trick is done by means of the Private Finance Initiative (PFI) and Public Private Partnerships (PPPs), which are scams for getting the cost of public buildings like schools and hospitals off the present government's books, and placing them on the books of governments ten or twenty years hence.

It's an inefficient way of providing public services, because you have to bind yourself to a private company, and the arrangements are ferociously complicated and one-sided. Just to draw up the PPP agreement for the London Underground cost £455 million to bankers, lawyers and consultants. In return they drew up a deal that allows consultants to fleece the taxpayer more or less indefinitely, forces us to borrow money at much higher rates of interest than we would otherwise have done, and leaves us carrying almost all the risk. Or rather, leaves our children carrying it.

In 1995, the Management Consultancies Association reported that its members, who only account for about half the industry, earned £196 million from the public sector. By 2004 that had increased by 850 per cent to £1,865 million, excluding the costs of developing IT systems. For our money, we get administrative chaos and spiralling management costs. But it does mean payment is deferred until the baby boomers are retired or dead.[9] The baby boomers, who have benefited far more from the welfare state than any earlier generation benefited or any future generation will benefit, do not wish to pay for it.

*

We have squandered the good times.

In the eighties, while one section of the baby boomers embraced Thatcherism as the best sort of freedom they could get, and another section buried itself deep in left-wing sectarian politics and forgot what was going on in the real world, successive governments made a bonfire of business regulation. We threw money at a few city folk, who became fabulously rich without expending much effort or taking any risks.

It was our children's money we were throwing at them. Shadow Chancellor George Osborne said in 2009, 'Every child in Britain is born owing £17,000 because of Labour's debt crisis.' Of course it's not just Labour's debt, and you can argue about the exact figure, but there's a substantial sum of money which our children will have to pay off, in order to finance the debts our generation's politicians have incurred. One day the great unregulated orgy of spending and speculating was going to lead to disaster. That day came in 2009, and our children are going to have to pick up the bill.

They are picking it up already. As Polly Toynbee noted:

Already 85 per cent of people aged between fifty-four and seventy own their own homes as wealth is sucked up the age ladder, leaving the young struggling harder than they ever did . . . With their demands for good care and good pensions, [the baby boomers] risk trampling on the impoverished generations that come after, making the employed pay for what the baby boomers have failed to fund in their own working lives.[10]

Yet even in 2009, a baby boomer government was putting the baby boomers at the head of the housing queue. In the 2009 budget, Chancellor Alastair Darling announced an increase in the tax-free savings allowance from £7,200 to £10,200. But only those over fifty were to benefit straightaway. It makes at least one economically literate young man of twenty-three to whom I have spoken feel angry. He says that he and his generation are expected to lead a recovery in the housing market, and find somewhere to live at the same time, despite most prices in London being way out of their reach. Yet mortgages now equate to only two-thirds of salary (we baby boomers used up the 100 per cent mortgages) so that first-time buyers have to save hard for a deposit. And then, when help is given to savers, only those over fifty – the baby boomers – are given immediate benefits.

When I left university, there was work, and places to live that we could afford. Our generation grabbed the housing, for investment and to help pay for its old age. And the baby boomers used their homes, not as places to live, but as ATM machines.

'The young are not to blame,' writes Polly Toynbee,

> but they are taking the hardest hit for the financiers' folly. Meanwhile we lucky baby boomers walk away with the bulk of the nation's wealth. We had everything done for us – a new health service, new schools and new universities, a burst of new and better jobs and the best pensions as we live longer. We bought homes cheap, and soaring untaxed property values made us rich, pricing out the young.[11]

Almost a third of young men between the ages of twenty and thirty-four – nearly two million of them – now live with their parents, mainly because of the lack of affordable housing.[12]

We did not know how dismal a legacy we were leaving the young, but we should have done, and our governments and industrialists should have done.

One half of the baby boomers was too busy to notice, and the other half too greedy to care.

*

It's not just money. We have closed off the freedoms we enjoyed as well.

'Suddenly, almost without warning, liberal Britain finds itself friend-less,' said an editorial in the *New Statesman* in June 2000.

> William Hague uses 'liberal elite' as a term of abuse, and the government doesn't bother to challenge him. Philip Gould, the Prime Minister's favourite pollster, warns that Labour, as the voters see it, is soft on crime (even though the prisons now hold record numbers) and puts asylum-seekers and minorities first; this, he says, must change if the party is to get back in touch with 'ordinary people'. An eccentric farmer who shoots a burglar becomes a national hero. Almost nobody can be found to defend teachers who think there is more to education than multiplication tables and spelling tests. The Secretary of State for Culture makes disapproving noises about nudity on Channel 5. In Scotland, a privately organised 'referendum' finds overwhelming public opposition to the repeal of Section 28.[13]

(Section 28 of the Local Government Act 1988 banned the 'teaching in any maintained school of the acceptability of homosexuality as a pretended family relationship'.)

It was back to the early fifties. 'Lest we forget, the fifties were awful,' wrote the magazine's then editor Peter Wilby, who is a war baby and remembers.

The freedoms the baby boomers fought for, they deny to their children. Their intolerance about clothing is far greater than that of their own parents. 'Hoodie' was just a name for a garment in fashion with children and teenagers, until it was demonised by politicians who were young in the sixties and defended their right to wear their sixties clothing, but who now want to create a shadow enemy they can fight on our behalf.

We even try to take away from the young the sexy clothing our generation pioneered and enjoyed in the sixties. Here is fashion writer Sarah Mower, also the British Fashion Council's first Ambassador for Emerging Talent, attacking short skirts worn by young women, and hoping (vainly, I fear) that her attitude is not 'the first sign of approaching old-trout-dom'. 'It's Slapper Summer,' she writes furiously. 'When I've tried to buy my teenage daughters the odd pretty summer dress that actually comprises a few inches of skirt, they've shrieked, "Ugh, frumpy, Mummy".' But did not we baby boomers pioneer the miniskirt in the sixties? That's different, says Ms Mower: 'Unlike the gamine minis of the Twiggy-ish sixties . . . this is not a charming, coltish look.' Instead, it's 'brash, sexy glamour of the most repulsive brassiness . . . Looking like trollops . . . Slapper-short . . . conformist mass uniform . . . I could scarcely believe it when I saw that the slapper dress had even invaded the audience at the Oxford Union last summer . . .' The worst thing of all, apparently, is that short skirts are cheap: they 'can be bought at any high street store for £29.99.'[14]

Here's a baby boomer trying to justify taking away from the young in 2009 what she and the rest of her generation used to enjoy, and justifying it with the idiotic suggestion that somehow we did it with more style. We didn't.

Ms Mower's sub-editors let her down: they illustrated her piece with a large picture of Girls Aloud, looking elegant and not at all slapper-ish in short skirts.

I realised when my children were in their teens how far we have closed off all the places young people used to go. Today, teenagers under legal drinking age cannot go anywhere – pubs and clubs are barred to them, far more effectively and efficiently than they were ever barred to us. So they hang about on street corners, and old sixties relics say their presence is threatening, and talk darkly of imposing a curfew on them.

And we are generally wrong, because we do not understand what is going on. In early 2009, I was on a bus in North London when a group of black teenage boys boarded, some of them in hoodies, all of them noisy, talking and laughing in loud voices, lounging about the seats. Middle-aged passengers felt a sense of unease. At the next stop, an elderly lady with a stick boarded the bus, and the two in the front instantly jumped up so that she could sit in the seat nearest the door. I realised I'd made a series of stupid assumptions. We baby boomers are making them about the young all the time.

Schools, after a quick burst of sixties freedom, are being sent back to the fifties. The sixties generation in government has brought back the school uniforms it rejected, and also the rote learning it rejected, in the form of a rigid national curriculum and a punishing regime of testing. Schools have been turned into forcing grounds in which chosen information is crammed into young heads, and in which there is no place for flights of fantasy or inspirational teaching.

After subjecting our children to a regime that we struggled to get rid of for our own generation, we then insult them annually at exam results time by saying exams have been 'dumbed down' since our day. They haven't been, but any fun there was in learning has been taken out by the new syllabuses. We might have got an extra few marks for a flight of imagination in an essay when we were young, but it couldn't happen now. Marks are awarded by slide rule.

And there is no hope of escape from the increasingly regimented schools we have given our children. The penalties for truanting are growing, with police now routinely frogmarching truants to their school. One of the arguments used in favour of school uniforms is that they help the police to recognise those who ought to be at school. We are forcing our children into prison uniform so they will be instantly recognisable when they scale their prison walls.

Sixties liberalism didn't always work, but it did not deserve the vitriolic denigration with which the baby boomers have, in their middle and old age, sought to discredit it. We have reinstalled the deference we rejected. Now we are in charge, politicians of the sixties generation realise that deference can be helpful to governments. So we are reviving it – only we call it 'respect', just as our parents did.

The baby boomers won those battles, forty years ago. We won the right not to be regimented into uniforms like prisoners, we won the right to make our own decisions about our lives, to live different lifestyles from the norm if it suited us. Then we threw our new freedoms away, because they no longer mattered to us. We were too old and conventional to enjoy them any more. We became puritans when we got too old to be libertines. We are like Lord Hailsham at the time of the Profumo affair, condemning sins we are no longer up to committing.

Baby boomer politicians worked hard to put the clock back. They even had the nerve to call for something like national service, because we, unlike the war babies, had never experienced its miseries. In 2006 Gordon Brown called for an expansion of the schools cadet programme to persuade pupils to volunteer to 'put on a military uniform to learn the meaning of discipline and pride in their country.' David Blunkett wants every school leaver to be forced to do six months of compulsory public service, to learn 'self-discipline, commitment, leadership and citizenship . . . A tough enough regime, overseen perhaps by recently demobbed sergeant majors.'[15] They are likely to get their way. It will be introduced by a Conservative government, because the baby boomers have used up Labour's chance.

We never treated the young with the respect that we expected – and often got – when we were young. We treat them as fifties products, not sixties products. But of course we still require respect for ourselves, and huff dreadfully when we do not get it. Here is Emma Soames, editor of *Saga* magazine, which goes to people who use Saga travel services for retired people (one of the few business areas that is booming these days), complaining about how shop assistants rush to serve her daughter 'who is young, blonde and pretty.' By contrast, Ms Soames herself has to hang around waiting for attention, and 'there's certainly no fawning.' From this she concludes that 'age discrimination is rife . . . silent, insidious, nasty . . .'

Ms Soames – who was young and pretty herself once, and no doubt extracted all the benefits to be obtained from it – concludes, 'As the authors of the greatest social and sexual revolutions of the last two centuries, we baby boomers are famous for kick-starting change and confounding prejudice. Well, we had better get on and add another revolution to the list.'

But the baby boomers are not the authors of these revolutions – they are the beneficiaries of them. What we are the authors of is the cult of youth. And it's come back to bite us.

*

The generation war has started.

Our parents knew they were bringing us into a new and better world. My parents, and many others, would often say, 'I want him to have the opportunities I never had.' Our parents may have grudged us our freedom, but they never grudged us their money, even though most had little enough of it.

Now the children of the sixties are parents and often grandparents, there seems to be a special venom in the loathing they show to their young. A popular car sticker around the turn of the century read triumphantly, 'Spending the kids' inheritance'. I hear parents of children in their late teens and early twenties say sourly, 'They've come home for another handout.' We sneer about them coming back to live with their parents in their twenties. 'The lure of the well-stocked fridge,' we say archly. But we have left them no choice. They would love to live out, but we took all the houses and mortgages.

At some level we know we have squandered the inheritance our parents worked to give us. It is as though the sixties generation decided that the freedom from humiliation and worry that they had enjoyed was too good for their children. The baby boomers kicked away their children's legs, and now they sneer at them for being lame.

*

Do our children resent the fact that the baby boomers destroyed their inheritance, and declined to show the same benevolence to the next generation as was shown to them?

To judge by appearances, not at all. They behave much better towards us, by and large, than we did towards our parents. Greg Dyke says, 'We walked away from our parents in a way that our kids are not walking away from us. We were sixties kids and we wanted to separate from our parents. We had no respect for wisdom and age and we were probably wrong. These kids like their parents.'

But if we think that, because they are nice to us, they have not noticed that we stole their future, we are mistaken. I wrote a piece making some of these points in the *Guardian*, and responses flooded in from young readers. Here are a few examples, from a great many that are very similar:

It's the victory of the Baby Boomers. They have had all of the benefits of the culture of the welfare state that was established by their parents. Free health care, schooling, state and company pensions and university education were all grasped with welcoming arms and have now been dismantled or removed for their children's generation, whilst ensuring that their children still cover them until their death.

Your generation is guilty of a lot more than that. You have pushed house prices beyond the reach of the majority. You have set private rents at levels that make the ordinary working young man or woman gilded slaves. You have failed to save sufficiently for your retirements and expect us to fund yours as well as our own. Quite how you're not all racked with guilt is astounding. The most greedy, self-obsessed generation we have ever seen.

You lot got the university degrees, got your first paycheck and then saw 'income tax' and almost cried at your parents' feet. When Thatcher trashed the grant system, you were so happy to get your 1p income tax cut from it . . . Now it's twenty years later and it's your kids that want to go to university, you cry and scream about how you are being forced to subsidise them and pay their rent . . . You spend your savings like crazy and expect us to pay for your retirement and pay for your cosmetic operations on the NHS. Your generation has had it so good and yet, you can't take responsibility for your actions.

I cannot believe that someone your age has actually told the truth about this painful subject. Could you go round and have a word with my Dad now please? In my darker moments I believe generational warfare is coming and almost wish for it. But the truth is generational warfare has already started – wars always begin economically and develop from there. Your self-ish and arrogant generation makes me sick. It's hard to tell my parents this though, as it's hard to catch them between cruises and excursions whilst I give half my income to the owner of my hovel.

They've noticed.

*

'On our watch in the 1980s and 1990s,' writes Polly Toynbee, 'the dysfunctional income gap grew . . . By rights the young should rise up and put us to the sword. Instead, they will work to pay for our pensions and care.'[16]

But in the coming battle with their children, the baby boomers start with an advantage. They have had power all their lives, and because this is a rapidly ageing society, they have it still. Greg Dyke says: 'As we grow older, there will be so many of us and we will be so powerful. And we have voted all the time for ourselves. You can see age warfare coming.'

Research from the thinktank Demos suggests that any government that fails to give the baby boomers what they want, even at the expense of younger generations, is in for severe punishment at the ballot box. 'Future governments will have to do a deal with the baby boomer generation,' say the report's authors. 'Attempts to encourage people to continue working without offering something in return will lead to a baby boomer backlash.'

According to the report, the baby boomer generation as it marches towards the grave is exercising its political muscle to ensure that it can spend its money trying to recapture the excitement of its youth. Two in three adults with the means to make a bequest said they 'plan to enjoy life and not worry too much about leaving a legacy.' Between 1994 and 2004, the average age of Harley-Davidson owners rose from thirty-eight to forty-six. Volkswagen camper vans and Hornby train sets are selling like hot cakes among the over-fifties. Many baby boomers are putting on backpacks and heading for exotic locations for a delayed gap year.[17]

They have money as well as power. At a time when newspapers and magazines are folding and cutting back everywhere, the exception is those magazines catering for older people like Emma Soames's *Saga* and my *U3A News* (published by the University of the Third Age.) We can still get the advertising, and here's why, according to the advertising agency for another such title, *Mature Times*:

> While, like any age demographic, the fifty-plus age group contains a wide range of socio-economic segments, in total terms it out-owns, out-earns and out-spends every other. Over fifties buy 80% of all top of the range cars sold. They buy 80% of all leisure cruises, 50% of all skincare products and they account for 35% of total travel spend. 80% of private wealth is owned by the fifty-plus generation and 85% of them have private pensions. They are the generation most likely to receive monies from an inheritance and have more income than previous generations. The over fifties account for 30% of total time spent online.

Launching a Demos report on the baby boomers in middle and old age in 2004, Gordon Lishman, Director General of Age Concern, said:

> A new generation of seventeen million older people are marching towards retirement with a clear set of demands. The boomers are unlikely to put up and shut up. If the political parties fail to listen to the boomers on priority issues like the provision of public services and retirement then they could be punished at the ballot box.
>
> We will also experience radical attitudinal changes, as the large post-war baby boomer generation reaches retirement age within the next twenty years. The baby boomers, having throughout their lives been at the forefront of radical attitudinal and social change, are different to current generations of older people and will redefine the meaning of retire-ment . . . The government is risking a 'baby boomer backlash' if it doesn't deal with the demands of a generation who plan to grow older very differently from their parents.

The Demos research finds that the baby boomer generation is defined by two distinct – and sometimes conflicting – attitudes: social activism and individualism. 'The defining character of the "new old" will depend on whether their individualism or social activism wins out,' Demos says. 'Baby boomers will either turn into "the selfish generation", which contrasts with the Dunkirk spirit of their parents, or "civic defenders" who push for wider social change.' The research predicts conflict as younger people, brought up in the far harsher world that the baby boomers have created for them to live in, decline to finance the sort of retirement that the baby boomers think is their right.[18]

We saw the class barriers coming down, and put them up again. If we really meant any of the things we said in the sixties, about peace, about education, about freedom, we would have created a better world for our children to grow up in, and earned the comfortable retirement we are now going to fight for. But we made a worse one.

Britain is now one of the worst countries to be young in, according to a league table of young people's wellbeing in twenty-nine European countries, compiled by researchers at York University for the Child Poverty Action Group (CPAG) using data mainly from 2006. They used forty-three criteria, ranging from infant mortality and obesity to poverty and housing. Britain came twenty-fourth; the only countries coming lower were Romania, Bulgaria, Latvia, Lithuania and Malta.

And we baby boomers have done that. For the New Economics Foundation calculated in 2004 that 1976 was the best year to be alive in Britain. It has been downhill ever since. They measured our material standards as well as levels of crime, family breakdown, economic inequality, welfare spending, pollution and the cost of living.[19] Things were good in 1976. We could have made them better.

*

No one who was there in the sixties and seventies can doubt that intangible things are worse too. We were young in a kinder society.

I know there is a danger of looking back fondly at a golden age that never existed, but there is something especially cruel about much of today's public discourse. Reality television and quiz shows are frequently built on sneering at ordinary people, and bullying them, and inviting us to laugh at their discomfiture: think of Jade Goody baiting and being baited in *Big Brother*, or Anne Robinson bullying contestants in *The Weakest Link*.

In 2008 a famous television presenter (whose fortune was made when Greg Dyke 'discovered' him as a 'talent'), live on air, rang an elderly actor and, pointing to the man standing beside him, said, 'He fucked your granddaughter.' (The elderly actor has a 23-year-old grand-daughter.) We were invited to laugh at this, because nothing is sacred, and many people did, rather uneasily, to show they were unshockable. But they are not unshockable: they would have been shocked if he had said something disrespectful about Christ, or Allah, or Buddha. We can hurt and humiliate ordinary, vulnerable human beings, but not the gods of our fathers, although, in the unlikely event that they exist, the gods of our fathers could hardly be hurt by our taunts, while human beings can.

Earlier generations knew that some things were just wrong, like torture and mass murder. They remembered Hitler and the death camps, and Stalin and the show trials. It was in the spirit of the sixties that a writer of the baby boomer generation could say, in the Communist newspaper the Morning Star, that while Stalin may have used 'harsh measures' readers might wish to ponder why 'hack propagandists abominate the name of Stalin beyond all others.'[20] We all know that our government is complicit in the torture of human beings, just as Stalin was. It does not seem to worry us, any more than it bothers that Morning Star writer. It should do. In the sixties, it would have done.

*

Why, when we were sure things could only get better, did they get worse? Partly because we missed what mattered. Perhaps making us fight for the right to grow our hair long was a very clever idea, because when we had won it, we thought there was little else to win. The baby boomers were fighting Beaumont and Fettes and The Leys and Christ's Hospital School when they should have been fighting for a better world.

Perhaps it was our lack of a sense of the past. The world seemed to us to have come into existence, fully formed – for some of us in 1956, for others 1963, for others again 1968. We complain that our children have no sense of the past, but they learned that from us.

Perhaps it was because we thought everything was easy. We had seen the battlements of the fifties collapse as we approached them: national service ended in 1961, the contraceptive pill made sex easy and safe, there was full employment, we did not have to fear our bosses.

We have not passed any of those advances, unsullied, to our children. Our baby boomer politicians want to bring back national service,

AIDS has diminished the power of the pill, the scourge of unemployment is back and our unions are no longer powerful enough to offer protection from our bosses. And we send the young to die in foreign lands fighting unwinnable wars.

The very kindest explanation was offered to me by the novelist (and baby boomer) Marina Lewycka:

> I think that stuff about the sixties spawning the asocial individualism of the eighties is a conservative slur. I think we were extremely pro-social, and many (most?) of us 68ers still are. I often feel I am pro-social to the point of prissiness . . . I think we were right about many things, but we were defeated by forces stronger and more purposeful than ourselves; unfortunately just at the point where the lawless cowboy world they created is beginning to crumble, we are too old and exhausted (and cynical?) and wedded to our hard-won comforts to seize the moment.

It is a good try, but not quite good enough. The real legacy of the sixties is New Labour. We said: never trust anyone over thirty, be modern, history doesn't matter, let people be free. We put style before substance. And we thought we were radical. We sneered at Harold Wilson who protected us from fighting in Vietnam, and elected Tony Blair who made some of our children fight in Iraq.

We fought the wrong battles, and often we still cannot see it. To this day, the London Freelance Branch of the National Union of Journalists has a strict rule preventing the chairperson from having a third year, and when in 2008 it was suggested they abandon it, the baby boomers, now grey and serious, pointed out that it was put there during the great battles of the eighties. It was part of the battle to defend the new left by preventing Bernard Levin and the Levinites from establishing permanent hegemony in the eighties, and you never know when it might be needed again, they said. It is still there. We fought government instead of making it our protector. G. K. Chesterton wrote a hundred years ago, 'The poor man really has a stake in the country. The rich man hasn't; he can go away to New Guinea on a yacht. The poor have sometimes objected to being governed badly; the rich have always objected to being governed at all.'[21] That's what government ought to be for: to protect the poor and the weak. That's why the richer the baby boomers became, the more they attacked what they called 'big government' and the less inclined they seemed to attack the real masters, those who control money.

*

Of course, not everyone who was born between 1945 and 1955 wanted the Iraq war, or the NHS turned into a market, or huge proportions of the nation's resources to be given to greedy bankers, or an increasingly illiberal society, or for the markets to rule. But the baby boomers' chance to change Britain for the better came, and it went.

It's attractive to blame Tony Blair for everything, and it's easy because he embodies everything that was shallow and hypocritical and meretricious about the sixties. But there was a bigger problem around than Blair: the spirit of the sixties itself.

When Bob Dylan was only moderately famous, at the end of the fifties and the start of the sixties, I was listening to the man I still regard as the greatest radical music-maker of my lifetime, the Harvard University mathematics professor Tom Lehrer. He saw the sixties coming and had no time for it.

You have to admire people who sing protest songs, he said – 'It takes a certain amount of courage to get up in a coffee house or college auditorium and come out in favour of the things everyone else is against, like peace and justice and brotherhood and so on.' His own take on the protest song, complete with Dylan twang, offered this:

> We all hate poverty, war and injustice
> Unlike the rest of you squares.

Lehrer got out of the sixties and returned to teaching mathematics, saying that when they awarded the Nobel Peace Prize to Henry Kissinger, he realised that a mere satirist could never compete with reality. We could have done with his stark, spare, intelligent voice in the sixties.

*

If and when the chance comes again, I hope wiser, younger people do not throw it away, as we did. In the meantime, the young need to try and preserve what the baby boomers have spared of the liberal Britain they inherited from the Wilson government, and the compassionate Britain they inherited from the Attlee government. The generation that has to clear up our mess must first ensure that Lord Beveridge's five giants may be prevented from awakening.

Here are some of the things we forgot, in the hope that they will remember them.

If the old are wrong, it's because they are wrong, not because they are old.

If the God of our fathers was a fraud, so are all the new Gods. If God exists, He is certainly not in a mood to tell us how to create a better world. We have to work that out for ourselves.

Money is not the root of all evil: poverty is. But you can't get rid of poverty except by redistributing wealth.

And radicalism is not a fashion accessory.

Notes

Chapter One: How the baby boomers got their freedom

1. Arthur Marwick, *British Society since 1945* (Penguin, 1982), p. 35.

2. Winston Churchill, *The Second World War*, Vol 1, p. 526.

3. Marwick, *British Society since 1945*, p. 22.

4. Julie Summers, *Stranger in the House* (Simon & Schuster, 2008), pp. xi–xii.

5. Peter Hennessy, *Never Again* (Vintage, 1993), pp. 159–60.

6. Hennessy, *Never Again*, p. 268.

7. Correlli Barnett, *The Lost Victory* (Macmillan, 1995), pp. 137–43.

8. H. G. Nicholas, *The British General Election of 1950* (Macmillan, 1951).

9. Francis Beckett, *Clem Attlee* (Politico's, 2000), p. 280.

10. Marwick, *British Society since 1945*, p. 44.

11. Andrew Davies, *Where Did the Forties Go?* (Pluto Press, 1984).

12. Quoted in Davies, *Where Did the Forties Go?*

Chapter Two: When we were very young

1. Greg Dyke, *Inside Story* (HarperCollins, 2004), pp. 37–8.

2. Arthur Marwick, *British Society since 1945* (Penguin, 1982), pp. 45–6.

3. Jonathon Green, *All Dressed Up* (Pimlico, 1999), p. 6.

4. David Lister, *The Independent*, 27 November 1997.

5. Peter Hitchens, *The Abolition of Britain* (Continuum, 2008), p. 83.

6. U3A News, June 2009.

7. Jonathan Croall, *Sybil Thorndike* (Haus, 2008), p. 394.

8. Peter Hennessy, *Having It So Good* (Allen Lane, 2006), p. 275.

Chapter Three: The cradle of the sixties

1. Dominic Sandbrook, *Never Had It So Good* (Little, Brown, 2005), p. 3.

2. Sandbrook, *Never Had It So Good*, p. 5.

3. Roy Hattersley, *Fifty Years On* (Little, Brown, 1997), p. 115.

4. Francis Beckett, *Stalin's British Victims* (Sutton, 2004), p. 146.

5. Francis Beckett, *Enemy Within* (John Murray, 1995), p. 134.

6. Alison Macleod, *The Death of Uncle Joe* (Merlin Press, 1997), pp. 99–100.

7. Douglas Hyde, *I Believed* (Heinemann, 1950).

8. Macleod, *The Death of Uncle Joe*, p. 177.

9. Francis Beckett, *Enemy Within*.

10. Dyke, *Inside Story*, p. 38.

11. Patrick Newley, *You Lucky People: The Tommy Trinder Story* (Third Age Press, 2008), p. 82.

12. Newley, *You Lucky People*, p. 90.

13. Newley, *You Lucky People*, p. 80.

14. John Wyse Jackson, *We All Want to Change the World* (Haus, 2005), p. 31.

15. Robert Tanitch, *London Stage in the Twentieth Century* (Haus, 2007), p. 166.

16. Sandbrook, *Never Had It So Good*, pp. 178–9.

17. *The Guardian*, 13 April 2005.

Chapter Four: The baby boomers go to school

1. Greg Dyke, *Inside Story* (HarperCollins, 2004).

2. *Daily Express*, 4 April 1960.

3. Robert Philp, *A Keen Wind Blows: The Story of Fettes College* (James & James, 1998), p. 90.

4. Francis Beckett and David Hencke, *The Survivor: Tony Blair in Peace and War* (Aurum, 2005), pp. 7–10.

5. Graham Wilmer, *Conspiracy of Faith* (Lutterworth Press, 2007).

Chapter Five: What if Mr Macmillan's out?

1. Richard Lamb, *The Macmillan Years – The Emerging Truth* (John Murray, 1995), p. 51.

2. Lamb, *The Macmillan Years – The Emerging Truth*, p. 27.

3. John Charmley, *A History of Conservative Politics* (Macmillan, 1999), p. 160.

4. Jonathon Green, *All Dressed Up* (Pimlico, 1999), p. 2.

5. Dominic Sandbrook, *Never Had It So Good* (Little, Brown, 2005), p. 48.

6. Sandbrook, *Never Had It So Good*, p. 48.

7. Alastair Horne, *Macmillan,Volume 2* (Macmillan, 1989), p. 178.

8. D. R. Thorpe, *Alec Douglas-Home* (Sinclair Stevenson, 1996), p. 257.

9. Peter Riddell, *Hug Them Close* (Politico's, 2003), p. 55.

10. Bernard Levin, *Run It Down the Flagpole* (Atheneum, New York, 1971), pp. 75–6.

11. Sandbrook, *Never Had It So Good*, p. 108.

12. Thorpe, *Alec Douglas-Home*, pp. 301–2.

13. Arthur Marwick, *British Society since 1945* (Penguin, 1982), p. 141.

14. *Daily Express*, 6 February 1960.

15. *Daily Express*, 20 April 1960.

16. *Daily Express*, 20 February 1960.

Chapter Six: The very model of a modern fluent technocrat

1. Dominic Sandbrook, *White Heat* (Little, Brown, 2006), p. 9.

2. Sandbrook, *White Heat*, p. 9.

3. John Betjeman, 'Executive', in *Collected Poems* (John Murray, 1958; reprinted 1992), p. 312.

4. Arthur Marwick, *British Society since 1945* (Penguin, 1982), pp. 161–2.

5. Richard Crossman, *The Crossman Diaries 1964–1970* (Book Club Associates, 1979), p. 100.

6. Crossman, *The Crossman Diaries 1964–1970*, p. 66.

7. *Mail on Sunday*, 14 January 2008.

8. Marianne Faithfull with David Dalton, *Faithfull* (Michael Joseph, 1994), pp. 40–8.

9. Faithfull, *Faithfull*, p. 70.

10. Alan Clayson, *Mick Jagger* (Sanctuary, 2005).

11. Faithfull, *Faithfull*, pp. 58–9.

12. Clayson, *Mick Jagger*, pp. 83–4.

13. Faithfull, *Faithfull*, p. 98.

14. *Sunday Times*, 16 March 2008.

15. Faithfull, *Faithfull*, pp. 98–9.

16. A. J. Ayer, *The Foundations of Empirical Knowledge* (Macmillan, 1940), pp. 1, 2.

17. Faithfull, *Faithfull*, p. 65.

Chapter Seven: The end of the adventure

1. Patrick Seale and Maureen McConville, *French Revolution 1968* (Penguin, 1968), p. 37.

2. Gerard de Groot, *The Sixties Unplugged* (Macmillan, 2008).

3. *The Guardian*, 21 May 2008.

4. *The Guardian*, 22 March 2008.

5. Marianne Faithfull with David Dalton, *Faithfull* (Michael Joseph, 1994), pp. 156–7.

6. Faithfull, *Faithfull*, p. 169.

7. *Mail on Sunday*, 14 January 2008.

8. Alan Clayson, *Mick Jagger* (Sanctuary, 2005), p. 15.

9. Jonathon Green, *All Dressed Up* (Pimlico, 1999), p. xii.

10. Seale and McConville, *French Revolution 1968*, p. 87.

11. Seale and McConville, *French Revolution 1968*, p. 102.

12. *The Guardian*, 22 March 2008.

13. Dominic Sandbrook, *White Heat* (Little, Brown, 2006), p. 709.

14. Faithfull, *Faithfull*, p. 168.

15. J. M. Kolbert, *Keele, The First Fifty Years* (Melandrium, 2000), pp. 144–6.

16. Robert Tanitch, London Stage in the Twentieth Century (Haus, 2007), p. 205.

17. Peter Hitchens, *The Abolition of Britain* (Continuum, 2008), p. 153.

Chapter Eight: How the baby boomers destroyed the trade unions and made Thatcherism

1. *The Guardian*, 22 March 2008.

2. Bernard Levin, *Run It Down the Flagpole* (Atheneum, New York, 1971), p. 11.

3. Gerard de Groot, *The Sixties Unplugged* (Macmillan, 2008), p. 437.

4. Martin Bright, *The Observer*, 3 February 2002.

5. *Mail on Sunday*, 14 January 2008.

6. Greg Dyke, *Inside Story* (HarperCollins, 2004), p. 50.

7. Denis MacShane, *Heath* (Haus, 2006), p. 63.

8. Quoted in Paul Routledge, *Scargill* (HarperCollins, 1993).

9. Quoted in Routledge, *Scargill*.

10. Jack Jones, *Union Man* (Collins, 1986), p. 261.

11. Andy Beckett, *When the Lights Went Out* (Faber & Faber, 2009).

12. Beckett, *When the Lights Went Out*, p. 177.

13. Jones, *Union Man*, p. 281.

14. Francis Beckett and David Hencke, *The Survivor: Tony Blair in Peace and War* (Aurum, 2005), p. 24.

15. Beckett and Hencke, *The Survivor*, pp. 23–9.

16. Beckett, *When the Lights Went Out*, p. 178.

17. Beckett, *When the Lights Went Out*, p. 229.

18. *The Guardian*, 13 August 2004.

19. Denis Healey, *The Time of My Life* (Penguin, 1990).

20. Beckett, *When the Lights Went Out*, pp. 335–6.

21. Beckett, *When the Lights Went Out*, p. 355.

22. Jones, *Union Man*, p. 326.

23. Beckett, *When the Lights Went Out*, pp. 434–5.

Chapter Nine: The radical conservatives

1. D. R. Thorpe, *Selwyn Lloyd* (Cape, 1989), p. 343.

2. D. R. Thorpe, *Alec Douglas-Home* (Sinclair Stevenson, 1996), p. 257.

3. Will Hutton, *The State We're In* (Cape, 1995), pp. 36–7.

4. Andrew Hosken, *Nothing Like a Dame: The Scandals of Shirley Porter* (Granta, 2006).

5. Hutton, *The State We're In*, p. 82.

6. Hutton, *The State We're In*, pp. 92–3.

7. Marianne Faithfull with David Dalton, *Faithfull* (Michael Joseph, 1994), p. 237.

8. David Childs, *Britain since 1945* (Routledge, 2001), p. 225.

9. Greg Dyke, *Inside Story* (HarperCollins, 2004).

10. John Betjeman, 'Executive', in *Collected Poems* (John Murray, 1958; reprinted 1992), p. 312.

11. Faithfull, *Faithfull*, p. 209.

12. Faithfull, *Faithfull*, p. 228.

13. Faithfull, *Faithfull*, p. 230.

14. Mark Garnett, *From Anger to Apathy* (Cape, 2007).

15. *Daily Telegraph*, 9 November 1979.

16. Peter Hitchens, *Monday Morning Blues* (Quartet, 2000), p. 155.

17. James Tooley, *Reclaiming Education* (Cassell, 2000).

18. Francis Beckett and David Hencke, *Marching to the Fault Line* (Constable & Robinson, 2009), p. 41.

19. Paul Mackney, *Birmingham and the Miners' Strike* (Birmingham TUC, 1987).

20. Hutton, *The State We're In*, pp. 2–3.

21. Hutton, *The State We're In*, p. 16.

22. Hutton, *The State We're In*, p. 24.

23. Martin Westlake, *Kinnock* (Little, Brown, 2001), p. 208.

Chapter Ten: The baby boomer Prime Ministers

1. *Daily Telegraph*, 9 April 1997.

2. Francis Beckett and David Hencke, *The Survivor: Tony Blair in Peace and War* (Aurum, 2005), p. 200.

3. Beckett and Hencke, *The Survivor*, pp. 182–203.

4. Greg Dyke, *Inside Story* (HarperCollins, 2004), p. 4.

5. Dyke, *Inside Story*, p. 330.

6. Charles Handy, *The Elephant and the Flea* (Arrow, 2002).

7. *The Observer*, 8 December 2002.

8. Tony Blair, *New Britain: My Vision of a Young Country* (Labour Party, 1996), pp. 50–1.

9. Quoted in Colin Leys, *The Socialist Register* (Merlin, 1996).

10. Roy Hattersley, *Fifty Years On* (Little, Brown, 1997), p. 385.

11. Alan Clayson, *Mick Jagger* (Sanctuary, 2005), pp. 187–9.

12. Cole Moreton, *Is God Still an Englishman?: How We Lost Our Faith (But Found New Soul)* (Little, Brown, 2010).

Chapter Eleven: The children of the baby boomers

1. *The Observer*, 16 August 2009.

2. *The Observer*, 16 August 2009.

3. Clare and Francis Beckett, *Bevan* (Haus, 2004), p. 84.

4. Francis Beckett, *Clem Attlee* (Politico's, 2000), pp. 251–2.

5. *Executive Intelligence Review*, 19 June 2009.

6. *Daily Mail*, 18 August 2009.

7. Chris Harrison, *In the Company of Friends* (privately published, 2010).

8. *The Guardian*, 21 August 2009.

9. David Craig, *Plundering the Public Sector* (Constable, 2006).

10. *The Guardian*, 13 May 2008.

11. *The Guardian*, 22 August 2009.

12. 2009 *Social Trends Survey*, published by the Office of National Statistics.

13. *New Statesman*, 19 June 2000.

14. *Daily Telegraph*, 8 July 2009.

15. *Times Educational Supplement*, 16 Feb 2006.

16. *The Guardian*, 22 August 2009.

17. *The New Old* (Demos, 2004).

18. *The New Old* (Demos, 2004).

19. Mark Garnett, *From Anger to Apathy* (Cape, 2007), p. 1.

20. Reported by Andy McSmith, *Independent on Sunday*, 2 March 2003.

21. G. K. Chesterton, *The Man Who Was Thursday* (1908; Penguin reprint, 1986), p. 128.

Index

Wilson, Harold *cont.*
  as Labour Party leader 77
  as Prime Minister 78–9, 80–81
  resignation of 139
  and trade unions 82, 109, 121,
    130, 139
  and United States of America
    33, 81
  and university expansion 81
  viewed by baby boomers x,
    82–3, 84

Wilson, Peter 26
Winstanley, Michael 56
'winter of discontent' 141–2
women
  in 1960s music 89–90
  and feminism 136
  traditional view of 74
Workers Revolutionary Party 123,
  156

Yarnit, Martin 112–13